EVERYTHING'S TRASH, BUT IT'S OKAY

MORE BY PHOEBE ROBINSON

You Can't Touch My Hair

EVERYTHING'S TRASH, BUT IT'S OKAY

Phoebe Robinson

PLUME

An imprint of Penguin Random House LLC
375 Hudson Street
New York, New York 10014

Copyright © 2018 by Phoebe Robinson

All photos courtesy of the author.

LIBRARY OF CONGRESS CATALOGING-IN-PUBLICATION DATA
Names: Robinson, Phoebe, author.
Title: Everything's trash, but it's okay / Phoebe Robinson;
foreword by Ilana Glazer.
Other titles: Everything is trash, but it is okay
Description: New York, New York: Plume, 2018.
Identifiers: LCCN 2018025958 (print) | LCCN 2018028615 (ebook) |
ISBN 9780525534150 (ebook) | ISBN 9780525534143 (hardback)
Subjects: | BISAC: HUMOR / Form / Essays. | SOCIAL SCIENCE / Essays. |
BIOGRAPHY & AUTOBIOGRAPHY / Personal Memoirs.
Classification: LCC PS3618.O33363 (ebook) |
LCC PS3618.O33363 A6 2018 (print) | DDC 814/.6—dc23
LC record available at https://lccn.loc.gov/2018025958

Printed in the United States of America
1 3 5 7 9 10 8 6 4 2

To Oprah. Like lit'rally every book should be dedicated to her. A'doy.

Contents

Contents

FOREWORD

I met Phoebe in the smoky basement of a hookah bar doing stand-up on the Lower East Side in 2010. It was one of those shows with, like, twelve comics, and each gets lit at six minutes, letting them know they have sixty seconds to wrap up. We were the only women on the show, and Phoebe was joking about getting catcalled, and how New York catcallers get creative. They'd guess her birthplace, "Jamaica! Jamaica!" or "Tanzania" or some African nation . . . but it was also probably because she walks around with a boom box blasting *The Lion King* music. I was in. After we finished our sets, we introduced ourselves.

Phoebe is one of those people you meet and think you've met before, like you went to high school with her, or made it through some shitty job only because she was your desk mate. She's got that Midwestern openheartedness yet the no-bullshit focus of a New Yorker. I felt so invited by Phoebe's unabashed nerddom—we were not smoking hookah in the basement, we had headaches, lol. And we were both one-drink sorta gals—drink tickets were our only pay, and it gave us a thing to hold. I loved how she wasn't trying to pretend like she didn't care about comedy, which a lot of comics—and, obviously, specifically male comics—do. No, she cared. A lot. And she was prepared to work her ass off for years and years, which I've had the awe-inspiring pleasure of witnessing to this day.

Phoebe is a woman who gets. Shit. Done. As a Jew with anxiety issues, I'm most in awe of her ability to shrug off hesitance or doubt, set the bar high for herself, and jump for it. And yet she's still like, "It's not brain surgery, we're not saving lives—it's comedy." And then will literally say "tee-hee." Like the thing she cares about most is still . . . what it is. It's empowering to be around, and it feels the same way reading her book.

In her essays, Phoebe gives herself over to her reader. I can tell you: It's like having Phoebe-the-friend in a book. When I was reading her first book, literal *New York Times* bestseller *You Can't Touch My Hair: And Other Things I Still Have to Explain*, I would truly lol on the subway because it was like having a mini Phoebe sitting on my shoulder, telling me realer, deeper layers I didn't know about her before, but the way she says it is hilarious. Phoebe's relationship with language is the absurdity of her comedy. Just in real life, I get texts with "abbrevs"—abbreviations—that have apologies attached to them, so the phrase ends up being ten times longer than if she had just written out the original word. Like "eems aka email—#Lol #NotWorthIt" instead of "email." But she'll play like that even when—or especially when—it comes to talking about race and gender and money and all the stuff that makes most people's butts clench. She invites us all to get straight to it, gets to her most intimate and vulnerable places, but you don't even realize you're going there because of how she dances with language, and she invites her readers to do the same. You'll find yourself adopting Phoebe's phrases because they truly make life more fun to live but also because they make it easier to hold, at the same time, the insane complexities of this world while also just giving a little eye-roll, a shoulder-shrug, and laughing that shit off.

—Ilana Glazer

Introduction

In summary: The world is currently one big "Previously on *Homeland*" recap that plays on repeat. Nothing but a bunch of dumpster fires and Claire Danes ugly-cries.

Despite a few glorious things—Beyoncé's historic Coachella performance and Solange's *A Seat at the Table*, Pamplemousse LaCroix, sitting in the window seat on a flight with an empty middle seat next to you—the world is *en fuego*, boo-boos (and has been for a while, to be honest), and I have the receipts to prove it. I mean, Brexit happened. And some of the people who voted for it were like, "Oops, J/K," and the Legal System responded, "Lol. Wut? This is literally how voting works. The thing with the most votes wins. I don't have time for your #Jokes-NotJokesButForRealWeHighKeyJokesLife, so please pack your bags." Then there was the De-Peening of 2017 aka very powerful men such as award-winning actor Kevin Spacey, legendary journalist Charlie Rose, comedian/auteur Louis C.K. watching their lives and careers implode following the uncovering of their sometimes decades-long sexual-deviant behavior, which ranged from harassment to sexual assault. And let's not forget the murder of Harambe, the gorilla, at the Cincinnati Zoo; Apple removing the headphone jack from their iPhones because this company is hell-bent on being the Nurse Ratched of our time; or the first black bachelorette, Rachel Lindsay, incorrectly choosing Bryan over Peter, thus denying the world some cocoa, gap-teefed babies. Oh! And remember a few years ago when a dude in the US legit had Ebola and went bowling and ate chicken wings with friends instead of quarantining himself because #WhiteNonsense? Say it with me: *Dumpster. Fire.* But far and away, the most telling sign that the world is in dire straits is the fact that in the past few years, the universe started killing off everyone who mattered in my childhood.

There was Carrie Fisher (White Jesus, why?), Prince (Black Jesus, why?), George Michael (Levi Jeans Jesus, I can't), and David Bowie (Alien Jesus aka the feathers from Björk's swan dress at the 2001 Oscar ceremony, *<squawk, blergh, blop>*—because y'all know Björk and anything in Björk's universe only communicates through sound). Oof. I don't know about you, but I was overcome with emotion at seeing so many pop culture icons pass. Utterly devastated. Heartbroken and beside myself. So I mourned like we all did. *Appropriately.* Okay, I didn't, but I tried. Well, I tried the way I do when the heater in my apartment is too high and instead of getting up to adjust the thermostat, I say to no one, "It's too hot," and then unzip my onesie down to my hips so that I end up looking like a caterpillar taking a cigarette break mid-metamorph-morph aka metamorphosis. #IgnorantAbbrev #SorryForWastingYourTime. Anyhoo, I did not try very hard *not* to be utterly inappropriate mere days after Bowie's death.

When he passed, I fell down the usual internet rabbit hole many of us are wont to do when someone famous dies. I read think pieces, bought any albums I didn't already own, watched old performances on YouTube. After about forty-eight hours of this, I became an unofficial truther of Bowie's personal life, hoping that in my quest to unearth all the last unknown details about him, this busywork would distract me from the reality that we're all going to die. And since this mission was rooted in earnest and profound love for the dead, I felt like Doogie Howser at the end of *Doogie Howser, M.D.*, just writing smart bon mots about what I'd learned. But I wasn't. My good intentions were quickly replaced by my just-below-the-surface hot-mess tendencies.

About three days after Bowie died and amid a particularly wide-eyed-and-awake-at-four-in-the-morning internet hunt, I typed this into Google:

Did David Bowie have a big penis?

I know, I know, *I know*! And it's not like I pulled up Googs's "incognito window," which wouldn't have recorded this question in my browser's history. I typed this question in the broad-as-the-Alaskan-daylight-during-midnight-sun season aka Google's regular search window, where anyone could track

3

what I'd done. To which, Google basically responded à la Danny Glover from the *Lethal Weapon* franchise, "I'm too old for this shit," and then set about unsuccessfully trying to save me from my trifling ways. I started with "Did David Bowie," and before I could continue, Google countered with this auto-complete:

> Did David Bowie wrote "My Way"

What in the hell kind of poor-grammar-of-a-troubled-youth-from-*Dangerous-Minds* voodoo is this? Can't lie, I admire the tactic, but this search engine knew not who they were messing with. In my twenties, I once had a girls' sleepover and made us watch *Showgirls*. Then we went to bed, and when we woke up, I convinced them to watch *Showgirls* again. Clearly, my ignorance is only matched by my determination. Googs sounding like the "Cash Me Outside, How 'Bout Dat" girl was cute, but no way was that stopping me.

So next Google tried to attract me with honey:

> Did David Bowie Have Pets

Suggesting there might be pictures of pets at the end of this search is the visual equivalent of a coworker telling you there are cookies in the break room. I'm intrigued, but I'm a grown-ass woman and can literally get cookies any time I want. Plus, I have an "in case of emergency" photo album on my phone called "Chocolate Puggle Puppies." I'm good, Google.

Starting to feel defeated and tired, Googs began throwing

haymakers, but it didn't have the strength, and as soon as I typed "a," I was met with this:

> Did David Bowie Have Any Siblings

Lmao.com/WhenSearchEnginesGiveUpAndStartSounding LikeAOneNightStandStrugglingToMakeConversationOverBreakfast.

And then when I hit the space bar after the letter "a" and typed "big," Google knew it couldn't save me from myself, probably did the sign of the cross, and mumbled under its breath, "Maya Angelou, I know you didn't work this hard so Phoebe could do this bullshit, yet here we are." I typed "penis." And pressed enter.

Yes. This. Is. Trash. And. I. Am. Not. Proud. But like I stated earlier, I'm a truther, and somewhere along the way of reading copious amounts of articles and learning the basic deets—why his eyes were two different colors (they weren't; they were both blue—it's just that one had a permanently dilated pupil after he got in a fight with a good friend whose fingernail sliced into his eye), the name of his first band (the Konrads), and checking out his and Freddie Mercury's isolated vocals on "Under Pressure" (if you haven't, please listen ASAP)—I stumbled across an old interview with one of his exes, who "casually" mentioned that Bowie was packing down below.

Three things:

1. LOL for the rest of my life over his ex "happening" to provide a State of the Naysh about his peen. It is

wack to kiss and tell about someone, especially if the person in question has moved on (Bowie married the love of his life, Iman), but more importantly, peen size never *casually* comes up in conversation. It's not like some dude is chilling at a house party, shooting the breeze about the latest home renovation he's working on, and goes, "Speaking of wood, the other day, I chubbed twice and measured once and whaddya know? I have a big dick." Real talk, discussing peen size in the press is an IHOP (Intentional Hijack Of convo vis-à-vis Peen) triple stack. She knew this was going to get her attention, so she did it.

2. I'm not even a size queen! Just like a nation hosting a hundred-plus countries at the Summer Olympics, after the countries proved your athleticism, if you qualify as sauseege, I'm giving you a thumbs-up, a team windbreaker, and a Target-sponsored sports bottle. I welcome all even if you have no chance of making the podium. *ANYWAY.* What I'm getting at here is that I didn't truly care what the answer was going to be re: Bowie's peen.

3. If a dude had Googled about Zsa Zsa Gabor's tatas after she passed away (RIP, boo-boo), I would have hollered to the heavens in the key of "Hell to the naw, to the naw, naw, naw," which is one key below Mary J. Blige's "I'm on my period, at Walgreens, and

they're out of Toblerones, so I can't get my chocolate fix" key. In short, I would have been livid and grossed out.

Yet there I was, trying to Lester Holt my way to the truth. Why? Because I am a trash person living in a trash world.

To be clear, I'm not calling myself "trash" because I'm fishing for a compliment. I'm saying this because I love myself. And you know what they say: Only with the people and things you love can you be truly, and sometimes brutally, honest. As funny, smart, kind, thoughtful, pretty, warm, and talented as I can be, I am also a ludicrous trash fire like the kind you see on *Naked and Afraid* when people sign up to be in the wilderness when they're barely capable of troubleshooting Mozilla Firefox, let alone making an actual fire from scratch, so they end up with fire that's the length, width, and height of *just* the hair part of a troll doll. Real talk though, if my allergic-to-manual-labor-with-the-upper-body-strength-of-an-eight-year-old self could find a dude who could make a fire as big as an *entire* troll doll (if not bigger), I would say adios to "spray and pray" life and yes to "leave it in and let our new lineage begin" life. (Mom and Dad, I literally do not engage in spray and pray; this is just jokes.) MOVING ON! What I'm getting at is that I can be a nightmare, but in case you don't believe me, here's a sampling of my trash from the past couple of months:

- I've walked into several stores mere minutes before closing and took my sweet-ass time shopping.

- I ordered and ate a small Papa John's personal pan pizza because I didn't feel like washing a Granny Smith apple that was straight chilling in my crisper.

- I misspelled my own name.

- I attempted to cancel my own going-away party one hour before it was supposed to start because it was raining. Not like disaster-movie rain, but what Seattle would call "Every day."

- Instead of telling my masseuse that I needed a moment, I eked out a fart in segments like it was a seven-course tasting menu at Spago. Oy. A fart is still a fart no matter how you try and dole it out over time to lessen its effects. I think the Dalai Lams said that.

- I rented *The Counselor* on iTunes even though it only has a 35 percent rating on Rotten Tomatoes just so I could look at Michael Fassbender's hotness. The movie—dis is where they fuq'd up—put his sex scene as the film's *opening* scene, so then I just watched that and turned the film off. Rude? Yes. A waste of my money? *Of course.* But also, everyone knows when you make a lame-ass movie, you put the sex scene like forty-three minutes in so the viewer will be too invested to peace out. So really, it was the filmmakers' fault for putting the sex scene up top, giving me time to abort mish and still catch the monologue on *The Late Show with Stephen Colbert.*

- I made my ringtone the "Somebody!" part from Smash Mouth's "All Star."

- I skipped going to Equinox because I didn't feel like walking the flight and a half of stairs to get inside the gym. Like I don't want to have to work out *before* working out. That's too much working out.

- I snuck a burrito bowl from Chipotle into the movie theater and made it everyone's responsibility during *Creed* to be a lookout in an after-school special and make sure I didn't get busted by one of the ushers.

- When I was behind on my student loans and the American Student Assistance would call me, I'd say, "Now's not a good time to chat." They'd ask when they could call back and I'd pretend to be earnest and give them a time, knowing damn well I wasn't going to pick up my phone at 4:45 P.M.

- Even though *The Bachelor* and *The Bachelorette* burn my toast with their antifeminist ignorance, I watched *The Bachelorette* when they cast their first black bachelorette, Rachel Lindsay, and I thought, *Ooooooh, this must've been what some white women went through when they chose race over gender and voted for Trump.* Literally. Not. The. Same. Thing.

- I had my sister-in-law, who lives in Cleveland, buy and mail me "rosé all day" white slip-on flats from

DSW that I barely wear because white shoes are a mofo to keep clean.

- When I started my period while on a working vacation on Vieques Island and only had two pads, I called Olga, my hotel's concierge, and she told me they only had tampons, which I've never used because I'm scared of getting toxic shock syndrome after leaving the tamp-tamp inside me for too long.[1] Anyway, she offered to call me a cab to take me to a convenience store about fifteen minutes away. I hard-passed on this suggestion and thought to myself, *Well, I guess I'll give this free-bleed thing a spin.*[2] Free bleeding is generally considered a feminist move, but in my case, it was just unbridled laziness. I didn't feel like going through the trouble of putting on pants, which makes me wonder: Is this what parenthood is? Something inconvenient happens with your kid and you must fight all urges to be like, "Peace out, dawg," and instead help them? Like if my kid came to me and said, "Mom, I need new shoes for school and the mall closes in thirty minutes," I can't respond with, "Okay, but I need to read this *InStyle* magazine profile about some white lady

---

1. Friends have assured me that I wouldn't forget there was a tampon in me, but I once forgot to pay my Con Ed bill for three months until the company sent me a "Hey, heaux, the only thing lighting in your apartment will be your white-ass teeth if you don't pay this bill," sooo . . .

2. For those not in the know, "free bleeding" is when a lady gets her period and abstains from using any sanitary products, instead saying to herself, "The world is my canvas and my vajeen is Jackson Pollock."

in Marrakesh—YOU KNOW, A PLACE I CAN'T AF-FORD TO VISIT BECAUSE I HAD YOUR ASS—doing a fashion diary and posing next to elephants that are like, 'Bish, why you have that goofy AF smile on your face when the back of my knees are like ashy celery?'" Point is, because I didn't want to leave my hotel room, I free-bled for two days, which were my super light days, so it was less a typical menstruation sitch and more like a few drops from a glass of V8 Splash spilling on a kitchen counter. Then on day three, I called Olga, she gave me one pad from her personal stash, and I went to the convenience store.

- THE FACT THAT I MADE THAT STUPID "SPRAY AND PRAY" SEX COMMENT WHEN I KNOW MY PARENTS ARE GOING TO READ THIS BOOK BE-CAUSE I WAS HOPING THE JOKE WOULD MAKE READERS LAF (TYPO, BUT I'M LEAVING IT, THUS MAKING THIS TRASH WITHIN TRASH. #INCEPTION).

See? I can be garbage! And it's okay. Because guess what? Everyone is garbage. *Everyone.* I don't care how great or altruistic or insanely talented a person is, there is something (or, if we're being honest here, some *things*) absolutely ridiculous that they do, think, feel, or say. Repeat after me: No one on this planet can completely rid themselves of their trash ways. Meaning you, me, your parents, the local nun, J. R. R. Tolkien, Selena (both Quintanilla-Pérez and Gomez), Langston Hughes, your auntie, all your cousins (but you already knew that tho), the entire bobsled team from *Cool Runnings*, the lunch waitstaff at Mae Mae Café who told me after I asked for the egg on my avocado toast to be scrambled instead of fried that they can only scramble eggs in the morning (so ig), Galileo Galilei, your boyfriend or girlfriend/husband or wife/side pieces obvs, manufacturers who make it impossible to open scissors packages unless you already own a pair of scissors, Lucy Liu, the movie *To Wong Foo, Thanks for Everything! Julie Newmar* (J/K, it is the most perfect movie that ever movied), poet Gwendolyn Brooks, Martin Luther King Jr., and the founder of the St. Jude Children's Research Hospital (we don't know their life). All of them have been low-key trash from time to time. Period. End of subject. No rebuttal required.

At this point, you're probably wondering, "Um, great . . . is that it? Everyone sucks or has tons of moments of suckery? Where's the moment of hope, the 'But It's Okay' that's in the book title? You know, something *positive*?" Right, right, right. Well, here's the thing. I think admitting to our "trashery" *is* a positive because it helps us see ourselves more clearly and makes it a *liiiittle* bit easier to deal with the Major Trash that's the world right now.

In summation: We have a president who proclaims that women need to dress like "women," meaning dressing for the visual consumption of straight dudes; who behaves as though all African-Americans live in the inner city; who endorsed Republican and alleged child molester Roy Moore during his 2017 campaign to become Alabama's newest senator; and who emboldened neo-Nazis to be out, loud, and proud in a way these groups haven't been in quite some time in America. The CDC aka the Centers for Disease Control and Prevention recently revealed that drug overdoses involving heroin tripled from 2010 to 2015. The latest version of North Carolina's bathroom bill completely fails to address which bathrooms trans people can use, thus making it impossible for them to feel safe using public restrooms. The Program for International Student Assessment (PISA), which measures skill levels in reading, math, and science every three years among fifteen-year-olds from dozens of developed and developing nations, has, as of 2015, concluded that the US placed fortieth out of seventy-one countries in math and twenty-fifth in science. Women's reproductive rights are still a contentious battle, as documented by that 2017 viral pic of Vice President Mike Pence and a sea of dusty-ass, evil-ass, and old-ass white dudes discussing whether maternity care should be covered by insurance companies. Jobs for blue-collar workers are drying up and have been for a long time, and some of us (myself included) have unfairly ignored this problem for far too long. According to the Center for American Progress Action Fund, one-third of Congress (182 politicians, to be exact) are climate change deniers, including Senate Majority Leader Mitch McConnell and Senator Marco Rubio; meanwhile, the Honey Nut Cheerios bee is like, "Every day, I'm legit buzzing the Bone Thugs-N-Harmony 'Tha Crossroads' melody because my family is dying thanks to humans, but a'ight, keep pretending Earth isn't on life support." And the list goes on and on. I don't know about you, but I find this amount of mess to be overwhelming and depressing AF.

Still, not all is lost. Far from it. For starters, all we need to do is look at history and remember that if humanity could survive the worst atrocities—famine, slavery, the Holocaust, natural disasters, corrupt political systems, inequality, Christopher Columbus, etc.—and still be here, then there's hope. We are stronger, smarter, and braver than we realize, and when we're deep in the weeds, we can override our trash instincts and help advance society further. And even in those moments when it appears that we've made less than honorable decisions (ahem, the election of Donald Drumpf), the pushback (the 2017 Women's March) has, time and time again, served as a reminder that everything will be okay. OKAY. I know that folks who live in the middle-class-and-above luxury of America and other first world countries and whose daily diet includes therapy and self-help books (I myself *love* me a good self-help book) and who have been raised on the notion of "living your best life" like Oprah has taught us might view the word "okay" as not promising. But life is fucking hard. Extremely hard for most. And that's why, to me, "okay" is not a state of settling (aka ordering Sprite at Wahlburgers, but all they have is Fresca and you're like, "Sure, I guess"—see also: dining at Wahlburgers in the first place); "okay" is a state of acceptance and then pushing forward (aka coming to terms with the fact that you were sober when eating at Wahlburgers, analyzing everything in your life that led up to that moment, and thinking to yourself, *I'm going back to school, I'm joining a gym, I'm completing my Alicia Keys music catalogue once and for all*, or whatever gets you back on the right track in life). In all seriousness, to me, waking up every day and not only contending with our baser instincts but also dealing with the multitude of curveballs that life throws our way and coming out the other side, perhaps a little dinged up but tougher and smarter and ultimately okay, is good. In fact, okay is great. Better yet, okay is for closers.

And I don't know about you, but I consider myself a closer. I've successfully talked (in Barack Obama's hypercorrect pronunciation) a karaoke staff into letting my friends and I have an extra half hour so we can do our rendition of Biggie's "Hypnotize"; I've gotten free Wi-Fi at a swanky hotel just because I treated the employees like humans and not indentured servants; and on more than one occasion, I've made a sick day 1000 percent more bearable by lunging to my Spectrum remote in time to press the start over button before the option went away so I could watch old reruns of *America's Next Top Model* from the beginning. To put this in perspective, I've never seen *Schindler's List*, but I've devoured seas three of *ANTM* no less than eight times. If my eyeballs could #Unsubscribe from my body, they would. In all seriousness, I know how to get ish done and motherfreakin' close. I'm sure you have your own coming-through-in-a-clutch moments that you use to remind yourself of your awesomeness. I'm also sure that you're nowhere near done closing on the regs, nor finished with the everlasting journey of accepting and dealing with your own trash as well as others'. I know I'm not.

I'm still battling self-doubt, trifling dudes, sexism in the workplace, people who hold up the line because they take forever to figure out what kind of latte they want, internet trolls, the barrage of depressing political news, homophobia and transphobia my friends and strangers are on the receiving end of, and the fact that I believe that "showering on the weekends should be optional AF for single people" falls under the umbrella of "civil liberties." Clearly there's so. Much. Trash. To. Contend. With. But all of it takes a back seat to the biggest problem of the day: getting this book into Viola Davis's hands so she'll read it and want to meet me. All right, all right, I should have written "the biggest problem of *my* day." Oops. But also I'm medium-key garbage, so you should've expected that I would pull some monkey mess like this.

Anyway. Why Viola Davis? Well, she's an acting genius, insanely gorgeous, and I love her. But my mom, Octavia? She *loves* her. I can't blame her. My mom is also a badass, so this is merely real recognizing real. And because my career in entertainment as a podcast queen, writer, and performer has taken off since I started ten years ago, I occasionally brush shoulders with the A-list. As a result, my mom has only one thing on her mind. Her Hoda Kotb–esque follow-up query to whatever career news I share is forever "Have you met Viola Davis yet?"

This is one of my favorite things about black parents, besides watching them cuss out their kids in public and witnessing the resulting fallout on their child's face. (Truly, getting read to filth in a Burlington Coat Factory will really make you have a mini existential crisis.) But getting back to my original point: Black parents typically have five to seven celebrities that they are impressed with—and this roster of celebs will never ever change, mind you, for as long as the parents live—and all the other famous people? The. Parentals. Could. Not. Give. Less. Of. A. Fuck. About.

Exhibits A to D of My Mom's Not-Giving-a-Fuckness

A. I worked with Kevin Bacon on the Amazon show *I Love Dick*, and by "worked with," I mean I had one scene with him where his character said two words to me and I tried not to vomit, smile hugely, or blurt out, "MOTHERFUCKING *FOOTLOOSE* IS TALK-ING TO ME!" I told my mom about being on set with K. Bake and she didn't care.

B. Jon Hamm, who is in the running to be America's Next Top Zaddy,[3] did the *2 Dope Queens* podcast I have with Jessica Williams, and he and I crowd-surfed while *holding hands* like this was the fucking end of *My Big Fat Greek Wedding*, *Sex and the City*, and *Roots* all rolled into one. I texted video proof of this sexcellent moment to my mom. No gahtdamn reply. A month later, I worked an event Jon attended

---

3. For the uninitiated, a "zaddy" is DILF-y but isn't necessarily a dad. I'm talking about your Idris Elbas (a dad), your Chris Pines (not a dad), your Jason Momoas (a dad), your Kit Haringtons (not a dad), and so on. Okay, now that I write this out, I see that a "zaddy" is basically any guy over thirty who's hot. And we already have a term for that: "hot." But my hunch is "zaddy" came about because there are folks, myself included, who don't like calling men "Daddy" in a sexual manner, so a "z" was slapped on as a replacement to make things better, kind of like when Michelle Williams replaced LaTavia Roberson and LeToya Luckett in Destiny's Child or the creation of Smartfood Delight, which is allegedly a healthier version of Smartfood popcorn that somehow tastes just as good. #LolForever #FakeNews

and chatted with him briefly. I mentioned this to Octavia, and she goes, "By any chance, did you bump into Viola Davis?"

C. I recently had the extreme privilege and pleasure of interviewing Tom Hanks for my *other* podcast, an interview talk show called *Sooo Many White Guys*, and he was a good sport and recorded the outgoing message on my voicemail. My mom's response? "But what about Viola Davis?"

D. I was a guest on a talk show to promote my previous book, and my parents flew out to attend the taping. Before we arrived to set, I was gabbing with the parental units about dream run-ins at the show and I said, "It'd be insane if Beyoncé was here. I mean, she never does TV, but it would be cool to be in the same building as her." My mom responded, "I wouldn't even say hi to her."

You did not misread. Octavia Robinson's reaction to Beyoncé Giselle Knowles-Carter is not an ugly-cry nor a squeal nor to ask for a picture. My mom's instinct is to ignore her like the two of them are a WASP couple midargument on *Big Little Lies*: just nothing but chunky knits and silent rage.

To be clear, there is no backstory. It's not like Yoncé and my mom were at Trader Joe's one time and Bey snagged the last Amy's Thai Red Curry frozen meal. Nor did Beyoncé cut her in line at

Starbucks and pretend like she didn't feel my mom staring her the hell down. And finally, no, it's not like Beyoncé and my mom are in the same baking club and B showed up with some dope-looking pies and casually said, "Oh, yeah, it's this new recipe my friend Patti let me borrow," and locked eyes with my mom real hard on the "my friend Patti" line to make it clear she's talking about Patti LaBelle, my mom's all-time favorite singer. And once everyone else in the club finished oohing and aahing at the pies, my mom showed her dessert, which was vegan oatmeal raisin bars, and she was met with some weak encouragement like she's on *Family Feud* and just gave an asinine answer.

My mom and Beyoncé have never met. There is no rivalry. It's just that Queen Bey did not make the cut of celebrities that my mom gives an eff about. So who did make the cut? Oprah, Barack Obama and Michelle Obama, Bruce Willis, The Rock, Patti LaBelle, and, of course, Viola Davis. So, dear reader, how about we make a deal? Throughout this book, let's acknowledge all the trash that's surrounding us (literal litter and also the state of American politics) and accept the trashery within ourselves that we cannot change (the way I eat chips, you would think a Sonos surround-sound system was installed in my molars) while fixing the garbage that can and should be changed (e.g., FaceTiming in public without headphones on so everyone can hear your friend regaling you with a story about her noisy neighbors like it's a Greek tragedy), *and* then please put in your prayer requests that I meet Viola Davis or, better yet, my mom and I meet Viola Davis together. In the meantime, let's do a search to unearth more Justin-Trudeau-looking-fondly-at-Barack-Obama pics because that ish is #Goals for whomever I marry. Sure, compatibility, sharing same values, attraction, and emotionally and financially supporting each other matters greatly in a marriage, blah, blah, blah. Whatever. If my future husb looks at me the way Trudeau stays looking at Obama, we won't have any problems. If not, there will be some dreadheaded n***** in the lobby, waiting on bae. #ChanceTheRapper-Reference.

I Was a Size 12 Once for Like Twenty-Seven Minutes

Since I was fourteen, my brain has been consumed with all the ways my body is not good enough, meaning not attractive to straight dudes and/or failing to meet fashion-industry standards. Even now, at thirty-four, and with a deeper understanding of how we've been conditioned to have unhealthy relationships with our bodies, I still remember what I weighed eight years ago as if that's important information. If you were to throw out a year at me, I could, without fail, tell you what size I wore. Ugh. Every day, I struggle not only with rewiring my brain to not equate self-worth with how my body looks but also with not letting men and clothing companies define my own gaze. But because the ole noggin has been busy accruing its ten thousand hours and then some in mentally Hadoukening me via negging about my physical appearance, there's so much knowledge I don't possess, and in its place a big chunk is dedicated to straight-male societal approval, but more on that later. First, I have to address the lack of information in my brain.

Remember when Mariah Carey shaded Jennifer Lopez with the now legendary "I don't know her" comment when we all know these beige beauties are on a first-, middle-, and last-name basis? Well, that's my response to everyday stuff because I (black-girl-in-an-argument hand-clap) literally (black-girl-in-an-argument hand-clap) don't (black-girl-in-an-argument hand-clap) know (black-girl-in-an-argument hand-clap) shit (black-girl-in-an-argument hand-clap): The metric system? I don't know her. Thirty-three percent of the names of former US presidents? I don't know her. Is saying "Candyman" five times in the mirror with the lights turned off just a ruse to scare the chillrens, or is it real AF? I don't know her, and I damn sure ain't going to test her, because living is one of my top three favorite things to do. What are the other two? Glad you asked: texting friends pictures of U2 and hanging with my niece and nephew. Anyway, as I was saying, women are conditioned to waste hours, days, weeks, months (although, truth be told, it's most likely years) doubting, undermining, and ultimately hating parts, if not all, of themselves based solely on "problems" with their bodies that can be solved by buying products from an industry that invented these problems in the first place. How fucking convenient. And when all is said and done, what is the prize for this self-torture? Fitting neatly within society's destructive narrative about the female body. Hmm, I don't know about you, but this endeavor seems like my checking account after I pay rent aka it's empty as hell. Yet here most women are with very complicated, time-consuming, and counterproductive relationships with their bodies, which helps explain why, at times, especially for me, straight men's opinions about us seem to matter as much as, if not more than, our own. Ooof. That last bit might be a tad scary to own up to, but it has certainly been true for me in the past.

Even though I'm a proud AF feminist who was raised by two super badass, intelligent, and fiercely independent parental units, I would be a liar if I didn't admit that, for many years, I used to watch *Bridget Jones's Diary*, in particular the scene where Mark Darcy tells the charmingly hot mess Bridget, "I like you very much, just as you are," the way LeBron James watches game tape. Just pressing rewind, marking X's and O's, and figuring out how to get the desired result of some dude thinking I'm so perfect that the way he sees me changes the way I see myself. Thankfully, I don't feel that way anymore. However, that's not going to stop me from telling you the closest I ever came to a Darcy/Jones moment IRL.

One night, I was platonically dining with one of my agents and explaining how I wanted to drop ten pounds before doing some on-camera work. He responded, "You're beautiful the way you are." Now Old Pheebs would've dined on this compliment for weeks—nay, months!—like when Thanksgiving has come and gone, yet your parents are still making you dry-ass turkey sandwiches as your school lunch even though it's Groundhog Day. But New Pheebs? New Pheebs is like, "Uh, duh, of course I'm beautiful, but also, like, I pay you 10 percent, so I cannot trust you." This is not to say my agent is not a great guy; he is top-notch and probably meant what he said to the max, but he also ain't trying to fuck up his direct deposits, so he couldn't really say anything to me that doesn't sound like a Bruno Mars lyric. The only difference is I was at a point in my life where I didn't care whether he, or any other dude for that matter, felt positively or negatively about my looks. All that mattered was how I felt. I wish I could say this shift in my thinking happened a while ago—it's only been a few months; thanks self-help books!—but my confidence made it seem like years, right? Well, it doesn't matter how new this confidence is; I'm simply thrilled that this next level of self-acceptance is here, so yay! But also snooze, because this'll make for a boring essay if I don't take a stretch-the-old-hamstrings break during this victory lap and go back to a time when, unfortunately, outside opinions mattered too much.

The year was 2010. Wait. To fully enjoy this story even though I'm not in the room with you, open a bottle of wine, get yourself in a 2010 kind of mood, and cue up "Empire State of Mind." Great. Ready?

The year was 2010, and this was me in a nutshell: almost twenty-six years old, had been doing stand-up for two years, lived by myself, had a decent day job as an office assistant to a couple of entertainment lawyers, and was hella single and could not understand why. Of course, now I do. I regularly wore a pair of square-toed Nine West pumps (stage whisper: I had no swag), I was still exclusively drinking whiskey sours and thinking that made me cool (normal whisper: I had no swag), and when I wasn't doing stand-up, I spent many nights watching "diet woke"[1] TV like John Quiñones's *What Would You Do?* (for the person looking over your shoulder while you're reading this in public: I HAD NO GAHTDAMN SWAG!). In fact, I literally just got swag about one summer solstice ago and I'm certain I just lost it because I measure time in solstices. But for real, who are these people who have swag in their twenties? Or in their teens? I'm talking about teens like the singer Monica.

She was young as hell when she sang about not messing with you romantically, spiritually, or emotionally while on her period in "Don't Take It Personal (Just One of Dem Days)" over a fire beat that had grown-ass women and men bumping it in their cars. Not only that, but It. Was. Her. Debut. Song. That's right: Monica Denise Arnold was out there in those streets from the beginning, standing in her truth in the Always Infinity with Wings aisle. And the pièce de résistance? She was only fourteen when she did all of this. When I was fourteen and had my period, I'd quickly and not so discreetly wrap a zip-up Eddie Bauer fleece around my waist after bleeding through my pants at school, and when anyone would ask me why I did that, I'd just say, "DON'T WORRY ABOUT IT!"

---

1. Yes, "woke" is omnipresent thanks to exemplary people such as Black Lives Matter and LGBTQIA+ activists working to make the world better, but there's a subset of wokeness that's not talked about as much—"diet woke." A d-dubs person is usually #TeamDoGooder in the sheets (thanks, social media warriors) and #TeamThisIsGonnaInconvenienceALittleBit #HmmLemmeGetBackToYou in the streets. Sometimes this dichotomy exists because people are simply getting through the day or they're multilayered and live in contradictory ways or they're lazy AF, like I can be sometimes. For instance, I'm anti-misogyny, but that hasn't stopped me in the past from basically busting out a rhythmic gymnastics routine complete with ribbon work when Jay-Z's "Big Pimpin'" comes on.

Anyway, after listening to me complain about being single, my mom suggested I try Match.com since the company I worked for owned it, meaning I could probably join without having to pay for a membership. Which, if I remember correctly, I did, so yaaas Gaga for free shit. I wrote my bio with the help of my friends, uploaded a bunch of pics, including my singular "hot" photo (me with a baby fro, wearing jeans and a vest, with a hot-pink hand-me-down Joe Boxer T-shirt underneath) that I'm sure dudes read less as hot and more as "tech avail[2] for background work in a Subaru commercial," and I set about finding myself a boyfriend to prove to myself that I was attractive because I was lovable and lovable because someone found me attractive. To be honest, my time on Match is mostly a blur to me as I was a member eight years ago, but there is one guy—let's call him Eric—who I remember vividly, the way you recall a particularly gnarly episode of food poisoning.

Eric was a teacher who lived in Philly. He was cute, seemed kind, and laughed at my jokes when we flirted on Match.com. After a few days, we eventually escalated to Gchatting frequently throughout the day, which is code for "I like you more than I like doing my work, which I need in order to keep my dental plan." #CurseOfPotentialNewPeenOrVajeen. We upgraded to phone calls, and then he said that magical sentence:

---

2. For non-Hollywood peeps, "tech avail" describes an actor/director/writer/etc. who would do a project if nothing more appealing comes through. I now apply this phrase to all facets of my life. Want to have brunch with a bunch of married couples at 11:45 A.M. aka early-as-fuck o'clock? *Tech avail.* In Pilates class when the instructor wants me to do eight more seconds of the Hundred? *Tech avail.* When checking out the $600 worth of clothes I have in my shopping cart on FreePeople.com, which is full of things I don't need, and the website asks if I can pay the balance in full? *I'm tech avail if U2 tickets don't go on sale on Ticketmaster on Friday.*

"I want to come to NYC so we can go on a date." Cue the confetti, lift my ass in the air the way Johnny Castle did Baby at the end of *Dirty Dancing*, and then let's go to the DMV so I can combine our last names with a hyphen. What I'm getting at here is that your girl, up until her last breakup, had a penchant for not only putting all her eggs in one basket at the first sign of interest from a dude, but chopping down the bamboo stalk, stripping it, weaving it into a basket shape, shellacking it, and outfitting it with crinkle-cut decorative filler paper, marshmallow Peeps, and Cadbury eggs. I had zero chill and held the secret hope that every potential suitor was going to turn out to be "the One." I blame romantic comedies and society (but not my parents!) for conditioning every straight woman to approach dating like it's a Black Friday sale at Century 21 while straight dudes are taught to be as relaxed as a black woman's hair during a 1960s Civil Rights march.

Anyway, Eric made plans, and I made sure to tell a couple of my besties, Karen and Jamie, about this upcoming date just on the off chance that if I went missing, they could do their low-budget Nancy Grace investigation into my disappearance and by "low-budget Nancy Grace investigation," I mean they would just call the police because they are an interior designer and an actress/comedian. The point is, my friends were on "Don't Let Phoebe Die" duty; meanwhile, I didn't tell my parents about this date because I didn't want to jinx the situation—if things didn't work out with Eric, Ma and Pa Robinson wouldn't have had to worry about adjusting Christmas dinner recipes to account for one less portion. #JokesNotJokes. I got ready for the date and met Eric in the city. He was just as cute as in his photos, and he picked a delightful restaurant for dinner. The chemistry was there, the food was great, and the conversation was fantastic. Well, mostly.

At one point, we were talking about stand-up, and he said something to the effect of "I don't think that many female comedians are funny, but you're really funny." If a dude were to say that to me now, on a date or otherwise, I would politely ask him to do humanity a favor and swan-dive down an empty elevator shaft into the seventeenth circle of hell aka Shaquille O'Neal's bare feet (Google that shit—it will make you want to get right with whatever God you believe in). But that's New Pheebs. Old Pheebs was knee-deep in the innocence of youth and open to teaching a sexist dude in the hopes that my bootleg and on-the-fly "Don't Have Turds for Brains/Women Are Awesome, Obviously" course was going to make him less a ding-dong and more husband material. I remained on the date, willing to overlook this red flag. The rest of the conversation was fun and free-flowing. He paid for dinner, we went for a stroll, and I suggested we hang out my place to watch a movie with the hope that we would make out with our tops off like Felicity was prone to do on season one of the show.

We arrived at my adorable one-bedroom Brooklyn apartment. It was minimally decorated with a bedroom set from Macy's and approximately 17,000 DVDs. You see, I was a movie and TV nerd, so I most definitely needed all six seasons of the ahead-of-its-time HBO prison series *Oz* and not a coatrack. #Priorities. So Eric and I chatted for a little bit and then decided to watch the 2005 comedy *Wedding Crashers*. Let's take a moment because I need to drag both of us for this foolish choice. I had 36,000 DVDs for us to choose between, ranging from cutesy (*Brown Sugar*), scary enough to make us cuddle close together but not enough to ruin romantic vibes (*The Ring*), and vintage sexiness with high drama (*Carmen Jones*), and we. Both. Still. Chose. *Wedding Crashers.* That'd be like getting ready to fight any of the X-Men by choosing from myriad superhero powers including invisibility, telepathy, and weather modification and instead going, "I think I'll use this dusty-ass musket that takes seven minutes to reload and was last used during the Civil War." Completely stupid, right? Sure, but ya know what? Eric and I still ended up making out, so I guess watching peak Owen Wilson and Vince Vaughn is enough to get my motor running, which is something I can't unlearn about myself. Derp.

At this point, I will fast-forward through details because (1) my parents are reading this, (2) from what I've heard, erotic novels describe hetero sex with a lot of nauseating descriptors, such as "her center," "flesh mound," and "the heart of her femininity," and so on, and I don't want to put you, dear reader, through that, and most importantly, (3) it's what happened after sexy times that matters.

Eric and I returned from the Bone Zone and chilled in my bedroom, surrounded by 45,000 DVDs and the faint sounds of *Wedding Crashers* dialogue in the background. We drank some water and engaged in some casual small talk while cuddling. A couple of beats of silence and then homeboy started up with a quasi-serious tone that Boyz II Men's Michael McCary had when he would drop his patented monologue during "End of the Road." Eric began, "Ya know . . ."

RECORD SCRATCH! Let's pause for a sec. If you're post-coi-coi aka post-coitus with someone and s/he starts a somber-sounding sentence with "Ya know . . . ," please understand that what follows will not be ". . . I think we should be exclusive," or ". . . Leah Remini deserves a Purple Heart and a lifetime supply of agave syrup for all the tea she spilled in her Scientology docuseries," or ". . . hotels should stop only putting grilled cheese sandwiches on the kids' menu. It's not a kids' food, but pure joy to be enjoyed by anyone." Instead, what's coming around the mountain, here she comes, will be such an outrageous pile of garbage that it will make Oscar the Grouch be like, "Lemme hit up my real estate agent and see if I can put a bid on this place."

Eric began, "Ya know . . ."

And then I began cautiously, "Uh-huh?"

". . . there are exercises that you can do to tone up your thighs."

NOOOOOOOOOOOOOOOOOOOOOOOOOOOOOOOOOOOOO OOOOOOOOOOOOOOOOOOOOOPE.

JUST FUCKING NOOOOOOOOOOOOOOOOOOOOOOPE!

Y'all, this the biggest nope I done noped in my entire life. Bigger than the nope I feel when I see a grown-ass dude wearing Crocs with socks. Bigger than the nope when my iPhone goes from 40 percent to 12 percent all because I played the game Two Dots for approximately three and a half minutes. And bigger than the nope I screamed when a pigeon drive-by-pooped on my arm and friends told me that means good luck. Sorry, but if birds messily taking dumps on me the way a pastry chef tries to finish icing a cake with three seconds remaining on a

MasterChef challenge is supposed to signal something good is coming my way, well, let me go on record stating that I would rather have a mediocre life with C-plus peen and C-minus cuisine. Anyway, Eric telling me, mere seconds after sex, that my thighs are subpar def belongs in the Nope Hall of Fame, but in that moment, I didn't have the strength or self-love to yell out a "Nope" or kick him out of my apartment.

Instead, I was stone silent, which he didn't realize was because he had deeply hurt my feelings. He wrongly assumed my silence meant, "Oh, really? Golly gee, let me pull out a tape recorder and notepad like I'm Peter Parker taking copious notes for my front-page story for the *Bugle*."

He continued: "Yeah, you could be more toned, but no worries, you don't need to lose weight. This is an easy fix."

Bitch, I wasn't worried. And unless your name is Bobby McFerrin, singer of "Don't Worry, Be Happy," don't you ever in your life insult my body and then drop a dollop of "no worries" on top like it's Cool Whip on a slice of peach cobbler. Besides, my thighs don't need fixing because they're not a problem to begin with! They're two cocoa-colored powerhouses that are strong enough for my niece to climb and hang from, yet tender and delectable enough to be the star of a six-piece drumstick box (no coleslaw, but double the mac and cheese, duh!) from KFC. So, if anything, you should be grateful AF that this Blackleesi even said yes to the sex with you.

Okay. Okay. I didn't actually say any of the above to Eric either, because when I was younger and someone was dragging with me to filth, my reaction time was that of Bobby Riggs when he played Billie Jean King in the Battle of the Sexes tennis match aka I was slow as hell. So instead of defending myself, I just savasana'd my behind in my bed, mentally reciting the Papa Roach mantra I use whenever I'm met with even the slightest of life's inconveniences: "Cut my life into pieces! / This is my last resort." And before I could collect my thoughts and respond to anything he said, the idiot JUMPED OUT OF BED, THREW ON HIS UNDERWEAR, AND LITERALLY DEMON-STRATED A SERIES OF EXERCISES I COULD DO TO, in his words, "MAKE YOUR BODY BETTER." If you made WhatDa-Fuq.Huh.co.uk the home browser on your computer, then you, indeed, reacted correctly to this trash pile demonstrating lunges, squats, and reverse lunges approximately none point none seconds after sexy times. And with that, let's add "telling someone the 'flaws' about their body that need 'fixing'" to the list of things you don't ever say or do to someone immediately after sex, which includes:

- "I killed a guy."
- "Train is my favorite band."

Annnnnnnnnnnnnnnnnnd THAT'S IT! Just three very sim-ple things to avoid upon exiting the Bone Zone.

All kidding aside, it seems after doing an informal survey with my straight girlfriends, the whole negging post-coit is commonplace. Some have been told they get "too wet" down there, take too long to come, are not thin enough to date pub-licly but are good enough for "sex on the DL," and one buddy of mine, who is not particularly into period sex but decided to go for it with encouragement from a guy she was dating, was told by him MIDSEX that he didn't really enjoy the way her vagina smelled while she was on her period. Are. You. Fucking. Kidding. Me?!

Unfortunately, women are all too familiar with this type of gross body-shaming; furthermore, it is behavior that, for far too long, some men have thought is perfectly acceptable. But before I get into how society has conditioned men to express all opinions, especially the hurtful ones, about women *to* women, let's return to #Thighgate2010, because every lady I know—whether she is gay, straight, or anywhere on the sexuality spectrum—has self-esteem issues in part due to outside sources like Eric. And us women all respond differently. Some do work out more. Or eat more. Or starve. Or feel unworthy. Or do the thing that I used to do, which I never, ever will again: mentally try to prove to him as well as to myself why my body and, to a lesser degree, why I, was good enough.

While this impromptu Legs by Eric demonstration continued, I got my Sarah Huckabee Sanders on, defending myself to myself. I went through the stats: I'm five foot seven, weigh probably 120, 125 pounds, am a size 6 in H&M clothing, which translates to "LOL. WUT?," and I can mostly eat what I want, in moderation, and not worry about too much weight gain. I know. I know. That is some cringe-y trash, because even at twenty-five, knowing how pervasive society's toxic beauty standards are, deep down those are the ones I was still measuring myself against to ensure I was "good." This iffy relationship with my body began when I hit puberty, but by my late teens, the relaysh had officially become complicated.

When I was in college, I was a size 0. I know, I know, woe is fucking me. But I was very flat-chested, had no hips, butt, or thighs; in fact, there were no curves to be found anywhere. Basically, I looked like one of those paper-thin, rectangular general-admish signs on day three of Coachella that have been abused by every breeze, burp, fart, and queef that had blown their way in the past seventy-two hours. In short, it was not my best look, and I was hella insecure about it. And it certainly didn't help when one of my college buddies explained I only got hit on by closeted gay men because my boyish figure was unattractive to straight guys. Talk about the call coming from inside the house! Better yet, this call was coming from inside my bedroom closet while I was reaching for my Aldo shoes. Who needs enemies when there are friends straight up willing to pinprick the tiny-ass ego balloon I had to begin with? Still, I hoped, in vain, that my insecurity would lessen as I began to fill out. But nope! Turns out I wasn't filling out properly.

By junior year of college, I had joined my school's improv team, developed a pretty banging social life that offset how much I was watching *Oprah* alone in my dorm room,[3] and happily put on some pounds. One weekend, a group of us improvisers were hanging out when one of the dudes I was chatting with took one look at my thighs (I was sitting down, and my thigh meat spread a bit as thigh meat is wont to do) and said, as

---

3. I would race home from class to watch Queen O, and one of the episodes that stuck with me is from 2005, when Tom Cruise repeatedly jumped on Oprah's couch and shook her and punched the floor and air, all to express his "love" for Katie Holmes. And we all kind of lol'd and were like, "He's an actor, so he's just being over the top," and then six months later, Tom Cruise continued doing the most and we were all like that GIF of Homer Simpson disappearing into that green hedge due to secondhand embarrassment. Well, I was a virgin at the time and thought to myself, *If this is what sex on the regs does to people, I think I'm okay with my vajeen being vacuum-sealed for life like a package of Sahale Snacks Honey Almonds Glazed Mix.*

a "joke," "I would never date a girl whose thighs spread when she sat down." Yeeeeeeeeah. As I'm sure we can all assume from my lack of response to Eric, I didn't say anything to this improviser either, but I will now.

Actually, this is not just for the improviser, but for all members of the sauseege party, so take note, mofos: This whole "one of the guys" concept of busting chops for funsies needs to die off like the evil twin on a soap opera. Why? Because some guys think it gives them license to just outright insult women's bodies, looks, intelligence, etc., as in, "I thought you were cool and one of the guys where I could say mean stuff to you, and you would take it as a joke because you're not like other girls and being 'not like other girls' is aspirational, or haven't you heard?" No. No more of that. If you want to be an asshole, then be an asshole instead of pretending women not being super down to be your punching bag means they don't know what real friendship is or, worse yet, implying that it's aspirational to reject whatever society has deemed unacceptable characteristics in women (feelings) in exchange for mimicking toxic male behavior (being a dick due to own lack of self-esteem). It's not OKAY, men. It's also not cool when clothing companies and stylists tag dudes out and take over reminding me of my body's supposed inadequacies as they did the day I discovered I was a size 12.[4]

---

4. I understand that for plenty of women being a size 12, 14, 16, and higher is not a new-normal kind of sitch for them, but an ongoing reality. But I'm now going to be writing from the experience of someone who started out their adult life as a size 0 and now waffles between a 10 and a 12. And no matter what size you are, I think we can all agree that if you've put on weight without necessarily clocking how much until the wear and tear of your thighs rubbing together has ruined your *third* pair of pants, then, in the moment, that shit can feel like a "Holy crap, e *does* = mc²" discovery. #DisrespectfulToAlbertEinstein.

IDK about you, but whenever I go back home to visit my family, I automatically get into Operation Stuntin' on These Heauxes, but it's just my parents, who gave me life; my brother, who supports me; and my sister-in-life, who is pretty chill and definitely not a heaux, so I guess it's more Operation Dressing Well Enough to Snag Myself a Divorced Dad at a Journey Concert. Whatever the case may be, when I visit my fam, I want to dress to impress, in hopes that my outfits convey the message that I'm doing more than all right in the Big Apple. And December 2016 was no different. I was fresh off the book tour for my first essay collection and had just completed minor on-camera work on a TV show, and with my Christmas trip right around the corner, I needed some new threads because I had been so busy working that I hadn't been shopping in months and OH, YEAH, THAT TELEVISION SHOW THAT I MENTIONED? DURING DOWNTIME BETWEEN SHOOTING SCENES, I SPLIT THE SEAM THAT WENT DOWN THE BUTT CRACK OF A VINTAGE JUMPSUIT AND HAD TO SHOOT THE REST OF THE DAY WITH THE FLAPS OF SAID JUMPSUIT FEELING LIKE SALOON DOORS SWINGING IN THE WIND ON WESTWORLD. For the first time in my life, I had ripped a pair of pants simply from bending over, and I assumed the clothes had magically shrunk instead of the obvious truth: I had put on some weight. Unfortunately, the realization that I was a size 12 wouldn't come until the shopping spree I went on before my Christmas trip in 2016.

I went to one of my favorite stores, Zar Zar Binks. For a person like me, Zara is amazing because it allows me to feel like what I think being European is like (eating buttery pastries, riding Vespas, loving Dame Judi Dench the way black Americans love Smokey Robinson, ending bitchy statements with the question "isn't it?" and no one calling you out for that, etc.) without actually doing the nonfrivolous things that Europeans do, like knowing two or more different languages, understanding degrees in Celsius, and not eating trash-ass baguettes and croissants from Au Bon Pain because French people def don't touch the stuff. Anyway, Zara is the jam, and the clothes are reasonably priced, so there was no reason why Operation Dressing Well Enough to Snag Myself a Divorced Dad at a Journey Concert wouldn't go off without a hitch. After all, about eight months after the Spanx snafu (more on that later), I was less sedentary and eating healthier just to have enough energy to handle my growing schedule, and ultimately, I lost weight and dropped down to a size 8. However, by Christmastime, I had put the pounds back on and then some as evidenced by the ripped jumpsuit. Still, I didn't register the weight gain, and while looking through the jeans pile in Zara, I grabbed a few 8s and headed into the changing room. I couldn't pull them up past my thighs, which I chalked up to maybe just being bloated from too much LaCroix. #NotARealThing. So I went back to the showroom and snagged some 10s. And, derp, I couldn't zip them up, so I had that Julia Roberts moment in *Eat Pray Love* where she is on the dressing room floor, cackling because she's having the gahtdamn time of her life in Italy, eating pasta, and oops! She put on weight and can't fit into pants, but it's all good because by the end of the movie, she's smashing Javier Bardem and wearing bejeweled tunics from Chico's. Except there was no Javier Bardem in my life, I hadn't had pasta in months, I was not in Italy but in SoHo during rush hour, with a line of impatient women behind me, and I was most definitely not laughing. I was pissed. What the hell was going on with these jeans and why were none of them fitting?! Once again, I exited the changing room and grabbed the next largest size, which also happened to be, as I later learned, the biggest size Zara goes up to—a 12 aka an XXL—which I was certain was going to be too big. But when I returned to the dressing room and pulled up those jeans, I was shocked not only to find that they *barely* fit but that I was rocking a fupa.

Sure, part of the shock was due to the fact that I had my very first fupa. And it's not like anyone warns you that it's coming. Life gets in the way: You're busy working, making plans with family, paying bills, visiting friends, dating, and you wake up one morning and realize that you have way more cushion for the pushin' than you realized. That's a mini annoyance, but the bigger frustration about becoming a pear shape aka small on top (34A) and bigger on bottom (soft and cute belly, fuller hips, thick thighs and booty) and reaching size 12 status was everything below my waist was officially damn near too big to fit into clothes at places like Zar Zar Binks. Sorry, but so many amazing things come in twelves: roses, eggs, cupcakes, the "Twelve Days of Christmas" song, the A.M. and P.M. hours, doughnuts, oysters . . . All right, so it's mostly food, but you get the idea. Twelve is a great number, but I had trouble finding clothes in that size. I thought and hoped it would be different if I had the help of stylists. I was (mostly) wrong.

Before I go any further, I will state that I've had the pleasure of working with a Blue Ivy–sized handful of amazing, talented, and body-conscious stylists (whaddup, Katya!—you're my fave!). As for the majority? It has been mostly a disaster. Whatever pieces of self-esteem I had walking into a photo shoot tended to be massacred the moment I tried on the clothes that were picked out for me. Yes, I understand that dressing someone for a magazine shoot is not easy. Stylists often have to work in tandem with the magazine, photographer, makeup artist, and hairstylist to create a unified vision. Also, stylists want to create the perfect outfit that not only matches the subject's personality and fashion tastes but also elevates it, so that the picture will grab readers' attention while they flip through a magazine. Plus, stylists tend to work with a limited budget and time window to get the clothing, and like with a lot of creative industries, the stylists sometimes don't get paid; the paycheck is being featured in the magazine. Not to mention the fact that the fashion industry is incredibly sizeist, so plenty of designers don't make clothes above a size 8. That's a lot for a stylist to contend with, but that's no excuse. There are designers and/or clothing lines that cater to a wider range of body types. These brands may not be the coolest, but they're out there and should be used as much as the same batch of household names many stylists and magazines rely on. But these clothing lines remain underused, so here I am with an all-too-familiar situation of a disaster fitting, which admittedly is the definition of a champagne problem.

Being body-shamed at an all-expenses-paid-for photo shoot is certainly not on the level of the Flint, Michigan, water crisis or soul-crushing minimum wage many Americans receive and must use to figure out how to pay all their bills in a timely manner. So if your first instinct is to tell me to stop the complain train,

I understand. But I would ask you to hop aboard as we journey to These Motherfuckers Must Be Out They Damn Minds Ville and Oh, I See Why She's Mad, Go 'Head and Stay Mad Town because underneath the trappings of a photo shoot, the recurring problems that I and so many other women in my position have had remain. We're still subjected to fashion and society's two-prong attack—physical (not making clothes in appropriate sizes that will fit) and psychological/emotional (making women feel bad/sad/guilty/ashamed/like failures for not being able to fit into clothing)—in the hopes that we'll change and adhere to the often unhealthy and unrealistic body standards so as to perform womanhood the way the patriarchy wants us to.

Below is a list of some of the embarrassing moments I've had to endure in the name of fashion:

- Often stylists will want to give women a Cinderella moment, dressing them up in a fabulous gown with high heels and making them the belle of the ball. But I don't necessarily want to be the belle of the ball; I want to be the basic bitch of a Raymour & Flanigan aka I'm all 'bout that comfort, 'bout that comfort, minimal effort. Truly, I'm a jeans, T-shirt, and Converse sneakers gal (or a fierce jumpsuit if I'm feeling frisky), so whenever I do a shoot and all I see are pants and, more importantly, a plethora of jeans, the black auntie who lives inside me is praise-dancing to Chaka Khan's "I'm Every Woman." And that joy was on full display at this one photo shoot that was to accompany an internet profile of me. The happiness evaporated quickly, however, when I saw that all the jeans were a size 29 and under (I vary between a 30 and a 33 if they are stretchy; am starting at a 32 if there is no stretch, which why would you make jeans without stretch, ya filthy animal?), and none of them had any stretch, meaning they would not accommodate my at-the-time size 10 butt, hips, or thighs. Still, I was told to fear not, because the jeans would work. Ya know, the only thing more annoying than being presented with clothes that don't fit and trying them on in front of strangers is a stylist acting as though I could fit into the too-small clothing if only I believed enough.

But I carried on because I don't want to be labeled as difficult. I struggled but managed to put on the fabulous blue jeans that were supposed to go with the fabulous designer top that actually did fit. Sigh. The jeans. Would. Not. Zip. Up. We each took turns gripping and straining, but the zipper wasn't budging and remained at the bottom of the crotch. I suggested putting on a different pair of jeans because duh. She dismissed me and replied, "But these are the perfect jeans to go with this shirt." Y'all. Y'ALL. Y'ALL. This is not a Michelin-star restaurant where no substitutions are allowed. These are blue jeans; they're everywhere, and so many of them look alike that you can't even tell the difference. This stylist didn't feel this way and instead had the genius idea of safety-pinning the ends of the zipper together all the way to the top of the jeans, reassuring me that this was fine because she's used this method before and they can simply crop the photo if need be. Wait. Wut? There's a possibility the final photo won't even show me in the jeans? Then why are we doing this? I could've been Winnie the Pooh'ing all up in this mofo from the get-go. Before I could say this aloud, someone told the photo shoot crew that the delay was due to the jeans not fitting, causing everyone to look over to see the stylist struggling to make her "solution" work. THANK YOU FOR THAT VERY PUBLIC UP-DATE BECAUSE THE CHERRY ON TOP OF THE SOMEONE-PERSPIRING-WHILE-FORCING-YOUR-BODY-INTO-CLOTHES-THAT-DON'T-FIT SHIT SUNDAE IS MAKING A DAMN CNN BREAKING NEWS ANNOUNCEMENT ABOUT IT TO EVERY-ONE IN THE VICINITY.

Anyway, the stylist eventually finished and I was pinned into the jeans. I stiffly walked over to sit down where the photographer wanted. As soon as I sat, the safety pins were like, "Abort mish," and snapped open, including one that flew like Mark Wahlberg does in an action movie when a bomb has gone off behind him. The stylist ran, picked up the safety pin, and there I was in front of everyone with my stomach doing its best Jack Nicholson "Here's Johnny!" impression from *The Shining*. And guess what? The picture ended up being cropped from my head down to the top titty quadrant. #TechnicalLingo.

- A recent photo shoot kicked off with the first hour of fittings composed of my least favorite greatest hits about my body—"You Ain't Got No Titties to Fill Out This Shirt," "Carbs, Carbs, Carbs, Carbs, Carbs I Do Adore (The Ballad of a Muffin Top)," "No, I Don't Need Help Trying Anything On/I've Been in This Changing Room for Fifteen Minutes Because None of This Shit Fits"—before there was an outfit that worked. We found a few more looks to make this shoot an overall success. However, the moment that sticks out the most is when, at one point, I was handed a size small top to put on. I said, "Oh, I'm not a small. I'm usually a medium and sometimes a large if the shirt is cut to be extremely form-fitting." The stylist's response: "Yeah, but the designer makes their smalls kind of big, so it's almost like a medium." Um, mofo, can the designer then just make a medium that is a full fucking medium? I don't need to be out in these streets dealing with all these smalls masquerading as mediums and lulling me into a false sense of security when there's only enough fabric allowance for you to have a food baby made up of sixteen peanut M&M's. These are the kinds of smalls where the bottom of the shirt rides up your stomach approximately 1.6 seconds after you put it on. And then you look like Will Ferrell in the "Need More Cowbell" *SNL* sketch.

- Look, I love me a jumpsuit. They are all the rage and have been for a few seasons. But everyone and their mom can tell the difference between a joyful jumpsuit that has you looking like a sexy auto-parts salesperson at Pep Boys and a jumpsuit a stylist has you try on as a catchall/last resort option, as in "catch all the non-toned, jiggly parts of your body." The difference being, the latter jumpsuit will fit most parts of your body well and then be tight as hell around your thighs so that it looks like you're smuggling two weeks' worth of lingerie out of Victoria's Secret. This outfit works the way that DMV employee did when she sat in her booth, spent twenty minutes eating a Chobani yogurt and chatting with her coworker who was actually working, and then locked eyes with me before getting up and leaving. All of this is to say: Don't just shove me into the most shapeless outfit you have because you don't want to be bothered with my body.

- I love doing a photo shoot with a friend. You get to have a partner in crime whom you can sneak side-eyes at when good ("Yooooo, can you believe they're blasting a U2 playlist?" #ThisIsGoodOnlyForMe) and bad ("Why is this hairstylist giving me a *Designing Women* bouffant?") stuff happens. No matter what goes down, it's tight to share such an equally luxurious and absurd experience with someone you'd be just as happy doing the mundane with. At this particular shoot, racks of clothes were on full display and lined up and ready to make us shine bright like diamonds in this magazine. My homie had gotten pretty used to glamorous shoots like this. I, on the other hand, had not. Sure, I had done smaller stuff for indie outlets, but this was my first one for a maj magazine and I was ready to pop my couture cherry, which is similar to popping one's sexual cherry because Sade is played in the background. Moving on. I scanned the designer labels and thought to myself, *Whoa, these are the fashion lines that goddesses like Mindy Kaling, Cate Blanchett, and Kerry Washington wear on the regs at fancy events. Oh, shit! Is that Christian Louboutin? Jimmy Choo?!* I felt like a character in a TV makeover montage. I whooped it up, got my cocoa-butter-lotion fingerprints on all the clothes, and took blurry, on-the-down-low pictures of different outfits to send to my fam.

Once that was done, my buddy and I set off to try on the clothes. As you can probably guess by now, quite a few of the clothes were unflattering on me. Luckily, there was one outfit that mostly worked except it was too tight and highlighted certain things I'm insecure about, most notably my belly, and made them considerably bigger. But of course, that outfit was the look everyone at the magazine loved. So that's what I was wearing, which I was told was no Jason Biggs aka no biggie because the fashion department had Spanx, which I had never worn before. I'm not saying this to brag. I get people wanting to look smoother and more toned in their clothes. But I'm just not into the idea of my body fat being stuffed and compressed like a comforter shoved in a too-full hallway closet. So, in real life, I either covered up my belly or just accepted that it was visible in whatever outfit I was wearing. But this was beyond real life. This was a national magazine. I was not too keen on opening it up and seeing my protruding belly. I knew that if push came to shove, it would be photoshopped away, but I didn't want to later regret not doing everything in my power to hide my soft stomach, so I said yes to wearing Spanx, and with that, someone left to find the magical garment that was going to make my insecurity about my body go away. Hooray! Then that person returned and handed me a size XS Spanx. An XS Spanx?!?! What in the sneak-into-the-bathroom-and-slip-off-your-shapewear-before-sex hell is this? WHY WOULD YOU GET ME A SIZE XS SPANX WHEN I'M A SIZE 10?!

Y'all, remember in school when you'd see that one black girl who straightened her hair to its maximum length, which ended up not being very long at all, and she gathered it into the shortest, barely there #StrugglePonytail where just past the elastic ponytail holder was the tiniest tuft of hair that looked like bristles from a Bob Ross paintbrush, and if you stood close enough to her, you could hear her overworked hair humming the Negro spiritual "Swing Low, Sweet Chariot" because it barely had the strenf to carry on and was ready to meet its maker? Well, just as pointless as it was for her to put her locks in a ponytail, it's equally as ignorant to make Spanx a size extra small. For what purpose? In case the person breathes in too much air at once and their stomach puffs out like a protective screen has been shoddily applied to a cell phone, so that all the air bubbles are smoothed out except for one? This is gahtdamn ridiculous!

So I said, "Hmm, this is an extra small, but I'm not. Can we get one in my size?" To which the magazine staffer replied, "Yeah, sorry. Earlier today we did a shoot with a few supermodels, so this is the only size we have, so you've got to use this." Coooooooooooooo oooooooool. I'm gonna just go in this corner, shove this up my vajeen, and slap it on my left fallopian tube to make it as thin as uncooked linguini.

But in all seriousness, c'mon! Not only do you not have clothes that fit me comfortably, but you can't even get Spanx in my size? It's not as if I rolled up unannounced like Steve Urkel coming over for Taco Tuesday on *Family Matters*. You knew I was coming here!

Real quick, for those of you who don't know the deal about professional photo shoots, it goes like this: Prior to the shoot, the stylist is given (1) your size (both clothing and shoes, and in the case of this one, they had a plethora of shoes, none of which fit, to which I was told, "Beauty is pain") and (2) measurements of various body parts to get a more exact fit. Measurements that in everyday life are fact but in fashion are often considered a rough draft to be improved upon. A what-if like, "So you say you're a 10, but what if . . . you were a size 4 like Halle Berry?" Hmm, welp, I would be wildly famous and had to dry-hump Billy Bob Thornton to win an Oscar, which is not a bad deal, per se, but alas, I'm little ole Phoebe Lynn Robinson, not famous, and have been dry-hump-free for well over a decade, so let's chill on the "what if" and instead deal with the "this is what is and that's just as good." But that seems to be the problem, right? That any woman above a size 2 or 4 would see her body as just as good as the body types media tells us should be the ideal, which, according to the person on set, I should be in discomfort in order to achieve. Trash, right? Of course. Yet thanks to conditioning, I fell in line by wearing the painful shoes and squeezing myself into the Spanx that didn't fit. And when I took them off, the imprint of the elastic band on my waist and legs branded me, as if to say, "Now you know better, so do better." Don't get me wrong, the picture turned out amazingly well, but I was not happy, so it wasn't freaking worth the physical pain.

- Before we move on, I have a PSA to share with all future stylists I may work with: AFTER I TELL YOU THAT MINISKIRTS DO NOT FIT WELL ON ME BECAUSE MY PEAR SHAPE CAUSES THEM TO RIDE UP, YET I DO YOU THE COURTESY OF TRYING ONE ON IN PRIVATE JUST TO APPEASE YOU, PLEASE STOP OPENING THE CHANGING ROOM DOOR WIDE-OPEN SO THAT EVERYONE SEES MY EXPOSED BOOTY CHEEKS CHILLING THERE LIKE STATLER AND WALDORF MUPPETS, JUST JUDGING THE HELL OUT OF BOTH OF US AND THIS IGNORANT-ASS SITUATION.

Whew! The above is just a bento box sampling and is by no means comprehensive of what I've gone through in the name of fashion and beauty. It stinks, but it's not actually about the clothing itself; it's much deeper and more systemic and has far-reaching consequences that affect all parts of women's lives.

It cannot be said enough how things are rough out there for the average woman (according to the *International Journal of Fashion Design, Technology and Education,* the median dress size for an American woman is a 16) in a sizeist society. Imagery in the media and societal conditioning from birth informs not only how women feel about themselves but also how they are treated, which then further reinforces how they "should" feel about themselves. So while it's "cute" that the prevailing thought is that being a petite woman is just about wearing the chicest outfit from fancy designers, it's for damn sure not about fashion. The truth is, being in the single digits means you're respected, allowed to be heard, deserving of love and a job, and more importantly, it's acceptable for you to have self-esteem. You are worthy and aspirational. And if you don't fall in line, then you're shit out of luck and a cautionary tale. So, no, size is not a matter of frivolity or self-absorption. Size, to me and a hell of a lot of women, is a question of: Will I have to fight that much harder to have the full, rich, delicious life I dream of and work for? Unfortunately, the answer is yes. Don't believe me? I have the receipts, and they are long AF, like the kind you get from CVS.

In November 2017, Fairygodboss, an employer review site for women, released a startling report after conducting a survey of five hundred hiring professionals about various hypotheticals when it comes to women in the workplace. One of the studies included showing participants a range of different body types and then asking them questions based solely on the images. And if you're assuming the results are about to be a landfill of Vanilla Ice CDs set on fire, then you are correct. Let's take a look at this trash, shall we?

- 21 percent of the hiring professionals viewed the heaviest woman as "lazy," and of course, this word was used far less frequently with thinner women.
- 21 percent also stated she was unprofessional.
- Only 18 PERCENT believed the heavier-set woman possessed leadership qualities.

- Worst of all, only 15.6 percent would even consider hiring the heaviest-looking woman.

This was in 2017. Twenty seventeen! Not during the sixties. Not the fifties. But present day as hell. The same present day where Elon Musk watched the original *Knight Rider* and was like, "Car doors that open up to the sky like a yoga teacher going from a forward bend into mountain pose? #Goals," and now we have Teslas. The same present day where you can use your bank's mobile app to deposit a check while taking a dump. The same present day where everyone at Burger King collectively got on board with chicken being French fries? All of these unnecessary luxuries are believable and fully exist, yet it is simply implausible to nearly 85 percent of employers to hire a plus-size woman?! Not only is this trash, but this is embarrassing and reprehensible.

This ignorance doesn't just exist in the workplace. It's everywhere. *Science* magazine, in 2016, released an article about relationships, and in a section about online dating it stated, "But when it came to body weight, men were less likely to browse the profile of a woman who was heavy-set." Arizona State University researchers in 2014 did a study about weight and friendship in school settings. Associate Professor David Schaefer said, "We found consistent evidence that overweight youth choose non-overweight friends more often than they were selected in return."

But we don't need studies and facts. We see how plus-size women are treated as a nuisance in public spaces like concerts and movie theaters, we read the vitriol spewed on their social media accounts whenever they post an image of themselves, especially if it's one where they are showing off their goodies ("You're promoting an unhealthy lifestyle" is a common refrain), and worst of all, we see (don't see/choose to ignore) how they are regarded as invisible. I cannot tell you the number of times I'm dressed down at the airport and men will "bump" into me, walk into a line I'm standing in and stand right in front of me, take up more than their allotted space on the plane, and every time, every single time, when I make my presence known, I always hear the same excuse: "Oh, sorry. I didn't see you there." Now, imagine if I were a plus-size woman. Or imagine yourself plus-size. Or if you are and you're reading this, you don't have to. You have lived with these indignities on a daily basis, and it is complete bullshit.

Thankfully, the tide is starting to turn, and I believe it has plenty to do with technology. Much like how Black Twitter can move the needle, whether it's political with #BlackLivesMatter or in entertainment with #OscarsSoWhite, Twitter, Instagram, blogging, vlogging, and many other forms of communication are allowing plus-size women, in particular, to celebrate themselves, provide clothing resources and support systems, and, most importantly, build momentum for the current wave of body positivity.

Models such as Ashley Graham, Precious Lee, Marquita Pring, Denise Bidot, and many others, as well as designers like Christian Siriano, who is renowned for dressing all body types, are at the forefront. Actress Danielle Brooks launched a plus-size clothing capsule collection last year for Universal Standard. Adele is one of the most successful singers in modern pop music despite early whispers that her not being skinny might harm her career. A new convention called theCURVYcon features fashion shows demonstrating how beautiful clothes designed for plus-size bodies can actually look, as well as panels on dating, business, confidence, etc. And while it is true that, especially in the world of beauty, white plus-size models like Graham have groundbreaking career success that plus-size women of color don't, it still doesn't change the fact that body positivity is powerful and is shaping a generation of women for the better.

Now I'm not writing all this, of course, to be the authority on body positivity or to claim my experiences are so unique or revelatory, as if to say, "Hey, everybody, let's now all pay attention to how women's bodies are discussed." There are people far more equipped than I to be a voice of the movement. What I'm more concerned with is that I had been so preoccupied with my own insecurities that I didn't pay attention to what my responsibilities are as an ally. That it wasn't until I put on weight that I was able to have the mind-set of "fuck this noise" and take notice of the responsibility I have to use my privilege as a woman who vacillates between a size 10 and 12 and can still move in certain places and be respected. And I'm not talking about writing a "Slay, queen" or "Yaaaas, bitch" comment on a plus-size beauty blogger's Instagram profile, although that is nice. I'm also not talking about me giving a middle finger to the Erics of the world who tell me my thighs are too big, although that also feels dope AF. I'm talking real actual shit. Instead of being silently complicit or only speaking up half the time, I'm talking about putting dudes in their place every damn time they think they can fat-shame women who are bigger than me. I cannot tell you the amount of times I've heard men, who think they are in a "safe space" with me, reveal what they truly feel about women who don't fall within societal beauty standards. Let me just say that "disgusting," "pig," "never would I ever fuck her," and many other objectionable comments often make the rounds. Furthermore, I'm talking about how if I can reject society's expectation of being the "respectable black person" (aka behaving in a manner to assimilate within white society and not ruffle feathers), then I can be just as adamant about rejecting the notion of the "respectable waif" aka a woman who dedicates herself to adhering to what the culture decides is beautiful. It's a damn shame that it wasn't until I became a size 10/12 that I truly realized the body-shaming spell I'm under. That we're all under. That all us women, plus-size or not, are dealing with the daily battle going on in our heads of whether we're going to comply with how the media tells us we should aspire to be beautiful. Well, fuck compliance. I repeat: FUCK. COMPLIANCE.

I don't want any of us to be compliant anymore. That's for suckers. Be defiant, or if you already are, continue to be so. And for those who aren't yet, let's eat, breathe, and sleep defiance until it becomes our daily routine to dare the fuck out of people and ourselves. Dare to reject the haters who tell you you're unworthy of love and basic human decency and a good pair of jeans because you have some or a lot of jiggle and cellulite on your body. Dare to challenge those who don't speak up on your behalf. Dare people like me to be the ally you deserve to have, meaning keep telling us some variation of, "STFU, listen, and go read a book" when we're hurting more than we're helping. Dare to push away your inner thoughts that want to sabotage you. Dare to expect better from whatever love interest you meet who thinks you should be grateful for compliments or act as if they're some kind of superhero for finding you attractive. Dare to roll your eyes at this person who thinks that pulling a Mark Darcy and telling you, "I like you very much, just as you are," should end with them bodysurfing out the room with a fireworks display going off in the background. Dare to do for yourself what Bridget couldn't do: Look at yourself in the mirror and say, "I like myself just the way I am."

Feminism, I Was Rooting for You; We Were All Rooting for You

⟿

Dear reader, ya damn skippy this essay title is inspired by the monologue Tyra Banks delivered to Tiffany Richardson after booting the model-testant from Cycle 4 of *America's Next Top Model*. The speech is iconic, and dare I write that, in particular, Tyra's "I was rooting for you; we were all rooting for you" is one of the most important quotes of our time, right up there with John F. Kennedy's "Ask not what your country can do for you, ask what you can do for your country," Michelle Obama's "When they go low, we go high," and the classic Ying Yang Twins rap lyric "Ay, bitch! Wait till you see my dick." . . . Y'all, this is like when Apple hints there's going to be a big announcement regarding the iPhone, so we all tune in to Tim Cook's live stream of the product launch, and he's just like, "The phone is slightly bigger," and we're all like, "Dat could've been a Post-it note message next to an empty bag of Chex Mix." Ying Yang, your dicks are like practically *all* of the dicks that have ever been seen, so calm down. But I digress. Back to Tyra and Tiffany. If you haven't seen this showdown, please bless your eyeballs with the once-in-a-lifetime clip ASAP. If you don't have time to find it online, I'll break it down for you now.

Like all reality TV, *ANTM* casting looks for people who can fulfill story lines that producers can easily edit together: the person seeking redemption, the caterpillar who turns into a butterfly, the comic relief, or the drama queen or king (think *The Real Housewives of New York City*'s Bethenny Frankel, who does all), and, most commonly, the underdog or rags-to-riches hero. Well, Tiffany hit the sweet spot of being a potentially rags-to-riches contender (like the average American, she was not flush with money), seeking redemption (she had competed in Cycle 3 but hadn't made it as far as she wanted), and having a charming personality plus a knack for being involved in drama, like in Cycle 3 when she got involved in a fight with a stranger in a bar and yelled, "Bitch poured a beer on my weave." Anyone who has ever worn a weave knows liquid being thrown on it is akin to Aaron Burr glove-slapping a dude to declare a duel, so naturally, Tiffany had to fight back. Anyway, later on, in a confessional, she regretted fighting and was determined to change her life for the better, which was probably music to the producers' ears, hence her being asked to come back to the show the next season following completion of anger-management classes.

Things were looking up for her during Cycle 4. To me, she was one of the judges' favorites. She was consistently killing it week after week with her photos, and she seemed more charming and likable than ever. The competish was hers to lose, which is why I think it was surprising that she was not only eliminated but kicked off in such a dramatic fashion.

On the episode that she got the boot, there was a challenge where all the models-to-be had to do an exercise as if they were reporting during Fashion Week, an exercise that required them to read from a teleprompter and pronounce various designers' names. Most fashion plates know that many of these designers' names can be tricky to pronounce when encountered for the first time, so the fact that the contestants weren't nailing them was to be expected. In fact, the contestants jacked up almost all the names. It was kind of like watching Nomi from *Showgirls* saying "Ver-sayce" instead of "Versace" on repeat for five minutes. It was adorable and funny. Except Tiffany wasn't laughing. She felt defeated because she messed up. The judges reassured her that *everyone* messed up and that the point of the exercise was to see how the women could roll with the punches and still have fun. Didn't matter. She was OverIt.Edu/None OfYourCreditsWillTransfer and made that clear to everyone.

Well, Tyra wasn't having it and launched into a stream-of-consciousness speech (punctuated with the "I was rooting for you; we were all rooting for you" line) that was engrossing, soul-shaking, dramatic, and should have won a Peabody Award for Extremely Wild and Incredibly Pertinent to African-American History and Iconic Television. Seriously, it's that good, and that's partially because, despite the reality TV genre's claims, we all know these shows rely on heavy scripting, cast manipulation by producers, and editing to create episodes and watercooler moments, which is why when an authentic one (or as authentic as one can be in reality TV) like the one Tyra offered up goes down, it truly *is* shocking because reality TV is finally accomplishing what it rarely does: capturing people behaving naturally as if the cameras aren't there. But more importantly, the real reason Tyra's monologue resonated with so many people, and especially other black women (myself included), is because it showed the outside world how many black moms read their chillrens the riot act when they get out of line.

To some, this may seem extreme or over the top. And, sure, is it occasionally true that reprimanding a child passionately can unintentionally veer into "No . . . wire . . . hangers" territory? Yes, but usually the rant isn't maniacal; instead, it's rooted in love and concern. Black mamas (and papas) know the chips tend to be stacked against them and their children, that their kids will have a tougher time getting their foot in the door than their white counterparts, and, furthermore, that they'll have less room for error once they get beyond the door. So even though Tiffany and Tyra aren't blood relatives, Tyra was, for a generation of black models-in-training, their "mother" who knocked down barriers (she was the first black woman to be on the covers of the *Sports Illustrated* Swimsuit Issue, *GQ*, and the Victoria's Secret catalog, just to name a few), thus creating an easier path for folks such as Tiffany. This is not to say that *ANTM* isn't fun entertainment—it is—but I'd argue that Tyra also had skin in the game when it came to Tiff and her future success, hence the blowup.

I imagine Tyra reacted the way she did because people such as herself, Beverly Johnson, Iman, Alek Wek, Roshumba Williams, etc., worked tirelessly to open up opportunities for girls like Tiffany. Thus, when Tiffany was intent on rejecting herself before anyone else could, it must have been like a slap in the face to Tyra. Furthermore, Ty-Ty knew that Tiffany's public display of self-pity was a luxury she could not afford, especially in an industry that, like many others, will, because of her skin color, mistake a common moment of weakness as a reflection of her character. Tyra, like all black parents, knew that the stakes, no matter how unfair, are much higher for someone like Tiffany than for a person from a different economic and racial background. So in that moment when Tyra yelled, "I was rooting for you; we were all rooting for you," everything I just described was probably racing through her mind, along with the realization that she perhaps wanted this for Tiffany more than Tiff wanted it for herself. And while Tyra might be the pop culture face of that realization and iconic statement, the truth is, that isn't just a black-mama feeling; it's a universal one we've all experienced.

At this point, you may be wondering what exactly this juicy moment of reality TV has to do with feminism, which is what this essay's supposed to be about. Well, if you just hold your horses, I'll tell ya. But what if I didn't? LOL. What if this essay was one big time-wasting switcheroo? Remember on *Sex and the City* when, as an apology for sending over her boyfriend Aidan to help an injured and naked Miranda (I'm talking Miranda's booty cheeks looking like two marshmallows that were supposed to be sprinkled in a cup of hot choc but ended up on the floor), Carrie came to Miranda's crib with bagels, but really it's an excuse to talk about relationship troubles with Aidan (AND,

I REPEAT, MIRANDA WAS ASS OUT LIKE THE COPPER-TONE GIRL[1]), which pissed off Miranda, who dubbed them the "bullshit bagels"? Okay, but instead of me pulling a Carrie and hooking y'all up with bagels, I just spent the past five pages temporarily turning my book into a *BuzzFeed* article about legendary reality TV moments. If I did something that trifling and you cussed me out like Robert De Niro did number 45 at the 2018 Tonys,[2] I wouldn't even be mad. I'd accept it the way ghosts accept being told to leave someone's home, which, by the way, is the dumbest shit I've ever heard. Ghosts, can't nobody see you! Just lie. All the time, as a kid, my parents would tell me to do my homework and I'd say, "On it!" Meanwhile, I was in my room continuing to live my life with my headphones on like I'm at a UN summit, listening intently to the radio so I could press the record button on my boom box at the right time to add Aaliyah to my mixtape. I mean, what goofy-ass ghosts are just out here telling the truth, packing up their night creams, and

1. Can we talk about the Coppertone girl for a sec? In case you don't know, Coppertone is a very popular sunscreen, and the company's signature image is, on a scale of 1 (waving at someone who was waving at the person behind you) to 10 (*Saved by the Bell*'s Screech awkwardly losing his virginity at AARP age), this uncomfortable mess was a 27, so buckle up! A'ight, so the image was of a dog pulling a little girl's swim trunks down with its teeth—great start—until most of her butt was exposed (because when you're drowning, why not tie bricks to your feet to ensure you'll end up in Sebastian the Crab's living room?), and the little girl didn't look horrified, like a child probably would. Instead she served us a coy face, as if to say, "Who, me? Whoopsies," like she was Marilyn Monroe getting ready to launch into a sultry rendition of "Happy Birthday" to JFK. To make matters worse, that "sexy baby" picture of her was used for *decades* with no objections. Raise of hands if this information makes you wanna disinvite humanity from the rest of your life.

2. Btdubs, entering rooms and cussing people out in my seventies is the new "get summer-bikini-body ready" for me. Just like getting in shape for swimsuit seas, I will spend the rest of my life woefully not preparing for it and then two weeks before my seventieth birthday, someone will eat the last of my applesauce and I'll naturally just drop f-bombs and somehow be ready.

moving out? Whew! OMFG, so many tangents just happened, people! Now you know what it's like to date me. My apologies. Time to get back on track.

Why am bringing up the Tyra speech and the best line from it? IDK about anyone else, but I am, at this particular moment, extremely confused and emotionally conflicted about the state of womanhood and feminism in America. While I was always low-key suspicious about feminism thanks to reading about the history of this country as well as being a black woman living in it, the election of Donald Trump as the forty-fifth president of the United States, thanks in part to the 53 percent of white women who voted for him, proved to me that we aren't living in a feminist country. And ever since the night that number 45 was elected, feminism has seemed to be in a bit of a state of emergency. Except that's not entirely true. Feminism, like any movement that's designed to challenge the status quo and strive for equality, has always been in some state of emergency. Has always had to contend with blowing out fires, both internal and external. Has always made strides in progress and reverted back to bad habits. It's just a shame that I and many others didn't understand that until that fateful evening of November 8, 2016, a night that rocked the nation and changed the course of American history and possibly international history.

It's rare for a single decision to alter the course of history, and it's even rarer to actually feel that seismic shift happen in real time. Not only is it rare; it's also powerful to seemingly be in tune with *everyone* when the shift happens and be able to feel all their feelings, especially the rawest ones that usually bubble below the surface. The induction of the "new normal" is scary, exhilarating, and so overwhelming that you might laugh or cry or be stunned to silence. Being that deeply connected to the energy vibrating from everyone around you is the stuff of comic book lore and almost too much for the human body to take while, at the same time, it's kind of exhilarating seeing how capable our bodies are. I can only imagine that the vibrations that made their way across the country on November 8 must have been similar to the ones felt when Lincoln abolished slavery or when women were allowed to enter the workplace. For the folks who were alive when those events took place, the takeaway might be that stuff was amazing or an abomination (or, in the case of the moon landing, a government conspiracy). As for the 2016 US presidential election, depending on who you ask, what occurred two years ago was either the worst, the best-worst, the worst-worst, or the best-best thing to ever happen, and the fallout was immediate. But I'm getting ahead of myself. Let me start a few hours prior to the result being announced.

There were Election Night viewing parties all over the cunch aka country, and I chose to go to a friend's house so we could celebrate the inevitable and only logical outcome at that point: Hillary Clinton being president. To be clear, I'm not implying that my homies and I voted for her because she was the lesser of two evils; on the flip side, we also didn't see her as a savior without flaws. She has many that have been well-documented for decades by the media, and people of color have mentally noted that her record when it came to race was spotty at best. Still, just like this pair of pants that I own—which are made of such temperamental material that, after I sit down for half a second, the now heavily wrinkled fabric around my crotch looks like the face of an unamused Chinese shar-pei, yet I wear them anyway because they flatter the rest of my figure perfectly—I, for one, had decided there was enough good there in the possibility of a Hillary presidency to outweigh the not-so-good. At the very least, she's highly intelligent and had the résumé to hold the office. So that night at my friend's Election Night viewing party, in addition to us celebrating what we thought was HRC becoming America's first female president, we were also toasting the fact that the three-ring circus that American politics had turned into, courtesy of Trump and the media, was finally coming to an end. Basically, my friends and I were like Whitney Houston, Angela Bassett, Loretta Devine, and Lela Rochon on the poster of *Waiting to Exhale,* just in flowy pajamas, laughing because the drama of men is over, while the song "Exhale (Shoop Shoop)" fades into the background, signaling a brighter future.

Cut to the end of the night. The flowy jim-jams had been replaced by black turtlenecks à la Simon and Garfunkel, and we were singing, "Hello, darkness, my old friend." It became clear that Clinton was not going to hit that magical number of 270 Electoral College votes, and the world as we knew it was over. That's not an overstatement. The hopes and dreams that Barack Obama had set in motion seemed to evaporate in an instant. Some of us cried. Others were so devastated that they *put down* the alcohol. There were also some who were angry. Most of all, we felt hopeless, helpless, and stunned.

I mean, none of us could have predicted the following confluence of circumstances that would allow him to win: (1) apathetic voter turnout (according to CNN, voting turnout was at a twenty-year low), (2) the unrealistic expectation that the number of black voters would be enough to overpower the disgruntled white working-class vote, (3) Hillary's refusal to make campaign stops in key states like Wisconsin, for example, which she ended up losing, (4) "whitelash" from racist people who loathed Barack Obama being in office for the past eight years,[3] (5) hella sexist voters, and (6) white women who wanted to protect their whiteness so much that they ignored the sexual harassment claims that have dogged Trump for years, including the *Access Hollywood* audio of him essentially bragging about sexually assaulting women with the poetic phrase "grab 'em by the pussy." Yeah, like I said, stunning. But more than just feeling shock, I was also disheartened because I knew there were plenty of people who were overjoyed at the outcome.

Then a thought popped up in the back of my mind that I couldn't ignore. Maybe I shouldn't have been so rocked by the election results. I mean, once homeboy launched his improbable campaign, which got more successful by the week in spite of his around-the-clock blunders, shouldn't I have seen it for what it was: an upgraded version of a bigoted Bat-Signal—the original one was a spotlight shining in the sky and projecting an image of the KKK's David Duke—that was a call to action for people of Trump's ilk (the racists, the sexists, the homophobes, the transphobes, etc.)? Therefore, I couldn't help but wonder, isn't the fact that I never fully believed Trump could be number 45 a sign that my stubbornness and naïveté prevented

---

3. "Whitelash" was coined by CNN commentator and host Van Jones on Election Night. It means that when there is significant racial progress, it is followed by a white backlash, hence "whitelash."

me from seeing America for what it truly is? Yes, but that's not entirely my fault.

To those on #TeamBarackObama #TeamYesWeCan #Team-EverybodyBlackBoutToWin, America appeared to have moved forward in a way that would make it impossible to return to the ignorance and racism of the past. Yes, he and his family faced an onslaught of racism during his tenure in office, he was routinely disrespected by his constituents, and he had to deal with roadblocks from other politicians hell-bent on making it difficult for him to get anything accomplished. But still. Despite all this ugliness, there was no denying that seeing this black man elected president—with that black-ass name of Barack Hussein Obama, married to a black-ass woman named Michelle, who not only was accomplished in her own right but also showed she had autonomy outside of being someone's wife, and together the two of them raised two black-ass kids—had lulled me into a false sense of security. It felt like a new era, and that anything was possible because there was proof of it every day inside the White House. It felt like actual, groundbreaking change, but now that this nation is two years and counting away from those glory days, I look back at the Obama years, and I see more clearly what that time represented for me. I spent those eight years living the way some people do during January 1 through 4.

You know what I'm talking about. Those glorious four days at the beginning of the year where people are high off the "new year, new me" vibes. I don't know what it is, but there's something about the calendar changing that makes folks stand in front of a mirror, *Dr. Phil'*ing themselves with tough love and tons of plans for grand transformations. And then right around 7:03 A.M. on January 5, reality sets in and with it the realization that a lot of work is required for personal growth to last, so #NewYearNewMe quickly devolves into #NewYearSameMe-StrugglingToDoTheBareMinimum. I'm not writing this from judgment; I'm not a New Year's resolutions person, but I get it. I just do this kind of stuff in other ways, such as the way I exercise.

Sorry to bring up weight again after spending the previous essay writing about it, but I'm an infrequent exerciser. I'll go hard for a month and then take two weeks off. Or two months of training literally goes down the drain because life gets in the way and my lack of discipline and dedication results in me not up in the gym working on my fitness for months and months. Point is that I'm inconsistent, but one thing that remains constant is my energy when I start getting into an exercise routine. I'll work out and do like twenty-three lunges over the course of two days, look in the mirror, and be like, "Oooh, look how toned I am," before calling Lloyd's of London insurance so I can pull a Heidi Klum and take out a $2 million policy on my legs. All kidding aside, just like the New Year's resolution makers and my fellow fickle exercisers, I got hyped as hell about the Obama presidency and rode the wave of happiness right into the 2016 election, believing that since we knocked down one barrier, our work was done, and like dominos, other barriers were going to come crashing down. I think a lot of feminists as well as the feminist movement itself felt that way.

After we make some progress (like director Ava DuVernay becoming the first woman of color in charge of a $100 million movie budget), we sometimes get excited as if the everyday microaggressions women face are now a thing of the past. And even if there *is* more structural change going on (i.e., the passing of Title IX in 1972, which is a law that states no person can be discriminated against on the basis of their sex at an educational program getting federal financial assistance), we still have a long way to go because it's clear that in plenty of instances, the #YesAllWomen doesn't apply to *all* women, even as we're in the age of #MeToo and #TimesUp, which are currently dragging the patriarchy out the door as it's kicking and screaming to stay in the past. Don't believe me?

Just this year, award-winning star of *Transparent* Jeffrey Tambor has been embroiled in controversy ever since he was accused of sexual harassment by two trans women, Van Barnes, his personal assistant, and Trace Lysette, an actress and Tambor's costar. Before an investigation could be completed, he quit the series, briefly disappeared from the spotlight, and re-emerged on a character-redemption tour of sorts, starting a promo run for the upcoming season of his other show, *Arrested Development*.

During an *AD* cast interview with the *New York Times*, Jessica Walter cried while recounting being on the receiving end of Tambor's verbal abuse. Instead of listening to her, the other male cast members downplayed what she went through and essentially chalked up his bad behavior to nothing more than "this is what having a job is!" Naw, bruh. "What having a job is" includes getting a lunch break or being paid overtime or indefinitely mailing out your Forever 21 returns via your job's UPS account because that one time your boss made you work three minutes past 1 P.M. on a Summer Friday like four years ago and you still haven't gotten the fuck over it. That, my friends, is what having a job is. Knowing you can act a fool because you're well respected in the workplace so no one will call you out—*that* is abuse of power. Obviously, many folks inside and outside entertainment agreed with this sentiment and rightfully came to Walter's defense, which, on the one hand, yaaas for having her back against verbal abuse and mansplaining, but on the other, the way people tripped over themselves like former track-and-field competitor Lolo Jones did over hurdles at the Olympics to assist Walter was kinda bullshit.

No shade to her or what she went through, but c'mon! Really? We're going to let Cis White Woman Tears be the "They may take our lives, but they'll never take our freedom" *Braveheart* rallying cry that gets people to act; meanwhile, when trans women Barnes and Lysette recounted in detail how they were SEXUALLY HARASSED, seemingly everyone got quiet the way kids do when they tiptoe across a creaky wooden floor in the hopes of spying on Kris Krings eating some chocolate chip cookies while dropping off some Christmas presents. There was no rallying cry to be heard for Barnes and Lysette. Aside from a few bloggers, no one in the media came to their defense. Most importantly, no one saw the irony in the fact that the show he was allegedly doing this behavior on was a show specifically designed to show the humanity of trans people, and yet when the women expressed how they weren't in a safe space, their humanity was ignored. As the great Lil Wayne once said, "Real

Gs move in silence like lasagna." I guess so do those who don't understand that in order for feminism to work, it *has* to be intersectional.

Look, I get that everyone is learning and we learn at different paces. Hell, *I'm* still learning. I don't always get it right. Far from it. I still accidentally misgender from time to time. I don't fight for sex workers and lower-class women as hard as I should. I've said things and made jokes in the past that I wouldn't even dream of making today. We all have; however, in the age of #TimesUp and #MeToo, when people are thrown the softball of defending trans women yet fail to do so . . . Say it with me, y'all: Feminism! I was rooting for you; we were all rooting for you! Sadly, this is a sentiment I have expressed often over my course of being a feminist, but I probably felt it most in the days and weeks following the Trump election.

I spent days after the election gathering my bearings. I would cry in Lyfts. Or get on the phone with my dad and talk to him for hours. Or do comedy shows because laughter is a great reprieve from anger. During this time, hurt, rage, restlessness, and a litany of other emotions layered on top of each like winter clothing during a ski trip, and pretty soon a call to action was formed. And not like the BS call to action like when a friend sends a mass email telling people to subscribe to their YouTube page, or the one I got recently from college friends whose ten-year wedding anniversary is coming up, so they're asking people to donate money so they can celebrate their marriage. And it's not like they just want a nice brunch where there's French toast with three kinds of butters. These mofos had the audacity to ask us to help them get overseas so they can do some in-depth activities like a tour of *The Lord of the Rings* and *The Hobbit* trilogy movie sets, a helicopter ride over the scenic parts of New Zealand, and a whale and dolphin safari. #NeggaPlease #RuthNeggaLegitHatesHerLastNameBecauseOf-AssholesLikeMe. But for real, that has got to be the most entitled married-people trash I've ever heard of. Like, bitch, I went to your wedding. Got you a gift. And now I gotta help pay for your anniversary present? Y'all had ten years to save for this trip and you're giving me six months. See? This is why some nonmarried people are salty towards some married folk. Single people don't ask for this kind of stuff. But there are those married peeps who act like their being legally together means they're allowed to keep asking everyone for money like they're an autorenewal subscription plan for Hulu. So ig, but if we're going to be ig, then can I get a gift for not being married to someone who's not a good fit for me? I have done that for more than ten years. Moving on. The point is the call to action following the 2016 election was all the way legit. If there were folks who were tired of the status quo and wanted a brash reality TV star to mix things up, there were also women who were tired of not being heard and they weren't going to take it anymore.

In Hawaii, a woman by the name of Teresa Shook created a Facebook event, inviting friends to march on Washington in protest. Quickly, similar events were created all over the platform by Evvie Harmon, Fontaine Pearson, Bob Bland (a New York fashion designer), Breanne Butler, and many others. Like a lottery to see a Broadway show for a discounted price, these invites inspired thousands and thousands of women to sign up to march, and smartly, Harmon, Pearson, and Butler teamed up, beginning the official Women's March on Washington. And because people of color don't sleep, meaning they didn't want this shit to be a Lilith Fair of whiteness in which the concerns of nonwhite and non-well-off women were swept under the rug, the demand that the march be led by women of different races and backgrounds was made and swiftly met. Vanessa Wruble, cofounder of the march and copresident of Okay-Africa, served as head of campaign operations and brought on Tamika D. Mallory, a black woman; Carmen Perez, a Latina; and Linda Sarsour, an American Muslim, to serve as national cochairs alongside Bland. This *Ocean's 8*–style crew was rounded out by former Miss New Jersey USA Janaye Ingram, also black, who served as head of logistics, and Paola Mendoza, a Colombian-American filmmaker who came aboard as an artistic director and a national organizer. Once the players were in place, the official name of Women's March on Washington was selected. And then it was off to the races. Everyone. Was. Getting. Mobilized. And. I. Was. Blown. Away.

Not because I believed the Women's March was destined to fail. It's more that, whether a get-together is as big as that march or as tiny as a threesome, I'm always impressed whenever anyone can organize a group event successfully. I mean, I struggle for weeks trying to plan a dinner with four busy friends from college, but *three* people can all agree to have sex with LED lights on? #RealTalk, if I had to bone two other people at the same time, the room would be dark AF with just one single candle burning, like the one that burned when Benny Franks dropped his sixteen bars on the Declaraysh of Indepennie late at night.[4] ANYWAY!

What I'm getting at is that seeing how smartly and efficiently the Women's March was being run from the beginning was inspiring and made me, and I believe many others, feel as though the march was going to *mean* something and *do* something. It was in the air. This march was going to be a *moment*.

It was going to prove that women cannot be silenced. It was going to show that women are not going to turn the other cheek as they have done for centuries. It would reveal the allies (i.e., some gay and straight men) who are unafraid to walk side by side with ladies to help amplify our message. It was going to take roll call and be all the evidence needed to show that if you're not with the women and supporting them by attending the march or if you couldn't due to extenuating circumstances (e.g., not being physically able, don't have the luxury of taking time off work, etc.), then you could show your support in other ways—donating to the ACLU and other women-friendly organizations, being more vocal in your everyday life with regards to womens' issues, etc.—and if you didn't do that, then you clearly weren't for the advancement of women. Rather you were silently complicit in keeping status quo or, worse, adamantly against women progressing. Pretty cut-and-dry, right? And given the complete upending Trump's ascendance signaled, acting partly on emotion and proverbially drawing the line in

---

4. Lmao. You are correct if you assumed that was the most ignorant way to say that Benjamin Franklin was one of the writers of the Declaration of Independence.

the sand like that might seem appropriate and rational . . . if you're a white woman. But I'm not.

I'm black. My decision to participate in the march wasn't as easy as 1-2-3. What the march represented, no matter how diverse its organizing committee was, is a far more nuanced and complicated thing to unpack for the average woman of color. And to be honest, the Women's March amplified a lot of what's wrong with feminism, including its main problem: protecting the institution of *white* feminism, even if, and in some cases especially if, it means sacrificing the needs, wants, and safety of women who don't fit neatly in the box of "educated, financially stable, straight, and white." I know I'm not the only feminist who, because she doesn't fall under the aforementioned category, has felt neglected by the movement. If you haven't been on the receiving end of the neglect, it stings and serves as a reminder of how despite all the "Rah-rah! Go #Team-Feminism," you can feel lonelier on the team than if you were never on it at all. I'll give you an example.

I still remember the first and only time I was called a "cunt" on social media. Aww! How touching. As you probably suspected, everyone reminiscences fondly about the first time they were called a "see you next Tuesday" the way they might look back on their nephew's christening or a horsefly air-dropping their doo-doo all over the just-opened container of chicken salad during a picnic. Being called the c-word is just that special, y'all. For me, this cherry-popping moment went down on Instagram.

If you don't follow me on Insta, here's a quick recap of what I do there: (1) marvel at the hotness of famous dudes like some do at double rainbows, (2) promote projects I work on, (3) post #TBT pictures of me from my high school and college years in which I somehow look like a forty-seven-year-old auntie trolling for peen at a church mixer, and (4) earnestly share content such as where to make charitable donations for various causes or express my opinions about certain social issues. One of those issues is #BlackLivesMatter, and except for black people named Kanye "Forward All My Mail to the PO Box Addressed: The Sunken Place" West, it's more than a hashtag.

It's a plea for people to see us instead of seeing *through* us, a "I think therefore I am," shouldn't-this-be-kind-obvious-by-now statement, and a call to action we hope will get stuck in the minds of everyone who hears it until it makes them want to help dismantle a system intent on policing and harming brown and black bodies by any means necessary. That's a lot for three little words to accomplish, but in an age when black men, women, and children are routinely murdered by police officers, who almost never suffer any real consequences for their crimes, and when black bodies are also routinely imprisoned for minor offenses that if perpetrated by their white brethren would, more often than not, lead to little more than a slap on the wrist, #BlackLivesMatter is, frankly, the thesis statement of a movement and also a reminder to black people that even though the world doesn't see it, we *do* matter, so don't fucking forget it or give up.

So two years ago, shortly before turning thirty-two, I was weary. A couple of men—Terence Crutcher of Tulsa, Oklahoma, and Keith Lamont Scott of Charlotte, North Carolina—were gunned down by police within the span of a few days. Like many people who were rattled by this latest in a long line of gut-wrenching deaths, I turned to friends and family, devoured as much news about these murders as possible until it was too much to stomach, and got online. I simply posted a ten-second video loop of #BlackLivesMatter in a rolling crawl. Within minutes, a white guy troll who was probably just searching the hashtag and spewing hatred on people's Instagram pages wrote: "Dumb cunt." A couple of internet strangers tried to silence him, and after a while, I just deleted all traces of this discord because infighting was not the purpose of the post. I was deeply sad and was using those three little words to keep myself from drowning in despair, and I was immediately made to feel as though I wasn't even allowed that. Now, that kind of berating as a form of silencing takes place all over sosh meeds and is nothing new.

I once saw a woman post a humorous and so-not-serious ranking of the components in Chex Mix and a guy called her a "dumb bitch." Makes ya wish you could nominate some dudes for vasectomies the way you can nominate a coworker for Employee of the Month, doesn't it? But in all seriousness, the point is that it doesn't take much for folks to needlessly and ignorantly go from zero to one hundred no matter if the subject is something as innocuous as a snack or as dire as black people being disproportionately harassed and killed by law enforcement. The aggression from trolls is all the same, but it is telling that almost any time a person of color comments on race on social media (or in real life, for that matter) they are *immediately* disrespected. What's also telling is the silence from the white folk who claim to be for equality.

Not to brag, but I know a lot of white people and specifically a lot of white women. As I often say, "To be asked the question: 'Should I get sprinks on this fro-yo?' is to know a white woman." And I've heard that question. *A lot.* So I know *a lot* of white dames. Yet when "cunt" was thrown my way, not a single one of my white girlfriends stepped in. There may be reasons for that.

It's common knowledge that it's best to *not* engage with trolls. Also, some of my white homies might not have seen this comment in their feed before I deleted it. While others, myself included, know that this, unfortunately, is considered light online harassment and is so commonplace that we might be a little desensitized to it. That's all plausible. Besides, I didn't expect a cavalcade to come to my rescue, as I can handle nonsense like that. In fact, that foolishness wasn't even what preoccupied my mind. What I was more concerned with is that not a single white girlfriend of mine commented *in support* of the post either. No "I can't understand all the way, but I empathize with your broken heart" or "YES! Black lives do matter. Your black life matters to me." All was eerily quiet on the internet front. I mean, I'll get a "yaaas" and/or a "slay" on a cute picture selfie I post, "lmao"s and "haha"s if I make a joke, but when I acknowledge the elephant in the room, which is that I know the world knows I'm black, meaning not only do I know that the deadly consequences for being black in America are lurking around the corner for myself, my family, and my black friends, but I know that information has forever altered the way I live my life because I don't live in the same America that many white people of a certain status do, that truth is too real to handle. Too uncomfortable to address. So people don't.

Often, I hear that many white people clam up when it comes to the topic of race because they're "scared of saying something racist" or they simply don't know what to say at all. Uh-uh. Nope. Not buying it. This isn't a Sadie Hawkins dance where the gals are nervous to ask the boys to grind to Sean Paul's "Gimme the Light." This is real life.

White people:[5] HOW. DO. YOU. HAVE. NOTHING. TO. SAY. AT. THIS. POINT? Black people are dying. Black people are being bullied. Black people are being blamed, silenced, told to get over it, told they're not fighting hard enough, and all this other bullshit designed to make them feel like they're not doing enough. Black people are being tasked with solely fixing a system of oppression as if it's not a societal problem that not only affects everyone but requires the efforts of everyone to achieve equality. Black people are made to feel alone. They're not. We're all in this bloody, depressing, trash pile of a mess together and we've been in it for far too long—centuries—for the excuse "I don't know what to say" to ring true at all anymore. So please, WP, find the damn words.

Not to get all Dr. Seuss on ya, but look for the words in a house. Look for the words under a mouse. Find the words and help a sista out. Have her and her brothas' backs to their speaking the truth and have their backs when some negative shit is going down. Have queer people's backs when they're routinely

---

5. It should go without saying that I, of course, don't mean *all* white people. I'm just using the collective caucasity of America because I'm not in the mood to bust out an H&R Block printing calculator and do some mathematicals to figure out the exact number of white peeps who are speechless when it comes to racism. All that matters is that the amount of WP who remain silent, even if it is one person, is one too many, so I have to address e'rybody. Cool? Cool.

the target of abuse. Have Muslims' backs when they're being harassed on the street in broad daylight. Have the backs of the children of color who are being ripped away from their parents by a heartless government, those who risk their lives and leave behind unimaginable circumstances to try to get into this country in hopes of a better life. Silence and putting your head down is flat-out unacceptable and only makes more *visible* the fact that you're trying to remain *invisible* in the face of atrocities. The middle-school fear of not wanting to be called on should be thrown in the dumpster along with beat-up Lisa Frank folders, dingy LA Gear sneakers, and watching *Saved by the Bell* with the same intense dedication that you might have for *American Horror Story*. But, can I be brutally honest for second (ha, like I haven't been already)?

Can we all agree that the whole "being at a loss for words" when it comes to topics like police brutality or having feminism benefit anyone other than well-to-do, educated, straight white women of a certain class, is a tired and weak lie? Maybe not a malicious lie in all cases, but a lie nonetheless. The truth is, white feminists have no problem finding the words. They speak up loudly and often whether it's at a march, in everyday life, or any time there's a microphone available, like when Patricia Arquette demanded equal pay during her 2015 Best Supporting Actress acceptance speech.

Ya know, I'd like to pretend that if I was ever in the position to give an acceptance speech at the Oscars where millions upon millions are potentially watching and could potentially share clips of me talking online for even *more* people to see, I'd be noble AF like Arquette and discuss a deeper issue. Use my platform for good, but honestly, I'd probably be ignorant. Just whipping out one of the chicken cutlets that are filling out my dress and waving it around in the air like I'm signaling the beginning of a street race, then I'd start calling out all the directors who *didn't* hire me ("I made it in spite of you, *Wes Anderson*"), and I'd then delay the ceremony because I'm doing the Tootsie Roll to the orchestral "wrap it up" music for about twenty-seven minutes. Pure, unadulterated ignorance. Luckily, Arquette's speech was not. In fact, it was the opposite and it went viral.

You might remember it. Meryl Streep was in the audience and taken to church—#Hozier—by Arquette's call to action. Plenty of actors and actresses joined her in cheering Arquette on. So did folks on social media. Arquette would later tell *Entertainment Tonight* that the speech cost her some roles though she still works, which is an unfortunate consequence that she had to endure, but seeing as we're now three years removed from her speech and equal pay is currently an issue that is front and center in Hollywood, which has resulted in many actresses earning salaries on par with their male counterparts, Arquette using her platform to address this issue was worth it as it was one moment in many that forced Hollywood to get to this point. What she did there was great. It's what she did afterwards that had me making that Tim "The Tool Man" Taylor confused-grunt sound.[6]

---

6. Do any young people know what the hell I'm referring to? That show came out when I was seven years old and I watched it on the regs. And I can't even use the excuse that I was really watching the show because I was into JTT aka Jonathan Taylor Thomas. Not. At. All. I was legit like, "Yaaas, bring on Wilson and his goofy-ass bucket hats." Who, at *seven*, is only showing up for *Wilson*? Y'all, I swear that on the inside, I'm a seventy-year-old with osteoporo-ro aka osteoporosis, rocking Patti LaBelle–themed compression socks and talking about how Jackie Robinson tried to holla at me when I was young.

Following her acceptance speech, Arquette elaborated on her call to action backstage in the press room and said the following: "It's time for all the women in America and all the men that love women and all the gay people and all the people of color that we've all fought for to fight for us now." No, no, no, Patricia, what are you doing?! You delivered a spot-on speech and then ruined much of the goodwill coming your way by calling out the very people who have been in the weeds with white women this whole time despite the historical attempts by white women to leave them behind?[7] Ay-yi-yi! The saying is "Quit while you're ahead," not "Keep going until you see Larry David chilling in the cut while the *Curb Your Enthusiam* theme song plays because you made shit so awkward." But that's exactly what Arquette did, cuing up the pomp pomp pomps of the tuba.

Immediately, on social media, people took her to task for the tone-deaf implication that (1) the struggle for queer women and women of color is basically over now in part because white people have done a sufficient job fighting for them (LOL forever), and (2) WOCs and queer women haven't been out here fighting for feminism since day one and now need to step up. Look, I'm all for tough love, when it's truthful. But what Arquette was saying? It wasn't adding up to me and many others,

---

7. For example, the ratification of the Fifteenth Amendment in 1870, which allowed men of all races the right to vote, did not please some in the suffragette movement. Like Anna Howard Shaw, the president of the National American Woman Suffrage Association, who said, "You have put the ballot in the hands of your black men, thus making them political superiors of white women. Never before in the history of the world have men made former slaves the political masters of their former mistresses!" Then the gloves were off and white suffragists made sure to push for the white woman's right to vote while purposefully not fighting for the voting rights of women of color.

and a backlash as well as a defense of her statement commenced.

Some chalked it up to her misspeaking (not buying it) or to people such as myself being hypersensitive and overreacting. While others wondered why anyone cared that a rich woman was asking for parity when the average non-wealthy woman is still fighting for the scraps she can get. That's absolutely true. The average woman is also underpaid. There are more important things than the salaries of the Hollywood elite, but that doesn't mean what Arquette said isn't worth discussing or analyzing or rightfully calling bullshit on when her statements are being used to galvanize the masses when, in actuality, they were tone-deaf.

Firstly, WOC and queer people *have* been standing alongside white women on the equal pay issue since the beginning, except those groups' contributions aren't typically acknowledged or appreciated by WW. Secondly, women of color and LGBTQIA+ folks make significantly less than white women and have let that information be known for *years*,[8] so it's not as though this isn't also an urgent matter for them. In fact, it's probably more pressing considering the median income is lower for WOC and queer people than it is for white women. So Arquette's demand that people who have always been in the fight need to step it up is not only ridiculous but it also shines a bright light on what happens when feminism isn't intersectional: the voices of the non-white, non-straight are ignored and the decades of work by the non-white, non-straight women is

8. According to *Business Insider*, white women make 79 percent of what white men do, black women earn 63 percent, and Latina women just 54 percent. ☹

erased from history. That's why I believe Arquette's comment burned the toast of many people. The notion that POCs and LGBTQIA+ folk aren't doing enough to change the system isn't just a belief held by an actress you can dismiss as "out of touch" if you want; it's held by the average, everyday white feminist who isn't standing in front of a microphone in front of the whole world on Oscar night but one who would most likely be participating in the Women's March and asking me to stand beside her.

Again, I understood that the march was being organized and run by a diverse committee, but no matter how hard I tried to focus on that fact, my hesitation remained as strong as ever. All I had to do was look around to see that my doubts were justified. Giant swaths of white women *only* mobilized after Trump was elected, yet they were eerily absent for #BlackLives-Matter demonstrations. Many white women were not speaking out in favor of trans women's rights or demanding that Muslim women in this country as well as non-white immigrants be treated humanely. Now, I can't know for certain why that was happening, but what I did know was that WW's inaction in movements that don't *directly* affect them proved to me that all those people are not a priority or viewed as fellow feminists who should be protected. But, still, I went to the march.

Even now, two years later, I'm not entirely sure why. Maybe a piece of me didn't want to miss a part of history. Maybe I want to be able to tell my niece when she gets older that I was there and didn't just sit in my feelings because white feminism wasn't as good as it should be. Perhaps another part of me just wanted to be with thousands of other people who were also devastated about Trump. Whatever the case may be, once I decided to go, I was all in. Not wearing pussy hats all in, because those were goofy-looking as hell. I was all in in other ways.

I booked my train ticket to Washington, DC, and shared an Airbnb with a friend. I encouraged others to speak up on sosh meeds; Ilana and I hosted a comedy show at the march and raised as much money as possible and donated all of it to the ACLU, in addition to my own private donation; I armed myself with as much knowledge as possible about what we could potentially be up against with a number 45 administration; I used my podcast *Sooo Many White Guys* as a way of having tough conversations with folks I didn't agree with on a plethora of issues, not just politics; as well as getting educated by the likes of political satirist Bassem Youssef and blerd[9] superhero Melissa Harris-Perry, who helped me see America and the rest of the world clearer. All these actions were lifting me out of despair, and I knew that going to the march was a key factor in feeling hope again.

IDK about anyone else who attended, but the march itself felt like a high school reunion minus the competition, a family reunion, and a spiritual rejuvenation. Listening to speeches by brilliant women ranging from politicians, activists, actresses, poets, etc. felt like earning a four-year degree in women's studies in one day without the sad Sylvia Plath parts. Seeing men there with their daughters and, more importantly, their *sons*, as if to say, "Boys, what's happening ain't a lady problem. It's an everybody situation." Watching folks get a kick out of

---

9. "Blerd" stands for "black nerd."

each other's signs and sharing snacks touched me. All these displays of humanity were saying something. What was mine saying?

This may be cheesy, but I believed my presence said to feminism, "Even though you don't always or even sometimes show up for me, I'm showing up for you." I hoped my chanting alongside other women conveyed the message of, "My feminism isn't conditional, because if it is, then how am I any different than those I have gripes with?" I needed my comedy and donations to say, "See how I'm fighting with you? Let that be an example that you can fight with me and for me and all the others you've forgotten about."

I'm sure some queer women and WOCs who didn't go to the march are probably rolling their eyes at these hopes and dreams of mine. Before I address that, let me just write this: I know that before, during, and following the Women's March, I saw white women online express their disappointment at the disgruntlement within the feminist community, claiming that those women of color and women in the LGBTQIA+ community were being divisive. Here's the deal: If you spill milk all over the floor, you can't then expect the milk to only go where you want it to go.[10] Meaning, feminism cannot be deeply flawed and exclusive yet expect everyone to show up and support it. Them's the breaks, kiddo. You can't have it both ways. So for those who are less than

---

10. Y'all, when I typed that colon, I was certain I was going to drop an amazing, instantly iconic Judge Judy–ism, like her classic, "Don't pee on my leg and tell me it's raining." Turns out, that's the kind of nugget you drop when you go to law school, become a judge, practice your craft for decades, and wear fashionable doilies. However, when you are me, you settle for pulling a semicoherent analogy out of thin air the way I pull a sweater out of a pile of clothes, do the sniff test, shrug my shoulders, and put it on.

satisfied with feminism or don't even identify as feminists as a result of its tendency to exclude, they are absolutely justified in *not* going to the Women's March. They are justified in expressing their displeasure. And they deserve to be heard. So listen to them and listen without speaking. Now, with that PSA out of the way, lemme return back to my being a damn Pollyanna.

I'm a relatively optimistic person, but even I'm shocked at how pie in the sky I'm sounding about my participation in the Women's March. After all, I cannot trust the preparers at Chop't to put dressing on my salad because I don't think any of them know how to not overdress my rabbit food, yet there I was praying that my moving in unison "Rhythm Nation" style with some feminists for two miles was enough to undo a lifetime of being okay with WW and society as a whole not caring about non-white feminists. That is a tall order, and my being there probably did none of what my daydreams would have liked it to have done. Or maybe it changed a couple of minds. I'll never know, and it's probably not my business to know. What *was* my business was how my relationship with feminism was changing. After being at the march, if I couldn't reconcile my mixed feelings about feminism, I could at least spend time figuring out what my relationship was going to be with the movement.

You know how sometimes when you're casually dating someone and you ask them to DTR aka define the relationship? That conversation usually goes one of two ways: (A) the person basically changes their name to "Boo, Your" on their driver's license, which is impractical but touching, or (B) the person drops a ninja smoke bomb and disappears, and while that hurts your feelings, you're also impressed because the old-school way of saying, "I gotta go," and then struggling to put on your pre-tied New Balances because they are tied too tight, is not the jam. Well, thankfully, when I asked feminism if it was going to step up and be there for me in the future, it responded, "Sure! And to help prove it, do you want to meet one of the movement's OGs, Gloria Steinem?" To which I responded, "Yaaas times infinity!!!"

"Great," feminism said. "Now go ahead and moderate a discussion with Steinem at the Massachusetts Conference for Women." OMG!

It goes without saying that nothing can prepare you for meeting an icon who has meant so much to so many people. So I did the best I could. I heavily researched her life, her writing, and her on-the-ground experiences as she, alongside powerful luminaries—such as bell hooks; Angela Davis; Dorothy Pitman Hughes, the cofounder of *Ms.* magazine (the other one being Gloria); Native American activist Wilma Mankiller, and many more—led the movement. And also, duh, I made sure I looked cute when I first met her by rocking a floor-length black dress with floral embroidery all over it that, if the front could talk, it would've said, "I make candles from scratch just because," while in the back, because the dress was backless, was like, "I'm a sexy-ass doula, so get out of the way so I can serve face while delivering your baby."

In a nutshell, my conversation with her was nothing short of amazing. She let me call her Glo-Glo, rolled with it when I said the word "peen," and she was dropping so many Tampax with pearls of wisdom—#PunNotWorthIt—that it seemed every five minutes there was an applause break. Hands down, my favorite part of our chat was when I brought up my mixed feelings about feminism, which are the result of its lack of inclusion. I could sense all the non-white women were like "Finally!" à la CeCe Peniston,[11] while it seemed there was a wave of white women in the audience giving off the vibe of "Oh no. Here we go again." There was a shift in the air, but I didn't care. The answers I was seeking were far more important than some strangers' discomfort.

Gloria immediately expressed her frustration with feminism being considered a white movement for a couple of reasons. First, black women have routinely lead the charge in fighting for *all* women. While acknowledging that #MeToo, which was created by Tarana Burke, existed long before white actresses such as Alyssa Milano got on board and became the leading voices of it, Glo-Glo went on to break down the origin of the term "sexual harassment." It was coined by feminists at Cornell University in 1975 and then a few years later, Catharine MacKinnon, a lawyer and feminist activist, figured out how to legally argue that sexual harassment was not only a violation of rights but a prime example of discrimination.

With this framework, three black women filed high-profile and successful lawsuits. Paulette Barnes and Diane Williams took on the US Environmental Protection Agency and the US Justice Department, respectively, while Mechelle Vinson sued Meritor Savings Bank after she was raped by her boss in a bank vault. Her case made history, as it was the first of its kind to go

---

11. In case ya don't know, CeCe Peniston is an R&B/dance music legend, and I blast her music a lot. See?! I don't just listen to Dad Rock . . . and no, you can't look at my iTunes account to see what's in there. You'll just have to take me at my word.

all the way to the Supreme Court, where the unanimous decision ruled that sexual harassment violated federal laws and that employers could be held accountable for the sexual misconduct of their employees.

"All three of these women were black," Gloria began. "And these black women now symbolize the fact that [sexual harassment] is certainly more likely to happen to people with less power in society than to people with more power."[12] She then stated that statistically speaking, black women are twice as likely to identify as feminist than their white counterparts.

Gloria also brought up the national poll *Ms.* magazine conducted in 1970, in which 60 percent of black women identified as feminist and supported the movement while only 30 percent of white women did. Then she continued by saying that considering that 53 percent of white women voted for Donald Trump during the 2016 election (91 percent of black women voted for Clinton), this was an example of how white women were still behind. What was notable about that moment was not Gloria presenting the receipts, although that was appreciated, but how the audience reacted. The women of color clapped loudly and proudly as did a few white women, but this truth bomb was not met with the rapturous applause that frequented earlier parts of our talk. Even when their icon, a woman they unanimously admire, speaks a truth *they* don't want to hear, there is discomfort. Gloria acknowledging that giving black women props for our historical contributions is long overdue—whether it's

---

12. Wish I had the kind of brain that could retain quotes like this, but thanks to the internet, I don't have to: Leah Fessler attended this conversation and wrote about it in an article called, "Gloria Steinem Says Black Women Have Always Been More Feminist than White Women," for Quartz, which is where the quote comes from.

#MeToo or those landmark lawsuits or turning up for Hillary Clinton (despite inflammatory articles like the one published in the *New York Times* with the heading "Black Turnout Soft in Early Voting," which was shady because we all know who the fuck did and *didn't* turn out)—was met with resistence.

So what are we going to do? How are we going to deal with the instinct to ignore the contributions of black feminists (as well as contributions from other WOC and LGTBQIA+ feminists) being alive and as strong as ever? How can we quell the desire to be agitated by the truth as well as the tendency to blame WOCs and queer feminists for the failures of feminism even though it has been proven time and time again that some white feminists will go against their best interests as women in order to maintain their class and race status? I mean, those are the million-dollar questions feminism has to be asking itself during these growing pains, and maybe part of the reason these growing pains aren't entirely apparent to all feminists is because they're being hidden underneath feel-good decorations the way I'd cover a wine stain on a couch cushion by using my Nicki Minaj "Miley, what's good?" throw pillow. Time-out because we *have* to talk about that question and how it was one of the greatest questions uttered in history next to Nicolas Cage's query in *Con Air*: "Why couldn't you put the bunny back in the box?"

Like many pop stars before her, Miley Cyrus constantly reinvents her image. Her current incarnation includes her singing chill love songs with a country-ish vibe while posing in meadows straight out of Allegra-D allergy commercials. It's all very innocent and quiet and well . . . white. This is in stark contrast to the Cyrus from a few years ago, who was wearing gold-plated grillz, twerking, hanging out with "thug-looking" black dudes and rappers aka using lazy and shallow stereotypes of black culture all to show that she was not a little girl anymore. This obvious cultural appropriation was hailed by mainstream media as cool and edgy behavior when we all knew that if she were black, this behavior would be considered nothing but ratchet. This fact seemed to haunt Cyrus during that period, but she was never forced to confront the truth until she and Minaj butted heads.

It all began when the 2015 MTV VMA nominations were announced. Nicki Minaj's highly popular and sexual video for "Anaconda" was not nominated for Video of the Year, so she cried foul by tweeting: "When the 'other' girls drop a video that breaks records and impacts culture they get that nomination." Taylor Swift assumed this comment was directed at her because her vid "Bad Blood" got several noms, Minaj assured her it wasn't, but implored her to speak on the issue of artists of color not being recognized. *Then*, Cyrus, who was completely not involved but decided to create some beef, ran to the *New York Times* (which has got to be the WHITEST THING TO DO IN A BEEF as I don't recall Tupac being like, "Lemme hit up *The Atlantic* so I can read Biggie Smalls to filth") and immediately reduced Minaj's comments to starting a cat fight. Right. Because the intelligent thing to do as a white woman when faced with valid criticism about what your privilege allows is to drag out the angry-black-woman trope. Not. Smart. The interview went viral leading up to her stint hosting the 2015 MTV VMAs.

Minaj took her moment to address the nonsense in the Minaj-iest of ways. She won Best Hip-Hop Video for "Anaconda" and closed her acceptance speech by addressing Cyrus with some-thing black people often say—"what's good?"—which is used as a greeting *or* to send the message of "We're not going to have a problem are we because if so, I might have to hand your ass to you." Everyone in the room, as well as the viewers at home, knew that based on the amount of stank Minaj put on "Miley, what's good?" this question fell into the latter category. And in that moment, we all saw Cyrus dropping her "street" persona and going full cul-de-sac. Y'all, her lip quivered like she was on *Days of Our Lives,* she stuttered out some congratulations to Minaj and said the media twisted her words, and let out a deep-ass sigh like "Golly-gee, this casserole is not going to be done in time for the *Frasier* marathon my friends and I are about to watch." Who knew that a simple and intense "Yo, what's good?" is the verbal version of "Bitch, you white" smelling salts that gets white ladies to cut their cultural-appropriating bullshit? I certainly didn't, but I'm going on a "What's good?" smelling salt spree to all the hair salons where stylists are putting *Battlefield Earth* dreadlocks on white girls. Okay. Back to our regularly scheduled programming of discussing why feminism's grow-ing pains aren't self-evident to all feminists.

Simply put, there are too many things distracting us. The pussy hats. Feminist T-shirts. Think pieces. Books. Pop stars ranging from Taylor Swift to Beyoncé publicly identifiying as feminists (who can forget the moment when Bey closed the 2014 MTV VMAs by standing in front of a giant, ten-foot-high lit-up screen that had "FEMINIST" on it?). There's no denying that feminism has been commercialized as a brand in a way it never has before. It's trendy to be a feminist, and that label serves as a catchall the way that "influencer" does for popular people on sosh meeds. Plenty of people, myself included, are thrilled that more and more people are identifying as a feminist because we need to keep building this army so we can make equality a reality. But much like when you're hosting a house party and the clock strikes midnight and you start looking around at the party crashers you don't recognize and mutter to yourself, "Who are all these heauxes and how did they get in here?," I'm a tad suspicious of some of these FPCs aka feminism party crashers who are claiming to be feminists.

Not that I'm the arbiter on who does and who doesn't get to be a feminist, but I have some questions about some of the behavior I'm seeing. I think a huge part of the reason questionable choices and comments are being made is because there is no one, correct, strict way to be a feminist. And sometimes, despite our best intentions, we all often fail to live up to what feminism should be and do for all women. Heck, celebrated author Roxane Gay even wrote a book called *Bad Feminist* in which she documented the complexities and complications with being a feminist, such as liking unsavory things in pop culture. I know I'm not the only one demanding that women not be seen as shrill, argumentative, and catty, yet I will watch trash reality TV featuring women who play up this stereotype. I know I have to grow and stop making thoughtless choices like consuming toxic content. I'm working on it. But not everyone is. Not all feminists are willing to get better or hold themselves accountable, not by trying to be perfect but by being conscious during their decision-making process, from the little things like bad television to the weightier sociopolitical issues. In fact, there are some pretenders out there, y'all. They might be hard to identify and there are several types, but these are the ones I've seen most frequently that I believe pose an actual threat to an inclusive feminism:

(A) FAUXMINISTS

Have you ever hung out with a woman and she, apropro of nothing, says something to the effect of, "Most of my friends are guys; I just don't get along with women, which is crazy, but I guess some women can't handle other women's success"? And you have to sit there with your face frozen in an uncomfortable smile like you just got some Bobo aka Botox? This is a typical fauxminist, or fake feminist, comment. I mean, sure, women get jealous, but so do men. Jealousy isn't gender specific. Also, when a statement like this is made, there's always an air of "I'm one of the exceptional women who can fit in with men," which is gross.

But what is really troubling about fauxminists is that their feminism is not only conditional (meaning they're for it unless what is being asked of them threatens their way of thinking and living), but it's also infused with patriarchal toxicity, so their big takeaway from feminism is not about equality and rights for all but that women should finally be allowed to behave as badly as men have for centuries. Hell no! I have no interest in having my turn to take a dump on progress. I want to elevate a room when I walk in it, not just keep it the same as it's always been. I want the world to be fundamentally different than the one my mom grew up in. So I refuse to get mine, so to speak, by reinforcing the patriarchy to my advantage. There is no point in perpetuating the same bullshit because it is somehow going to taste better going down because it's coming from a woman. Poison is poison no matter who serves it to you.

(B) FEMINISTS WHO ARE ALL ABOUT THAT MERCH

These are the ones who, inspired by the Swifts and the Beyoncés and any other public figure, get pumped. They'll go to concerts and wear the shirts and watch female-helmed and female-led movies and TV shows because that's the fun and easy work. However, when it comes down to the nitty gritty work, they're nowhere to be found. This is kinda like when I was in my twenties and was all hyped for my friends moving to a new apartment, so I sent them links to Target or West Elm products, but when they sent a text like, "I'm moving next Saturday at noon, can you help me?" I'd immediately think *Nope*, but didn't want to seem like a jerk, so I'd wait until 6:57 P.M. on that Saturday and write the classic lie of, "OMG! I just saw this text. Sorry! How did the move go?" Sorry to spill the beans, but no one misses texts. People see every single one the way I have seen every *Step Up* movie. So if you ask for a favor and your friend doesn't respond, they are treating your request like spam emails from LivingSocial.

(C) WRAPPING-PAPER FEMINISTS

They kind of remind me of my niece, who for a long time gave zero fucks about the presents people gave her and only cared about the paper it was wrapped in. I'd be like, "Olivia, you like this book I got you about black astronauts?" No reponse because she'd be off staring at the wrapper paper the way people tripping on mushrooms look at the evening sky. Same with some feminists who only listen to a feminist message if it's being delivered in a certain package. I can't tell you the number of times I've seen sex workers online talk about the failings of feminism only to be dismissed because of their profession. The notion that if you don't look (read: appropriate kind of white woman) or act a certain way then you aren't "one of us." And this is not saying that the white women who are making valid points shouldn't be making them. Of course they should. But, for example, while it was nice for actress Brie Larson to use her time while accepting the Crystal Award for Excellence in Film at this year's Crystal + Lucy Awards to address the lack of diversity in the field of film criticism, it was strange to see how viral this moment went. I mean, queer people and WOCs have stated for years that they don't have the same access as their white counterparts to screenings and aren't hired by bigger media outlets, which are intent on keeping that profession mostly white, male, and straight. Yet no one gave a damn until a famous, wealthy white woman said something. Nope.

(D) APOLOGY-TOUR FEMINISTS

These are probably the most popular of the four. They move through the world in a reckless, Steve Urkel sort of way, routinely causing trouble, busting out a "Did I do that?," offering up a nice enough sounding apology, and then carrying on with the same action that got them in trouble in the first place.

Clearly there's a lot of masquerading going on, which can lead to infighting that's counterproductive to progress as well as hurt feelings and women wanting to give up and stop rooting for feminism. Well, I implore those who want to give up to not do that. Don't let the disappointment be the only imprint feminism leaves on you. There are too many people who came before us, who fought tirelessly for us, so disappointment wouldn't be a stain on our lives like perhaps it was on theirs. But this isn't my biggest plea. I'm saving that for feminism.

Feminism, you honestly just have to do better. I know you've heard this a million times and a million ways, but you have to figure it the fuck out and do better. Yes, *you*. The onus is not on those you've consistently excluded to fix this. And trust me, it needs fixing, and I'm not talking about relying on repeating the same "remedies" of the past. Meaning, I don't need the sorries. I'm not interested in the #NotAllWomen defense. I have no desire to engage with your expression of guilt as a sign that the state of things bothers you. *Show* us it bothers you by behaving differently. Act as if you understand that inclusiveness is what feminism should have been about since day one. And not because you're hoping you're going to get a pat on the back for doing what you should've done in the first place. Okay?

Normally, I would attempt to lighten the moment right now, but sorry, not sorry, I can't. Feminism, I'm deliberately hard on you the way Tyra Banks was hard on Tiffany. The way my parents were on me when I was growing up, which used to piss me off, but as I got older, I understood it. They loved me the most, which is why they demanded the excellence they knew was within me. So, feminism, I say this to you: You're one of the things I love the most in the world, which is why I expect the most, because I know you have the potential to be everything you should be. Give me something to root for. Give me and all women of color, queer women, trans women, lower-class women, something to root for. Most importantly, give us love, because while you've been hard on us, the love has been in very short supply. Give us the love we deserve and we'll root for you forever.

LOL. Wut?: An Incomplete List of All the Ways Being a Woman Is Ridic

~~~~~~

Soooooooooo, if you haven't picked up on it by now, the lady experience can be complicated and frustrating. Obviously, it has its pluses (such as being capable of having multiple orgasms; on average, we live longer than men; and according to *Time*, women are more likely to obtain a college degree), but it definitely has its cons, and the negatives can feel oppressive at times. Remember when Leonardo DiCaprio was trying his damnedest not to be human tartare for that giant-ass bear in *The Revenant*? That's pretty much how many of us, especially those in the middle-class bracket and above, are about the biggest and, more often, the *tiniest* problems or inconveniences we face. So, to deal, we frequently dip into our complaint attaché cases[1]

---

1. Do you really think those who have the luxury of venting on the regs are walking around with a leftover Craftsman tool kit from a Father's Day sale? Hell no! We're gonna put our grievances in a fancy leather bag with this directive inside: "In case of my death, send to the cast of *The Real Housewives of New Jersey* because they will (1) know how to drag out these problems for years, (2) pepper the complaints

to use tools that help us defend ourselves when it may seem, in the moment, that our lives, core values, sense of selves, or even just our valuable time are on the line.

And yes, everyone has their very own monogrammed complaint attaché case. I don't care how nice you are. You complain. *Regularly.* Firing off a snarky tweet that garners tons of faves and retweets, spending money on retail therapy or actual therapy, or simply expressing frustration in hopes of either finding a resolution or blowing off steam? I've been there, done all of that, and most likely so have you. In fact, so have many Americans, as we are quick to bust out the case at the first sign of discomfort.

Don't get me wrong; sometimes the complaints are necessary. Like in 2015, when now-disgraced founder and former chief executive of Turing Pharmaceuticals Martin Shkreli raised the price of the drug Daraprim, an antiparasitic commonly used to treat HIV patients, from $13.50 to *$750.00* a tablet. Naturally, this sent shock waves across the country, people were rightfully outraged, a litany of think pieces were written, and months later, Turing lowered the cost to $375 for some hospitals, hailing this 50 percent price decrease a "victory." Yeah, no. This is a victory in the way when I'm at Dunkin' Donuts and I ask for *some* ketchup packets for my hash browns and they give me just one packet that's as wrinkly as Brad Pitt's baby character in *The Curious Case of Benjamin Button.* Undoubtedly, what Shkreli and his company did was full trash, so people voiced their disdain because being silently complicit would've been

---

with the appropriate amount of f-bombs, and (3) sprinkle in a few disingenuous 'sending you love and lights' to taste."

inappropriate. But! For every one of these glaringly outrageous situations, there are thousands where going for the complaint case is just ignorant.

Take, for example, that 2013 viral video of a lady going off on a Los Angeles Apple store employee because she thought she could roll in there sans an appointment and get replacement parts. Raise of hands if you've *ever* gone into an Apple store that wasn't insanely crowded. For real, every time I go to Apple's Genius Bar, I just see a line of Old Roses from *Titanic* who were formerly young hipsters, talking about how "it's been eighty-four years" since they first walked into Apple, seeking help for their technology woes. Of course, waiting for something to be fixed when you weren't planning on waiting can be annoying; however, losing your mind over something that insignificant is abuse of the complaint attaché case.

Now I, on the other hand, know how to hit that sweet spot of complaining only when necessary and only for legitimate grievances. J/K. I vent way too much over the littlest things. Maybe it's the Seinfeldian influence of grumbling and pointing out the "what's the deal with . . ." in life, which elicits laughter from friends, family, and audiences. But more than that, the truth is, I, like many people, *love* complaining. And the more innocuous the offense, the better.

For example: Commercials automatically playing when you open a page in your web browser? Most people probably take half a beat to register that's a little irritating. Not me. I turn this nonissue into a bit if someone is in the room with me or not. I mean, think about it. A commercial casually starting up like that is the most presumptive shit I've witnessed since the creation of the *Baywatch* spin-off *Baywatch Nights,* where the characters were . . . fully clothed the whole time, thereby completely getting rid of the reason folks watched *Baywatch* in the first place. I mean, Lol.nasa.gov/IsPlutoAPlanetOrNah. Never in my life have I been like, "Ya know, what would really set this Lululemon online shopping experience on fire? A pop-up video automatically playing Denis Leary's gravelly voice—which sounds like he gargled seventy-two pebbles from the *Fraggle Rock* set, by the way—as he yammers on about the torque on the new Ford F-150."

And if you think that commercial nonsense is bad, then don't even get me started on baths. Okay, actually, get me started on baths. L. O. L. at myself for caring, but seriously, what *is* the deal with baths, y'all?! I don't care about bubbles or how many bottles of champs are on the bath sill or whatever Janet Jackson baby-whisper songs you have playing in the background; the fact remains that a bath is just marinating in your own filth like you're a piece of oxtail in a stew. Let that sink in for a moment. There are people chilling in their own body broth, then going out into these streets, ordering a salad at Pret, and sitting next to me, pretending they're fresh as a bouquet of gerbera daisies. These people live in a web of lies, and I want no part of that mess.

If you haven't picked up on it by now, your girl has lots of opinions about the minutiae, which, full disclosure, besides making people laugh, also helps pass the time, and considering the self-starting dumpster fire that is the world right now, focusing on the minutiae can be especially soothing and a welcome distraction. But I also get worked up about weightier issues, and when something messed up or awful happens, making jokes helps me cope. And it should be no surprise that much of the time, the weightier issues that are a thorn in my side revolve around the onslaught of ignorance and discrimination that women face. Yes, yes, life is hard for everyone, but I can only write with authority from the female experience, and I think we can all agree that there is a lot thrown at us.

We fight to be taken seriously and viewed as fully realized people as opposed to objects for consumption. Then there's the societal pressure we feel regarding beauty and/or relationship status. Striving for equality in a world that was, by design, built on the foundation of inequality. And so on and on. However, it's not just these life-defining and lifelong battles. It's also the little things, like when I used to work in an office building.

Most of the dudes were strolling around in dress shirts and slacks; meanwhile, all the women would make it known that the interior Jack Frost (aka air conditioning) was nipping at our noses, toes, and elbows. As per usual, we'd get teased about constantly being cold, but trust me, women don't wake up thinking, *You know what would be tight? Spending eight hours huddled in my office/cubicle, sipping coffee and shivering while rocking a coon-fur coat like Kurt Russell in Quentin Tarantino's* The Hateful Eight. We don't want to live this life, dudes, so chill—heh— with all the jokes about women being cold at work because it's all your fault, buddy boy! Yeah, *you*, dude! The *Journal of Applied Physiology* conducted a study, and it turns out that men's metabolic rate is, on average, 23 percent higher than women's; furthermore, *Nature* magazine did some research and reported that most workplace thermostats are set based on a model developed in the 1960s (which conveniently hasn't been updated to acknowledge that women are in the workplace), which, as you probably have guessed by now, only recognizes the metabolic rates of *men*.

This range of BS has had me reaching into my complaint attaché case with more frequency as I age. And while I don't have the power to resolve these problems, I do have the power to vent about them and make us all laugh to stop ourselves from crying while we deal with big problems, small inconveniences, and everything in between. So, without further ado, here is a by no means all-encompassing list, in varying order of importance, of some funny and not-so-funny things that are absolutely boo-boo about being a lady.[2]

1. Elastic hair ties that practically leave signs of the stigmata when we wear them on our wrists for even the shortest amount of time. Look, if I'm wearing one all day, fine, the little hair tie can brand me like I'm some cattle a rancher added to his farm before the hard winter that's a-comin'. But that's not the case, is it? The least these hair tie companies can do is make it so that when I take a tie off my wrist, it doesn't leave an indent in my skin the way my sweatpants do on my stomach when I have two Christmas dinners and desserts in one day while home for Christmas vacation.

---

2. Please note that I'm writing from a cis, straight black lady perspective, and this ain't meant to reflect everyone's experience. I know you know that, but I just wanted to say it.

People will say, "What's the big deal? Just leave it down or, if you *must* have a hair tie, toss one in your purse and pull it out when you need it." Um, mind your fucking business, Carol. Even if your name isn't Carol, that was some unhelpful Carol-ass shit to say. First of all, I don't want my soup to taste like it has traces of Shea Moisture shampoo in it because when I bent over to eat some, I accidentally dipped my hair in it, nor do I enjoy my neck feeling like it has a layer of Crisco on it because I'm wearing my hair down when it's hot outside, so no, I won't just leave my hair down. Second, that whole "just toss some hair ties in your purse to find later" thing does not work. They either get lost and the next twenty minutes of my day turns into a damn *Cold Case* episode of me trying to find where they went before I give up, or they get coated in old ChapStick residue, crumbs, and melted gum that has oozed out of its wrapper. So, like the Tony Hale to Julia Louis-Dreyfus on *Veep*, I gotta have the ties on standby. On my wrist.

1A. I can fully admit this might not be commonplace, but I'm sure some of my sistern out there can relate to the following: head hair winding up in your butt crack. A few times a month, I'll be taking a shower and discover a few hairs from my head sticking out from between my booty cheeks like baguettes popping out of a basket on a Parisian person's bicycle. How. Does. This. Happen? I just don't understand. I assumed the hair from my head and my butt had minimal contact, but little did I know that my body is hella like *Downton Abbey*, with my head being aristocratic while my butt is more servant status and the two are interacting all the time! I'm not sure how to fix this nuisance, I just thought that on behalf of ladies everywhere (and maybe some dudes), I'd start a dialogue in hopes that we can come together and think-tank this issue and figure something out.

2. There are few things more laughably ludicrous than women being asked if they're okay when the only difference in their appearance is that they're not wearing makeup that day. I generally only wear makeup for public appearances, while in my day-to-day life as well as on my social media posts I'm often sans makeup, so most people know what the real me looks like. Still, there are those moments where someone assumes I'm tired or am in the middle of a crisis because I'm not beautified. And that "someone" is usually a guy. I don't know about you, dear reader, but I'm constantly seeing grown-ass men dressed in the "You are not the father" starter pack wardrobe (ugly polos or baggy dress shirts, khaki pants, run-down shoes, etc.), so maybe dudes can pump the brakes on women having to look perfect? I mean, I get that faces are the first thing we tend to see about each other, but society has trained

us to believe that women wearing layers of makeup is a beauty standard worth aspiring toward.

Sure, there are instances where some ladies paint themselves to the point of being unrecognizable without makeup. And in that case, it's fair to, *in your mind*, turn into Hercule Poirot in hopes of figuring out what's going on. There are also those on social media who photoshop or Facetune their pictures to look like impossibly perfect versions of themselves. But for the most part, women are not waking up looking like Huey Lewis, then shellacking on makeup and walking out the door looking like Leona Lewis. Rarely is a bait and switch going down. People are just rude and behave as though if a woman doesn't fulfill her "duty" of looking flawless, then she must be in the middle of a breakup or is unemployed or depressed. Look, not walking around dolled up like a model 24–7 doesn't mean I'm going through anything, a'ight? This is just what my skin looks like without the help of Fenty Beauty. Without foundation on, my skin can look like a couple of compare-and-contrast paint swatches at Home Depot; some of my pigmentation is dark in certain places, lighter in others. I have a few acne scars, and my eyebrows can look like a mechanical pencil eraser that's one-third of the way gone. I'm more than perfectly okay. I'm just being me, and ain't nothing wrong with that.

3. Let's be frank: Summer is either a heaux stroll for a
   lot of single people looking to catch some strange or
   simply an opportunity to break free of the chains of
   itchy, chunky knits and show off some skin. You
   probably guessed by now, but my heaux strolls have
   never been successful. Usually, I just wear breathable yet comfy sacks that don't show off my body at
   all or I'm rocking jorts aka jean shorts that turn my
   crotch into an Easy-Bake Oven. Thus, I've never
   picked anyone up and just settle for keeping track of
   my steps via my Apple Watch. Still, I have my moments where I get it right and look cute in a romper
   or skirt. Then I'll take public transportation, sit
   down, and part of my bare cheeks make contact
   with the seat.

   You ever have a dry heave push its way to the
   front of the line of your bodily reactions the way a
   hungry actor does at an audition for a Broadway
   musical? That's what happens to me during my
   butt-to-seat sitch in New York City. Don't get me
   wrong, I love NYC so much, but that love will not
   blind me to the fact that the subway trains and buses
   are hotbeds to a whole host of germs. So whenever
   my bare tush touches the seat, I wanna tell my butt,
   "Well, butt, we've had a good run. We went to some
   art gallery shows and understood none of what we
   saw, mastered dipping it low to a few Rihanna
   songs, and looked amazing in that one pair of pants
   that we wore all the time," and then donate it to a

plastic surgeon's office for some patient to use for their booty implant. Then I remember soap exists, and I, like most people, use my cell phone while using the bathroom, so I mean, I'm always a skosh dirty anyway.

4. The following is a biggie, and I'm writing it as much for other ladies as I am for myself because I'm guilty of this behavior. In fact, I just did it a week ago. I had ordered an Uber messenger to pick up a package from my manager's office and deliver it to me at my home in a part of Brooklyn that is not conveniently located. It sucks, but I was a broke mofo who freelanced when I needed a new place to live, so I couldn't be choosy. It was either move to that apartment or back home to Cleveland, Ohio. And over the three years I've lived here, I've gotten used to the distance. Other people like this Uber messenger? Not so much.

As I expected, it took him more than an hour to bike to me, and when he arrived, He. Was. Not. Happy. It was a blustery afternoon in March, so I knew the breeze was inspired by the Prodigy song "Smack My Bitch Up" and was not kind to his face. Feeling guilty, I immediately wanted to make up for weather I couldn't control by being extra cheery when I greeted him. His response: "Man, you live so far away. If I had known you lived so far away, I wouldn't have taken this job." No "hello" or movement to hand me my package. It's as if he just traveled an hour to tell me that my apartment is in a garbage location. Um, yeah, dude, I'm reminded of that whenever most of my friends take a magazine they'll barely have a chance to flip through during their short train rides while I'm schlepping around the entire *The Lord of the Rings* collection in my book bag like some nerd version of CrossFit because it takes an hour and a half to get to my hair appointment. I'm fully up to speed on the suckage that is the location of my apartment. Yet he continued venting his frustrations about his travel time and how he had to get on the train because he was sick of riding his bike. I patiently listened, and then before I could even stop myself, I apologized. This seemed to please him, because he handed me my package. End of transaction, right? Wrong. He *continued* griping and laid this whopper on me: "You know, this trip was so bad, it kind of ruined my day. I don't even feel like working anymore. I might just go home. I mean, I was feeling pretty good today and then I came here." *Bitch, huh?* But I knew that calling someone you don't know "bitch" is a surefire way to getting cussed out, so I just apologized profusely, and he stood as if there was something else I was supposed to do. A beat passed; I apologized a *third* time, and then he left. Just to recap: Not only did I apologize to him three times, but I could tell by the way he was pausing and staring at me that he was expecting an apology. How fucked up is that?! Even though I did nothing wrong, it was my fault. He knew his starting point as well as my address and still took the job, but again, it doesn't matter. It was my fault. And apparently, I agreed with him.

That was not an anomaly. Some days are peppered with moments of feeling bad for taking up space or having an opinion, and I subconsciously think that in any interaction with a man, I'm taking up valuable time I'm not worthy of. I'm not alone in this. All my girlfriends have dealt with these thoughts and I'm sick of it! Women have to stop apologizing for things they don't need to apologize for. A guy bumps into us, we apologize. In a pitch meeting, a man cuts us off while we're talking, and we say, "Sorry. You were speaking. Go ahead." Society conditions women to believe that their baseline for operating ought to be gratitude. Not gratitude as in appreciating being alive and healthy, but gratitude as in, "You should feel lucky we're even taking a chance on you. Don't fuck it up." Society's like some shitty club we got dressed up to go to because we've been convinced it's amazing even though, truth be told, da clurb needs *us*. The bouncer's an asshole, makes some snide comments, reminds you that he normally wouldn't let you in, and then, once you're inside, the DJ is just playing the Black Eyed Peas and Hoobastank all night, and you and your girlfriends look at each other like, "I went to some bougie spa and let my vajeen get steamed like it's an eight-piece dumpling appetizer at a restaurant for *this*?"

We've been sold a bill of goods, ladies! This notion that we must have an apology locked and loaded at all times has been perpetuated by weak people whose only source of strength is planting seeds of self-doubt in others. Well, I, for one, am putting on my gardening clogs like a Martha Stewart minus the talent and ripping all that insecurity out by the roots, then putting down new topsoil, and . . . I'm sorry. I truly know nothing about gardening outside of the fact that Annette Bening's character in *American Beauty* did it and then smashed a real estate agent played by Peter Gallagher and his sexy-ass eyebrows. So what's the moral of the story? The days of me behaving and believing that my life is an imposition on others is over. And I want that to be true for every woman alive. We belong here, society, so get used to it, or *you* can take *your* sorry ass home.

5. The fact that the stand-up comedy field is male-dominated and, therefore, seedy and sexually inappropriate goes without saying. Over the past year, we've seen famous and revered comedians have their careers crumble due to their bad and offensive behavior coming to light. And while it's nice to see certain folks answer for their past crimes, that doesn't mean that the industry has cleaned up. It

hasn't. Big offenses are being taken more seriously now, which is wonderful, but the truth is that sexual assault isn't the only pervasive problem. There's also harassment, which is what allows the culture of sexual assault to exist. Thankfully, I've never had to deal with the life-altering crime of rape or sexual assault, but I've had my fair share of harassment.

I remember one time, early in my stand-up years, I walked down the street to a comedy club. A comedian I knew was standing in front of it with a couple of fellow male comedians. He repeatedly yelled at me, "Hey, slut! What's up, slut! Look at you being a slut!" Of course, all of them laughed. Once I got within earshot, I let him know that he was not going to be calling me a slut in public or otherwise. "Whoa, whoa, whoa," he said. You know that fucking Joey-Lawrence-from-*Blossom* "whoa" BS men like to do when they've done something messed up and behave like you're overreacting? This fool came at me with a few "whoa"s and claimed he was joking and figured I could be "cool." In what world is a white man backed by a group of white men screaming a sexually derogatory term at a black woman a joke? Damn sure not the world that neither of us are living in. What he was doing wasn't for jokes, but to intimidate, however, he and his friends messed with the wrong chick and quickly learned they will never treat me like that again.

Often that kind of bullying is what female comedians deal with in order to do their job. And we're warned that bad behavior comes with the territory, that we just need to have thick skin and not let it bother us. It's screwed up, but that's what so many of us do. We know that any time we're in a predominantly male industry, harassment is done to test us, to make us feel insecure, to throw us off our game, and to challenge our strength. But other times, it's done because a dude is a motherfuckin' creep.

About seven years ago, I was at a rooftop party with a bunch of comedians. It looked like a rooftop party from a music video except all the dudes had soft bellies and there were PBRs instead of bottles of champagne. Not glamorous, but there's something charming about a bunch of newbies who don't have money and feel as though blasting music from a crappy speaker is all that's needed for a good time. There was a bit of a lull in the party, so I snuck off to a corner table and called my parents for a quick chat. A few minutes into the convo, a male comic who had been in the industry for a while came up to me. Let's call him "Richard." Richard and I had been on maybe one or two shows together and had been on friendly terms. So it was nice to see him, and I said a quick hello. But him being a comic, he immediately and rightly teased me for being on the phone while at a party. I laughed and wrapped up my call and we chatted.

"What's the situation?" he asked. I assumed he was asking about the party and he corrected me: "No, what's the situation . . . down there?"

"Excuse me?"

He looked down at my crotch and raised his eyebrows.

I was pissed off, but I didn't want to cause a scene, so I simply told him what he was doing was disgusting and to knock it off.

"Oh, come on," he started. "It's not like we're colleagues or anything." Oh, hell no! Because I was a newbie comic and not on the same level as him professionally, it was totally fine in his eyes to sexually harass me. Screw that! You should respect me whether this is my first day in stand-up or I'm a legend like Wanda Sykes. I stood my ground, he backed off, and I never talked to him again, and thanks to us being at different stages of our careers, we were never really on the same shows much after that.

Until a few years later, when I arrived early to a gig and saw that Richard was also on the lineup. Seeing his name caused that uncomfortable moment to come rushing back to me. *Fuck.* I tried to keep my cool. All the comics on the show eventually trickled in one by one and were greeting each other with hugs. Then he appeared. I didn't know what to do, as I was sure he didn't remember what he said to me all those years ago. So I did what a lot of women are conditioned to do: I thought about the situation from every possible angle, considered what his feelings might be if I acted a certain way, and then decided his comfort was more important than mine. I hugged him and said it was good to see him. It wasn't. It sucked, but *I* didn't want to make *him* feel weird if everyone hugged him except me, so I "took one for the team." I know, I know, but in that moment, I couldn't overpower what society had conditioned in me. I hugged him even though I didn't want to touch him, let alone be in the same room as him. His presence reminded me of when I was new on the scene and male comics would test the waters to see if they could disrespect, harass, or intimidate me. I felt small again. And that's the thing people forget about harassment's real power.

Harassment is not designed to be temporary; it's intended to stay with you, keep you in line, never allow you to fully relax and be calm. That way the perpetrator doesn't even have to do the work of oppressing you. You'll inadvertently do the work for him long after he's forgotten what he's done. So that instead of remembering how you stood up for yourself and using that memory as strength to propel yourself forward, you'll be taken back to when you felt weak. Harassment is not just about harming you that one time; it's about lingering around for every time afterwards and chipping away at you without you realizing it.

To be honest, that kind of treatment is sort of the norm for this business. Women starting out in stand-up are subjected to demoralizing behavior, and there's no HR to report it to. Furthermore, you can't tell other male comics because they won't believe you or they'll pretend to believe you and then go behind your back and do a smear campaign against you. So, us ladies confide in one another, sharing tales of horrific comments, inappropriate touching, innuendos, etc. And like me, some of us struggle with how to handle mistreatment and its aftereffects. I am happy to report that as my career has advanced and I've hit certain milestones, I'm no longer on the receiving end of this kind of behavior, but isn't that kind of sad? That simply because I'm a woman, I'm not afforded the baseline of respect as a coworker that's afforded male comics. I have to *earn* it, and by "it," I mean my humanity. That's fucking ridiculous.

6. This is related to the above but is a far lesser offense. I'll be in a crowded place and a guy is trying to get past me, so he places his hand on the small of my back. Ick! Way too intimate. Rule of thumb, straight boys who think that women don't deserve autonomy over their bodies and aren't well equipped to decide who is and isn't allowed to touch them: If

you don't think it's appropriate to invade another man's space, then you don't a woman's. Or, in other words, if you're not putting your hand on the small of Chris Christie's back when trying to walk through Buffalo Wild Wings, then keep your filthy paws off my silky drawers. #RizzoHadBars.

7. Noncontroversial statement alert! I've had it up to here with Aunt Flo and her indecisive nonsense. I'm specifically referring to when you think your period is done-zo, so you stop using tampons/pads/Diva-Cups/Thinx, and then the next day, your period starts back up again and all your clothes get ruined. Da hell? This is kind of like that song "Damaged" by girl group Danity Kane, which, if ya don't know, is an early-aughts classic. It's three minutes of pop perfection, and just when you think the song is over because they stop singing, Diddy comes in and talks nonsense and keeps the song going. Periods, don't be like Diddy.

8. I know that purses are the jam, but sometimes I don't feel like carrying one and instead want to roam the Earth like a stoner dude at a Dave Matthews Band concert, meaning I wanna rock pants that are more pockets than actual pants. So, clothing companies, throw all us ladies a freakin' bone here and stop with fake pockets in pants. Even worse than fake pockets are the tiny pockets that only go

knuckle deep, so instead of being able to relax my hands and arms comfortably, I'm now engaging my biceps, triceps, and traps in order to rest my fingers in pockets they'll never fit in anyway. What in the huh is this P90X class that I didn't sign up for about?

9. IDK if this terminology is used or not anymore, but when I was growing up, I was a certifiable tomboy. I was not into wearing dresses or makeup. I freely burped and farted (still do). I played pick-up basketball, tackle football with my older brother and his friends (side note: we also played badminton—lol times infinity). Most importantly, I watched wrestling, basketball—both professional and collegiate— ditto for football, tennis, track and field, baseball, and almost anything else where there was a clear winner and loser. And I mean it about the almost anything.

Golf? Naw, dawg. Golf takes place at basically all-white country clubs (except for the staff, who are "conveniently" 95 percent people of color) and consists of a lot of middle-aged white dudes walking in pleated khakis for long stretches of time while a person of color carries all their shit and an umbrella to shade them from the summer heat. Y'all, I ain't got time in 2018 to see a bunch of rich white dudes try to low-key bring back the cute parts of colonialism the way fashion is like, "Hahahaha! Everyone forget about the crack epidemic of the eighties and just focus on us putting shoulder pads back in women's blazers so you all look like Melanie Griffith in *Working Girl*." No. Fucking. Thanks. Golf.[3] So to recap, I like most sports except golf and, while we're at it, NASCAR (but I think it's obvious by now why I wouldn't be into that one either). But that's not the point I'm getting at.

What I find highly irritating is that when you're a woman *and* a sports fan, dudes want you to prove that you're really into the game before they'll believe you. Whenever I tell a straight guy I love a particular sport, I'm always met with an "Oh, yeah?" or a *"Really,"* and an up-and-down look. This is, of course, followed by a litany of questions, testing my knowledge. I'm sorry, unless you're wearing a blazer with elbow pads and drink minestrone soup out of a camping thermos (I literally have no idea what teachers eat and am basing my knowledge solely off of *Clueless* and *Boy Meets World*), please do not launch into a pop quiz, especially since it's not to help me pass a class but to validate me in the eyes of a nonfactor in my life who is under the misconception that I care about his judgment.

---

3. And don't even be like, "What about Tiger Woods?! He's black and plays golf." If you were walking down the street and saw one pomegranate seed sitting atop a pile of shit, you wouldn't go, "That's a parfait!" You'd register it as doo-doo and Electric Slide yourself to the right and out of harm's way. Not the most eloquent example, but you get the point. Woods's presence and the period he dominated doesn't erase the racism that has been woven into fabric of the sport.

News flash: According to a 2015 Gallup poll, sixty million women in the US watch sports on the regs. And no, we're not doing it to fit in and be "one of the guys." And no, we're not doing it to get a guy to like us. And no, we're not just jumping on the bandwagon of whatever team is hot at the moment (and let's be real, tons and tons of men do that, too, so let's stop thinking that is gender-specific behavior). We don't have to prove anything to anyone, especially some jabroni we met five minutes ago. So, all sportlovin' dudes, the next time a woman says she's into a sport, don't say shit. Well, actually, don't say *nothing*; that would be awkward. Just save your incredulity for the guy who talks about the New England Patriots and constantly uses the word "we," even though he's not on the team. Sir, *they*, not *you*, won the championship as *they* play on the team and you do not. In fact, the closest you've gotten to "playing" football is the fantasy league in which you and your pals mostly just sit around, rank professional athletes, and risk paper-cut injuries printing out stats. But, sure, the Patriots couldn't have done it without you wearing that old-ass jersey that stinks of BO and having a Roth IRA that's maturing at a reasonable rate.

10. Health care and reproductive rights. Like I mentioned earlier in the intro, the fact that members of the House Freedom Caucus (a group of white men

led by Vice President Mike Pence) were the only ones in the room where it happened and were deciding what women are allowed and not allowed to do with their bodies is upsetting. No matter what progress is made, women not only are greeted with resistance but also are dealing with legislators and insensitive folk who are determined to make society go backwards. Don't believe me? Then check out this sampling:

Roe v. Wade happened forty-five years ago, yet there are still *seven* states that only have one clinic left that provides health services for women including abortions. According to the World Health Organization, depression is the most common mental health issue for women, and for those under the age of sixty, suicide is a leading cause of death. A 2017 article published in *Marie Claire* revealed that black women are more likely than other women to receive the wrong treatment for breast cancer. Many conservatives in the GOP seem hell-bent on making life difficult for poor and low-income women (twenty-five million to be exact) by rolling back Medicaid, which is how many of them get primary, preventive, specialty, and long-term care services. But they're not the only ones feeling the GOP's wrath. Working mothers are also at risk, as conservatives are trying to make it so that insurance companies are no longer required to offer maternity care in their health packages. And Quartz reported with the backing of research from the *Lancet* medical journal:

> With an estimated 26.4 deaths for every 100,000 live births in 2015, America has the highest maternal mortality rate of all industrialized countries— by several times over . . . More women die of childbirth-related causes in the US than they do in Iran (20.8), Lebanon (15.3), Turkey (15.8), Puerto Rico (15.1), China (17.7), and many more.

Clearly, we are amid troubling times. Women's lives and health simply aren't valued. Our very lives are disregarded and viewed as an irritation. I mean, how else do we explain why politicians have no qualms about rolling back Medicaid, which would affect millions of low-income women, or that the medical industry hasn't fully acknowledged suicide as a leading cause of death for women under sixty years old as anything but a national crisis? No sufficient answer exists because this is categorically unacceptable. But if cis women think they have it bad, let's take a second to think about what trans women go through.

I'll be the first to admit I hadn't really, fully, and *intentionally* thought about the ins and outs of what a trans person's life could be like until I interviewed trans activist, public speaker, and former adult film star Buck Angel. Prior to speaking with him, I knew the grim, broad strokes: Trans people are more likely to be unemployed, harassed, sexually assaulted, homeless, and murdered. And when you throw race into the mix, it's grimmer. I also know that nontrans people have an unhealthy preoccupation with the anatomy of trans people. And, finally, I know that folks such as Janet Mock, Trace Lysette, Munroe Bergdorf, Chaz Bono, Laverne Cox, and countless others are inspiring *everyone*, not just transgender people, to live bolder, more well-informed, and compassionate lives. However, I was clueless about a whole list of things, including the medical industry's lack of research when it comes to hormone replacement therapy.

Turns out no one, including doctors, knows what the long-term effects of HRT are. Trans people, who made the vital decision to live their lives as authentically as possible, could be at risk because medical professionals don't deem it necessary to figure out if the hormones they are prescribing will cause harmful effects down the line. As Diana Tourjée wrote in an *Out* magazine article entitled "Hormone Therapy is Lifesaving—But Why Is No One Studying Its Long-Term Effects?":

> The medications trans women use to suppress their testosterone have not been designed for that purpose. Spironolactone is a diuretic, used to treat high blood pressure . . . There have been few studies

looking at the long-term effects of HRT. While observational studies have retrospectively reviewed trans populations and declared hormonal transition to be safe, trans medicine has not had the kind of clinical research that is typically conducted for life-saving medicine.

Wow. And while this is downright shocking to me, many in the trans community like Angel have been vocal about the fact that trans health being poorly researched is indicative of American culture not prioritizing the health and safety of trans people. Is it perhaps naive of me to think that the US medical industry would be any less biased than society when it comes trans people? Perhaps, but at least I'm not anymore. This information, just like what I listed earlier about women's depression, breast cancer, and maternal deaths, is all out there, begging to be consumed and then used to help dismantle the systems in place.

I write all this not to scare anyone. Well, maybe I *do* want to scare people. I want to jolt them. I want them to feel what I feel, which is rage. I want everyone to move through the world constantly arming themselves with knowledge that can benefit their lives and, more importantly, can help change the life of someone else. Like Mr. Rogers said his mother told him, "Always look for the helpers. There's always someone who's trying to help." There's more helpers than we think. Look for them. I'm one of them. And so are countless others.

11. I'm sure this is not unique to my industry, but it really burned my toast when I was confused for a guy's significant other when I showed up to work at a comedy club. It doesn't happen much to me these days, but when I was starting out? All the time. For those not in the know, when you start out doing stand-up, you make your friends, often traveling in packs to open mics so you can practice your material or perform on proper shows. It's common to see a group of four or five guys arrive at a club. Same for a group of women itching to test out their new material. However, when it's a mixed gaggle of folks, sexism often rears its ugly head.

I'd show up to the comedy club with a couple of buddies, and the dudes running the open mics (shows in which comics workshop their material in front of each other) or real shows would ask some variation of "Hey, man, this your girlfriend?" That's right, they wouldn't address me, but ask the guy next to me to explain why I was there. "No," I'd chime in, "I do stand-up." Then the guy would stutter and be like, "Oh, yeah, right, right." Rinse and repeat because this garbage would go down frequently.

Hey, fellas, here's a two-part idea to prevent you from Hugh Grant stammering your way through a conversation with me or any other woman in a professional setting: First, quit behaving as if the only justifiable reason for a woman to show up at a place of employment is because she's boning somebody. We work just like the fellas do, kick ass like the fellas do, so get used to it and step the fuck aside. Second, and more importantly, stop assuming every woman you meet is straight. I know you've been lied to and told the world revolves around you so all ladies must be into your Jimmy Dean peen, but guess what? For some women, the mere thought of a dong makes their vajeens let out the driest of coughs. #WheresTheRicola.

12. The concept of the walk of shame. I'm not going to even go into a whole diatribe at this point because we all know it's ludicrous that women face a "walk of shame" after boning someone they're not in a relationship with, yet men are freaking heroes for hooking up with some strange or familiar strange. Truth is, no matter who it is, if you got it in last night and are in these streets the following morning looking disheveled, you should be doing forward rolls into yoga mountain poses that are met with rousing applause à la Willy Wonka when he made his grand entrance at his chocolate factory. Congratu-fuckin'-lations on going to the Bone Zone.

Dear reader, that's it! Well, it's not. I mean I could go on and on and on about the ignorance women put up with nearly every day of their lives, but then this book would be the length of every Judd Apatow movie combined. Hey-O! Don't get me wrong, I love his films. I'm just saying, homeboy hasn't met an ending that he didn't put a chloroform rag on and go, "That'll do, pig," and then carry on for another thirty-five minutes. Anyway! If you're a lady reading my frustrations, I hope you served Civil Rights realness aka yelled a bunch of "Amen"s and stomped in black patent leather, square-toed heels. If you're a man, I'm optimistic that maybe you learned a thing or two about the female experience (okay, the whole head-hair-caught-in-a-butt-crack thing may not be lady-specific, but I'm pretty sure Michael Jordan's bald-headed self never had to deal with this and miss a jump shot because of an irritating rogue hair squatting in his bum like a hippie in an abandoned house). But honestly, it doesn't matter who you are, we all are now up to speed on at least thirteen things, big and small, that are the banes of many women's existences. Let's get to work eliminating this trash because I don't know about you, but my complaint attaché case is feeling a little heavy. So help a sister out, cool?

Some Thoughts on Interracial Dating from Someone Who Is a Motherflippin' Pro at It

⌒

Full disclosure: I've been single for two years. And while there are tons of pluses to singledom—I can do what I want when I want, traveling the world solo is empowering, and rocking Nature's Long Johns (aka leg hair that's as long as Kenny Loggins's hair during the seventies) keeps me warm during winter—I would be lying if I didn't admit it's sometimes difficult to be out in these dating streets in my early thirts. For one, my eggs are dying. Now, when I say that, people are quick with the "No! You have time!" Totes preesh the positivity, folks, but let's get real. My eggs *are* dying. That's just a biological fact. Sure, it's not over for me. Not by a long shot. I'm thirty-four. However, let's not pretend I'm walking around with farm-fresh eggs. They ain't. My insides are like a leftover frittata from Sunday brunch that has been chilling in my fridge, so I sniff it, am on the fence about whether I should eat it, but then I remember how good it was when I first had it three days ago, so I tell myself, "Fuck it. I don't need to see how *The Handmaid's Tale* ends," roll the dice, and eat it anyway. Point is, what's in my fallopes is pretty much a delicious *Barefoot Contessa* dish. And I'm more than fine with that since I'm not planning on having kids. But just because motherhood isn't on the foreseeable horizon doesn't mean I'm not open to the possibility of my mind changing in the future. I am, so I would be a fool if I weren't at least aware of the countdown on my biological clock. But that's not the only crummy part of being single right now.

Other things that suck about being single? Holidays can be a little depressing. There's no one to split bills with, which is a financial burden that's felt more deeply in expensive-ass New York City than in other cities. When something really cool happens career-wise, I don't have that special person to share in my success. Loneliness. And this is a biggie: lack of on-demand physical affection. I mean, I would be lying if I didn't admit that fantasizing about riding Michael B. Jordan's D like it's a toboggan down the French Alps has gotten me through many a cold night. Unfortch, being boo'd up with MBJ is not my reality; my reality is late-night jam sessions where I change the words to Tom Petty and the Heartbreakers' "Free Fallin'" to "Free Wal lin'," which is about me forgetting to bring underwear to the gym, so after I shower, my lady walls are unprotected in my jeans. #DisrespectfulToThePettyEstateAndMyLevis. Back to the matter at hand. Being single is rough stuff on occasion, and the worst thing about it is other people. More specifically, *getting to know* other people is the true bummer in the summer.

You know when you can't find your remote so you're like, "I guess I'm just going to watch this *Supernatural* marathon until my butt cheeks go numb"? That's kind of what being single is like for me. I'd rather just chill then get up and get out there. Five percent of that is because I'm lazy, but the rest of my inertia is legit. Getting to know another person can be nerve-racking because I'm worried if my small talk is up to snuff, if we like each other equally or at all, and if my butt is going to sound like the opening twenty minutes of *Saving Private Ryan* all because I forgot to "sneak take" Gas-X at the table before digging into the meat-and-cheese platter, etc. Simply put, there's a lot of anxiety that goes into finding a romantic partner, and while some of it is self-inflicted (I should just eat a damn burger on a date if I want to!), some of it is because I'm older, which means I'm much more aware of red flags, and when you're more aware of red flags, your dating pool shrinks significantly.

When you're in your twenties, red flags are like the Microsoft Word paper clip that pops up on your computer screen, asking if you need help, yet you click the X immediately with an "I got this, boo" confidence because you think you can and should be able to date anybody and you'll walk away unscathed and in slow motion like George Clooney did from the car bomb explosion in *Syriana*. However, by the time you hit your thirties, it's different. You. Take. Dem. Red. Flags. To. SeriousTown. Suddenly, you and your friends become Woodward and Bernstein, fact-checking, calling on sources who shall not be named, going over all the evidence any time the person you have designs on does the smallest questionable thing, like not calling when they said they would. It might be a sign of the person's flakiness, but usually it is just an honest mistake and falls under the category of red flag false alarm. But then there are situations that are so bad that not only does a red flag appear, but it's accompanied by "Ironside," the siren song Uma Thurman hears in *Kill Bill* right before she fucks some shit up.

A dude being secretive about the little things? "Ironside." A gal being hella rude to her parents for no damn reason? "Ironside." Your current beau cheated on their previous partner . . . with you. "Iron"-motherfreakin'-"side." Meeting a white dude on a dating app and his idea of making conversation with me is asking for my Ancestry.com family tree chart in hopes that I'm mixed? "Ironside" with a dash of "Go die in a fire; I'll bring the marshmallows" because that's something that happened to me when I joined Tinder, and if you're thinking, "Well, Pheebs, joining Tinder shoulda been your red flag, LOL times infinity," you can shaddup. Desperate times call for desperate measures, and at that point, your girl was hella desp. Let me set the scene.

It was like the beginning of every Yelp review ever: It was Monday night and it was raining. I was at the crib, sipping wine, scrolling through Debra Messing's Instagram, and started liking *all* her pics. This is not how a thirty-one-year-old should spend her evening! I should be parkouring around all the sweet, sweet D being tossed my way. Instead, I was looking at a pic of Messing[1] and fellow actress Catherine Keener wearing scarves and saying aloud to no one in my apartment, "Yaaaaaaaas!!!" I knew it was time to take the plunge. I signed up for Tins and immediately started judging people solely on a couple of photos and a short bio that is supposed to summarize

---

1. Do you sense a running theme here? I love Debra Messing, Laura Linney, Loretta Devine. Basically any forty- or fifty-plus actress that your mom and, more importantly, your single auntie loves, your girl Pheebs loves.

an entire life. This is a flawed system, but it's a system nonetheless. Before I go any further, I should explain Tinder for the readers lucky enough to not have experienced it.

Tinder is basically for people who, on some level, want to be like Ruth Bader Ginsburg and judge the hell out of others even though they're barely equipped to judge a chili cook-off. That might be fun for a while but, eventually, being on Tinder can feel kind of like a rock-bottom moment; however, because I was using the app on my iPhone, I still felt like I was #Winning instead of like that old black dude from that infamous crelling (combo of crying and yelling) scene on *Intervention*. Anyway, once you set up the profile, you get to swipe left (hard pass) or swipe right (I'm interested), and if you both swipe right on each other, you can start messaging. Aaaaaaaaaaaand this is where things pretty much fall apart. I'm not sure what it's like for men, but women get lots of variations on "Wanna hook up?"; dick pics (none for me yet, thank goodness); a lowercase "sup," which is universal for "Me horny, you a warm body, let's. Do. *Dis*."; awful answers to innocuous questions like "Hey, I'm on vacation with a bunch of girlfriends. What cool things should I get into while in town?," which elicited this response from an upstanding citizen: "Me, probably." HOW, SWAY, HOW?! #ReferenceOnlyPOCsAndMillennialsWillGet.

How am I supposed to get *inside* you, dude? Like what is the science on that? I can't even stop my laptop from overheating after using it for too long, but I'm just supposed to hit up Ms. Frizzle, borrow her magic school bus, and waste that shape-shifting technology all so I can shoot up your urethra? Listen, if you just stated something that would make Education

Secretary Betsy DeVos in her faux folksy voice go, "That makes a whole heck of a lot of sense to me," then what you said is literally such a crime against the English language and humanity that retired human rights activist Desmond Tutu must dust off his bishop robes and get to work to save us from you.

Then there are those bros that make the above seem like amateurs because this next type of fella sees no opening yet still attempts to shove his square peg self into a round hole, like this dude, who, after I told him earlier in the evening I was celebrating a career achievement with some girlfriends (my podcast *2 Dope Queens* hitting number 1 on iTunes worldwide), took a few hours to workshop his response with his sauseege before sending the following three messages within the span of one minute at 1:13 A.M.:

"I'm Home Chillen"

"Should have came here"

"1 mile away?"

Firstly. MOTHERFUCKER, 👏 I 👏 CAN'T 👏 EVEN 👏 GET 👏 A 👏 "GRATS"?! 👏 I wasn't even expecting or asking for the full word at that point. That's how low my standards are in this disappointing and commitment-averse dating world. I'm aware that a stranger sending another stranger "congratulations" is akin to Tom Cruise telling Renée Zellweger, "You complete me," at the end of *Jerry Maguire*. It's far too early for a moment of sincerity. But, dude, put in some effort and be a little bit more like fictional serial killer Patrick Bateman . . . which is something that I never, ever thought I would write. I, of course, don't mean the criminal part of him, but rather the part where he played the long game. He wasn't like, "Down to get fucked and chopped into tiny pieces?" No, he *feigned* interest like a gahtdamn gentleman for two point two seconds and engaged in what people were saying to him. Just pretend you're happy for me so the conversation can continue. Is that too much to ask? I thinketh not.

Secondly. "Should have came here." "Should have *came* here." "SHOULD. HAVE. CAME. HERE." You had *one* job! Just get the damn verb tense correct. If you're unsure, use a *Who Wants to Be a Millionaire* lifeline or something. I wouldn't judge your journey. But to be this sloppy makes my vajeen and I quote the great scholar of our time, music producer/*American Idol* judge Randy Jackson: "It's gonna be a 'no' from me, dawg."

Thirdly. Sowwie not sowwie, but last I checked, my name is not "White Girl Murder Victim in the First Five Minutes of *Criminal Minds*," so, no, I will not be taking a Lyft to your crib so I can be murderized. Coretta Scott King didn't go through all she went through for me to go out like that. In my mind, she worked her tail off so I can work my way onto the Obamas' holiday-card recipient list. In all seriousness, this is the kind of grossness hetero broads deal with no matter the dating app— Tinder, Match.com, Bumble, Raya, etc.—but I decided to not let it discourage me completely, and I remained on Tinder for another week. That was dumb.

I met a guy—let's name him "David." David is a white dude and private chef in New York, New Jersey, and Miami, which makes him sound like the star of a why-doesn't-this-exist-already Bravo reality TV show called *Playing with Fire* where he runs his own business and has a long-term girlfriend he can't settle down with because he's afraid of commitment. Anyway,

David and I matched and began texting off and on for hours. Everything was perfect until he hit me with, "What's your background, btw?"

Apparently, I'm Naive McGee because I told him I'm from Cleveland, Ohio, and he said, "Lol. What's your ethnicity?"

Hmm. There are five photos of me on Tins. It's obvious I'm black, so I wrote back, "Black."

"Caribbean or American, etc."

"American. Sup?" Please note that this "sup" has an upper-case *S*, so this was not a "sup" as in "You down to party in my pants?" It's more of "Boy, please don't test me." But, y'all. He did. He straight up dropped a blue book exam on my desk like I was back in ninth grade and had to break down the themes of *Lord of the Flies.* David wrote back: "Lol. Nothing. Lol. Just asking. You're hot regardless."

Hold up. "Regardless"? *"Regardless"?* That word is Gorton's fisherman fishy. It's as though this dude is letting me know he still thinks I'm attractive despite being black American and not something more "exotic." How patronizing and self-absorbed of him to think that I need or will only feel relief if I receive external reinforcement from a guy I barely know; furthermore, he's participating in the racist and historically damaging fetishization that a black woman is only beautiful if she has a diverse background. But what's even more infuriating is that in the span of me staying on Tinder for another week, David was the *fourth* guy who tried to see if I was indeed not African-American. Another white dude clumsily asked me about my background, as did two black men. The only difference is that the black dudes were much bolder about their displeasure in who I am. In fact, one black guy and I were getting along well until I told him I'm African-American and he stopped talking to me altogether. The other one? "Jamaican or black?" was his question straight out the gate. I responded "black," and not only did he end the conversation, but I assume he unmatched me because I was never able to see his profile again.[2] Suffice it to say that after this trifling-ass week, I deleted my Tinder account, but still, I must ask: What in United Colors of Benetton is this fucking fuckery? If y'all dumb heauxes cannot tell that I am black AF and/or are hoping I'm mixed with something so I'm low-cal black, y'all can choke on the peacoat Rosa Parks wore when she told that white dude, "It's gonna be a 'no' from me, dawg"—#Callback—and stayed her behind in the front of the bus.

Unfortunately, this background check is all too familiar with every single black woman I know. We've heard time and time again that black women and Asian men get asked out the least on dating apps. Well, the OkCupid blog did something about these rumors and analyzed their own data in the 2009 OkCupes's blog post "How Race Affects the Messages You Get," which is still, to this day, often cited because the numbers haven't changed that much:

> Men don't write black women back. Or rather, they write them back far less often than they should. Black women reply the most, yet get by far the fewest replies. Essentially

---

2. Just a reminder to the world, you can be both Jamaican and black, but based on the dude's reaction, he not only did not know that, but he clearly thought being Jamaican is better than being black.

every race—*including other blacks*—singles them out for the cold shoulder.

But my pals and I didn't need this data to confirm what we already knew. We relied on our own dating experience and what we constantly hear every day. There's the black guy on Instagram under the moniker Maserati Rick who stated rich athletes don't marry black women because "most of the sisters were raised in broken homes . . . the biggest difference is a white woman knows her position and accepts her role as a woman and let[s] her man lead. Black women believe it's 50/50 and you have to be uneducated to ever think such a thing." There's also the black woman on Facebook who told me that a guy wouldn't let it go and asked if she was *sure* that she is only African-American because she's beautiful. Or a white girlfriend who was confused as to why I get so many fewer messages from guys than she does. And, by the way, this is not just a hetero problem. OkCupid confirmed that black gay men get 20 percent fewer responses than all other races, so the problem is widespread. And the website pointed to the fact that Latinx and Asian women are often heavily fetishized when interacting with men on dating apps. Depressing and upsetting, ain't it? Not my intention, just trying to present the lay of the land here before we dig into my dating history.

So, to recap: (1) Being single is fun sometimes (assuming the starfish position in bed without having to worry about bumping into anyone is #Goals), and at others, it blows (Doing chores by yourself is trash. I have to do dishes *and* dust my bookshelves? LOL.co.uk/BloodyAwful). (2) Dating apps make it tough for black ladies (and indeed all ladies) to find a quality partner, and (3) being in your thirties means you inspect all potential romantic entanglements the way Detectives Stabler and Benson do a crime scene. Now about me.

We all remember the story from earlier in the book with the dude who told me I should tone up so I would look better? I don't want to say #NeverForget, as that hashtag should be reserved for legit tragedies, but maybe #GrabSomeNeosporin-BecauseDatsGonnaLeaveAMark would work? Hmm, not catchy enough. What about #RememberTheTime? Fine. That's a Michael Jackson song. Perhaps #YourMindWillMakeYouThink-AboutThatMomentWhenLiterallyEverythingIsGoingWellIn-YourLifeJustSoYouDontGetTooBigForYourBritches. All right, that is less a hashtag and more just an accurate description of what my brain likes to do to me for funsies. Whatever the case may be, it happened and we ain't forgetting about it anytime soon. Thankfully, that is the most humiliating thing I've encountered while dating, so yay, we got that out of the way. The rest of my dating life has been normal: crushes, unrequited love, being dumped, falling in love, and doing the dumping.

To be more specific, here's the Lipton tea: I went to a predominantly white private high school; my college's writing program only had two black people in it, including me, in my graduating class; and as a stand-up comic/writer, I work in a field that has a lot of Jewish and non-Jewish white guys. In short, from the time when dating typically begins for people (high school) up until now, my dating pool has mostly consisted of white dudes. So I've got a decent amount of experience dating outside my race, and more to the point, I have a good amount of experience dating white dudes (two significant relationships have been with white men) . . . which, depending on who you are and if you care, that might make you SMH, side-eye, or judge me in a multitude of ways.

To be clear, my stating that I've dated my share of white dudes is not meant as a form of braggadocio the way Kanye West rhymed that he balls so hard that his girl can "order fish filet." (LOL. Wut? You can buy a four-pound bag of tilapia filets from Walmart for $10.98. Buying fish filet is not baller; it's literally the foundation of Blue Apron's practical business model so that basic Bs like me can feel like *Iron Chef*'s Morimoto for an evening.) Neither is my stating that I'm asked out by (noncreepy, nonracist) white dudes somewhat regularly. It's not the sign that some in society believe it to be: that I'm dating "up," or have been "chosen" to hang with the "cool" kids. It happens since white dudes and I inhabit the same social circles.

I also do not state this apologetically, as if to imply that I've merely dated outside my race *only* because I've been asked and not because the interest level was mutual. As in, "Y'all, listen. I normally avoid nonblack dudes the way you do when you don't want something, but when you're offered it for free, you'll take it." White dudes are not the JPMorgan Chase bank keychains of my life.

Finally, I am not mentioning that white guys are interested in me as a tit for tat because black men date nonblack women, but that seems to be some people's perception.

Whenever I'm in an interracial relationship, I get emails or queries from black dudes wanting to know why I'm not with a black guy (funny, when I'm single AF, these same black dudes aren't asking me out, and most, if not all, of them are now happily boo'd up with nonblack—usually white—women). Look, I'm #TeamBlackLove. It's beautiful, gives me warm fuzzies, and on the rare occasions when I fantasize about having babies, it's with MBJ, and we have little Lindt chocolate truffle balls of adorableness, but there seems to be a double standard where I have to have a Nation of Islam vajeen while black dudes can be out in these streets dating whomever they damn please. (Note: Just to be clear, I know that black men who date outside their race, or any person who does, get a lot of mess thrown their way, and also that black/white couplings aren't the only IRCs [interracial couples], but I'm speaking specifically about my experience, and white men have been the only nonblack dudes I have seriously dated.)

And my experience along with my friends' includes a lot of outside opinions. You know how the Winter Olympics roll around and suddenly everyone at your job is talking about slalom all. Da. Damn. Time. And it's like none of them have ever, ever, *ever* skied before, let alone competitively, but they're now all experts in how the US needs to step up their skiing program to be medal contenders in slalom? That's what interracial dating can feel like sometimes. Seems like plenty of people have ideas about it, many of them negative, and want to let everyone know about it. Despite the Pew Research Center revealing that IRCs are more common than ever (12 percent of all US newlyweds married someone of a different race), when a celebrity, friend, or family member is in an IRC in HD IRL—#TooManyAcronymsButThisIsMyBookSo-FuckIt—it becomes the topic of focus, controversy, and conversation. Serena Williams, Constance Wu, and Jordan Peele have all been questioned for having partners outside their race.

Out of all three of them, I am most dumbfounded by the rage I saw from black men on social media about Serena being married to the half-Armenian, half-German Reddit cofounder Alexis Ohanian. Some claimed that she is a sellout, that she couldn't handle a black man, and that she is no longer a role model for young black women. If I remember correctly, she has publicly dated black men, but more importantly, throughout her entire career, I have witnessed black men on social media call her a monkey, say she is too manly, claim she is ugly and disgusting, assume that she couldn't handle a black man (Common and Drake) and that's why those relationships ended, and a litany of other insults (to be fair, nonblack men have historically dissed her as well), so for a lot of these black men to turn around and behave as though it is a grand betrayal that a black woman they didn't respect found love with someone who, I assume, RESPECTS her is patently absurd. Unfortunately, those aren't the only sort of comments. The following is just a smattering of what she and other people, like me, in IRCs undoubtedly have heard from people:

- "What do their parents think?"
- "Is this the first time s/he is dating outside of his/her race?"
- "This is probably a phase."
- "Looks like someone has jungle fever."
- "Oh, I used to have an [insert race different from the speaker] boyfriend/girlfriend in college."
- "Is the sex different?"
- "Is it weird to date someone of a different race?"

- "What do you two talk about?"
- "So what holidays do you two celebrate?"
- "Your kids are going to be so beautiful. You're having kids, right?"

The last question is always asked, of course, as if there is no other reason to date someone of another race if you're not going to make a Gap ad baby. Honey Bunches of No, y'all. I said it once, but I will say it again: Fetishizing or thinking that a mixed-race person is better because they fit within the arbitrary "exotic" box that society designed to create disharmony within racial groups (after all, we all know that race is a societal construct as well) is harmful and perpetuates the notion that those who don't fall under the category of "white" are not multidimensional people, but objects without agency that people can project their thoughts, opinions, and desires onto without consequence. Whew! That was a mouthful, but it bears repeating because no matter how many times some people encounter interracial couples, they still treat them as if it's something they've never witnessed before and do their version of John Stossel investigative reporting. News flash: If you do that, you're treating these IRCs not as human but as zoo animals to be analyzed. Obviously, I understand that plenty of the questions I just listed and more are born out of curiosity and unintentional ignorance, but a fair amount of the inquiries are fueled by anger and hatred. Despite progress, there are still plenty of folks who prefer everyone stick to "their own kind," so the dialogue tends to be nothing but vitriol. Take this, for example. When I was still dating my ex, an Italian, this is one of the lovely message I found in my "Others" folder on Facebook:

Conversation started Thursday

11/5 6:28pm

ialmost sent u a frien request thank god i looked a ur pictures ur the fucking ennemy u r sleeping with the ennemy damm lilgirl u have tobe a lilgirl inur brain

First of all, #FixYourSpaceBar #FixYourLife. And secondly, what is this two scoops of foolishness? This stranger cannot talk to me because I've dated a white guy? Riiiiiight. After receiving this ignorant message, I moseyed on over to his Facebook page, and half the black people in his pictures are lighter than a pair of baby Timbs. So clearly, there were some interracial sexy times going on in this guy's family at some point in the lineage, but somehow it was objectionable that I'd gotten in on the fun. Because I am sane in the membrane, I didn't write back to this buffoon, but I started to notice that, at times, it seemed that no IRC faces quite the same kind of scrutiny as white man/black woman (this may be colored—hehe—by my personal experience, but I'm sticking with it)—not even black man/white woman couplings. Of course, folks will run through the tried-and-true greatest hits album of racism (Mandingo myth, rebelling against one's parental units, etc.), but with WM/BW, in addition to the racist snark, there's also, a lot of times, confusion. People will have a blank look on their face like they're a 2002 MacBook buffering while attempting to load a ten-minute cat video. Like, "Why are *you* together? What could possibly be the reason?" Take, for instance, Ann Coulter.

I know. I *know*. Ann Coulter is one sparkly, spandex brief away from being a WWE heel in that 90 percent of the things she says fit into her brand of being the villain and may not always reflect what she truly believes . . . and yet her spewing nonsense in the public sphere does provide a voice for the ignorant voiceless who agree with what she says. Like when she appeared on a 2012 episode of *Fox & Friends*[3]—*DERP*—and stated that TV personalities Bill Maher[4] and Lawrence O'Donnell are "freedom riders" because they date black women. As if they get off on white guilt and this is the only plausible reason they would want to date BWs. I mean, certainly white men like O'Donnell are supposed to be getting their BAs in I Hang with White Ladies All Day, E'ry Day University. So what is going on? What is the "upside" for a white guy?

Guess what, folks, it ain't about any false narrative of an "upside." Some white dudes just—gasp!—find black women

---

3. Y'all. I. Freaking. Know. *Fox & Friends* is an unmitigated disaster, so when something objectionable is uttered on this program, it should not come as a shock. It should be taken in stride the way you do when you're reaching for your second dessert during the holidays and you're confronted with the ancient Aunt Corrine-If-You-Don't-Shut-Your-Damn-Mouth-thian proverb: "Once on the lips and forever on the hips," and, instead of cussing her out in front of your cousins, you laugh like Denzel Washington in every movie ever, stare her in the eyes, and double down on the Cool Whip.

4. Y'all. I. Freaking. Know, the sequel. Coulter lumped Maher in the group, so I have to honor that, even though we all know Bill Maher is the trash that Native American Iron Eyes Cody was crying about in the 1970s "Keep America Beautiful" antipollution commercial. And yes, I know that Iron Eyes Cody was an Italian dude the campaign pretended was NA instead of hiring a real Native American. #HollywoodIsIg. Anyway, Bill Maher is problematic AF, and it's kind of fitting to use trash to describe other trash.

emotionally, intellectually, and physically attractive. And isn't that the real problem? Thanks to the historical treatment and perception of black women, that's not supposed to happen. Black women aren't supposed to be considered beautiful by the mainstream. Not desirable. Not to be pursued romantically, at least not publicly. It's fine to have her as a side piece, but to bring her to functions? Tsk-tsk. And yes, we have the Tracee Ellis Rosses and Beyoncés and Lupita Nyong'os who break through and are celebrated, but for the most part, for the average black gal, media and society would like to have people believe that no one in their right mind would view a black woman as a partner unless that person dating her is also black. Even then, the notion exists that that's only until, as Kanye West rapped in "Gold Digger": "And when you get on, he'll leave yo' ass for a white girl," as if black women are a placeholder as love interests until black men can date the actual "prizes" aka nonblack women. But back to nonblack dudes, and specifically the white ones, for a second. Ultimately, some behave as though they cannot believe a WM would give up high status (being with a white woman) to be low status (being with a black woman). Heartbreaking, but that is often the message when they see a WM/BW couple. Don't believe me?

When *Scandal* premiered in 2012, it made Kerry Washington and Tony Goldwyn household names, but more importantly, it caused an uproar. The central conflict was that DC fixer Olivia Pope (Washington) was embroiled in a steamy affair with the very married president, Fitzgerald Grant (Goldwyn). While many people were transfixed by this love story, some immediately likened their relationship to the nonconsensual one of Thomas Jefferson and Sally Hemings. Hmm. That seems like quite a stretch. After all, Pope and Grant are two grown adults and this "star-crossed lovers who can never be together" is an ancient plot device that many a TV show and movie has employed. What's the difference here? Perhaps it's that people are letting race and the ugly history of white slave owners raping black women inform their perception of the Pope/Grant relationship. Because when other contemporary shows have nonwhite guys or black men in interracial love affairs, they weren't accompanied by a litany of think pieces. Not much of a peep was uttered about *Jessica Jones*'s titular character linking up with Luke Cage, ditto for *Unbreakable Kimmy Schmidt*'s Kimmy falling for Dong Nguyen, and *Brooklyn Nine-Nine*'s Jake Peralta and Amy Santiago didn't make waves at all. However, when the characters are a white man and a black woman, as was the case with Pope and Grant, she was constantly reduced to a person without agency, and some viewers claimed Grant partially likes her because he "owns" her.

Look, I understand the historical context, and due to slavery, black women have endured centuries of sexual assault and abuse at the hands of white men. There is no forgetting that; however, viewing all WM/BW couplings through that lens is just as unfair as Coulter's position that white men who like black women only do so out of white guilt. Sorry, but in my experience, the foundation of my interracial relationships is not giving middle White America (and the rest of America, for that matter) a heart attack. When my ex and I started dating, he didn't say, "Pass me that Johnston & Murphy catalog. I need to pick out a pair of wingtip shoes so we can march down to Washington, DC." He said, "Hey, you're cute"—a'doy—"let's go out to dinner," and I was two hours late. And before you can say, "Colored People's Time," it wasn't, I swear! It was "Selfish Stand-Up Comic Not Wanting to Reschedule a Show for a Date with a Cute Boy Because My Momma Raised Me Better Than Putting Sauseege First." Let's forget my tardiness for the moment. What's imperative for me to state is that making WM/BW relationships about how white men are rebelling against white people, rather than about a human connection, shows people's inability to see that not everything is defined in relation to whiteness *or* blackness. And as someone who has dated outside her race, I figured there is no better time than now to bust out my version of "Excuse me, sir, do you have a moment to talk about our Lord and Savior Jesus Christ," aka keep you hostage a little while longer to provide some information about the still mysterious world of interracial dating in hopes that the barrage of questions will cease or, at the very least, the dumb-dumbs will STFU.

FIX YO' FACE: THERE'S AN INTERRACIAL COUPLE COMING YOUR WAY

Hi there! Like Ferris Bueller said, "Life comes at you real fast," and in this case, we are already fifty-one years removed from the landmark *Loving v. Virginia* ruling, which not only invalidated laws banning interracial marriage but paved the way for sessy—#Lisp—ass cinnamon angel and MLB Hall of Famer Derek Jeter to be born and his hotness to warm our loins on disrespectfully cold winter nights. What I'm getting at is we've come so far in such a short amount of time, and we should give thanks for IRCs being able to live their lives how they want. Hooray! Yeah, yeah, you said, "Hooray," but I SEE YOU. Your face looks like how mine does when my bestie is being a drunken hot mess and forces me to record her attempting to hit Beyoncé's low-ass register on "6 Inch," and now I'm using up all my damn LTE connection to send her this boo-boo video so she can upload it to Instagram. Anyhoo, fix yo' dang face because this is the new normal. You might as well get used to it and understand that love is love is love is love. Thanks for that one, Lin-Manuel Miranda!

1. First and foremost, it's VERY important to note that everyone who has ever been in a black/white inter-racial relationship still harbors the hope that Seal and Heidi Klum will get back together. They had outlandish Halloween parties, and until their di-vorce, they renewed their vows with the frequency *Hawaii Five-0* airs at my gym. I mean, isn't planning weddings super stressful? These two made it seem like it was as cazh as planning Taco Tuesday dinner in Duluth, Minnesota. #OldElPasoOnFleek. Any-way, I know their reunion will probably never hap-pen as both have moved on, but they are the black/white IRC's version of Ross and Rachel, so it's prob-ably best not to bring Seal and Heidi up as it's a touchy subject.

2. Earlier, I touched on the "interracial couples making beautiful kids" thing coming off a way to fetishize people. Obviously, it's awful to make folks feel like objects, but more importantly, for every Dwayne "The Rock" Johnson or Olivia Munn, there are 372.6 busted-ass looking biracial or multiracial people. That is so much pressure to put on an IRC. Creating a hot person from scratch is harder than competing on *The Great British Bake Off,* and unlike the judges on that show, people are not sympathetic when ish goes wrong aka when folks are ugly. Frankly, there are too many variables that affect someone's future hotness— such as luck and genetics working together like green eggs and ham—so let's not make that yet *another* thing IRCs must do in addition to dealing with racism and ignorance. I know that in my case, if I do end up with a nonblack dude, I'm less likely to make a ridiculously attractive human being than I am to unnecessarily bring up slavery as to why we must watch *RuPaul's Drag Race* live ("Harriet Tubman would want this!") instead of hanging with his friends. Nothing gets between me and my Ru!

3. Memo to delivery personnel and movers: If I'm in a relationship and living with someone nonblack, I need y'all to stop referring to us as "roommates," like you're going to catch the vapors if you acknowledge that IRCs exist. Let's just be real about it, a'ight? There is one bed and one bedroom in the apartment.

That's simple math: One bed + one bedroom = our intertwined bodies looking like a cup of Baileys Irish Cream.

Store clerks: Treat a woman of color with respect *before* realizing that the white dude down the aisle is her beau. I can't tell you the amount of times I have entered a store with my ex and his friends only for us to separate, with ex-bae and his homies browsing on their lonesome, and employees swoop in to offer them assistance like they're the mice Bert, Mert, and Luke helping Cinderella fashion a dress for the ball. Meanwhile, in my aisle, it's just me and a dented box of Crest White Strips and doggone tumbleweeds like I'm on the set of *Unforgiven* because no one is helping me. But then a couple of the employees would see ex-bae walk over to me, kiss me, and place an item in my shopping cart, and they'd ask me how I'm doing and if I'm finding everything okay.

My name ain't Julia Roberts and I don't want to be *Pretty Woman*'d. You should be nice to me regardless of whom I'm dating. Behaving as though I'm only worthy of attention once my boyfriend is beside me is NYCSanitation.gov/TrashCollectionSchedule.

4. Don't "Halle Berry at the 2002 Academy Awards when she won Best Actress for *Monster's Ball*" an interracial couple. Meaning, don't start sobbing uncontrollably about how you're proud of them for not seeing color and being together and how their

relationship is for all "nameless and faceless" IRCs that came before them. There are few things more uncomfortable than someone trying to force a heart-to-heart when you and your bae just want to stuff pigs in a blanket in your mouths.

5. Just because I am dating [insert race], do not ask me if I know any other people I can set you up with from that racial group. Humans are not spare Mophie cell phone chargers lying about my crib, waiting to be passed out.

6. Remember that 2012 Fox News segment entitled *At Home with the Romneys,* in which they showed a clip of Mitt knocking over the Jenga tower his family had been playing with the second he comes near it? That's how quickly people get awkward when they assume an IRC aren't together and decide to hit on one of the people in the couple. Mofo, this dude and I are hella close to each other and practically moving down the street in unison like we're the North Korean army busting out high kicks. WE. IZ. TO-GETHER.

7. The next person who says something to the effect of "What's the sex like though" should just do us all a favor and ctrl + alt + del their reproductive organs so they don't have kids and raise them to be ding-dongs who ask inappropriate questions like that.

8. Parents, relatives, and friends: Be the Tony the Tiger you want to see in the world, and when your child brings home a bae of a different race, just say, "Grrrrrrreat!" and keep that shit moving. Ain't nobody got time for you to be stuttering like Roger Daltrey when he sings "My Generation." Haha. That is the most old-ass reference I could use. This is what happens when you've had a white bae and gone to hockey games.

All righty! That's a pretty sufficient primer for how to interact with interracial couples. It's really not that difficult if you just treat them like any regular old couple. You just have to see them that way. Trust me, I'm a pro at it. Despite having all this experience, I still have no idea who the hell I'm going to end up with, which is kind of exciting as long as I stay off dating apps. Maybe a black guy, but maybe not. Regardless, there is one certainty in my love life: Michael B. Jordan, the offer still stands to make some cocoa babies, so holla at your girl before it's gone. Oh, who am I kidding? Even if I lived in Idaho, married with seven kids whose births had effectively turned my womb and vajeen into an open-concept kitchen under renovation, and MBJ slid into my DMs like Tom Cruise slid across the hardwood floor in *Risky Business*, I would be like, "Husband, there are enough Lunchables in the fridge for the chillrens," chuck up the deuces, and get on the first Southwest flight to the land of This Definitely Gonna Fuck My Entire Marriage Up but #KanyeWestShrug.

The Top Ten Non-Trash Moments
of My Life

⁓

Life has two categories, trash and non-trash, and I like to
believe I'm an unofficial expert at identifying for myself, as
well as for others, which moments ought to be tossed in a Glad
garbage bag that'll end up at landfills (aka Earth's junk drawers) and what should be held up like Simba at the beginning of
The Lion King while one sings the Zulu intro to "Circle of Life."
I'm *that* good. Not to get all *Game of Thrones* on ya, but you can
call me Phoebe of the House Robinson, First of Her Name, the
Blerd, Drinker of Rosé and Also Chardonnay When Rosé Is Not
an Option, Khaleesi of Ignorance, Breaker of Chains, and
Mother of Trash. You're probably wondering, at this point, what
my qualifications are. I'm so glad you asked.

Peep the stats: (1) I'm alive, which means I've had enough
experience dealing with the good, the bad, and the ugly to
know what sucks and what doesn't, (2) I've watched one and a
half seasons of *Friday Night Lights*, so I understand what it takes

to lead and assess a situation in mere seconds: wear khakis, always be hot like Kyle Chandler is, and have some hella emotional music cued up when saying something poignant, and (3) sometimes when I give friends advice, I end it with, "but IDK tho," so that way if my advice Hindenburgs their lives, I can point to the "but IDK tho" clause so they can't cuss me out completely. You know the saying "Those who can't do, teach?" Well, in my case, there's the following saying: "Those who identify trash can do so because the double helixes of their DNA are made out of the plastic rings that keep together a six-pack of Fanta."

My résumé may be a tad iffy; however, I don't need a PhD to properly analyze the moments that make up our lives. For example, having to do a number two *after* showering? Trash. Finding an outlet in a store while running errands so you can charge your phone for ten minutes? Non-trash. The fact that Maxine Waters probably put her 1991 game of spades with Ruby Dee, Cicely Tyson, and Alfre Woodard on permanent hold to become a US representative for California? Simultaneously, trash and non-trash. I mean, thank you for your service, Maxine, but I really wish you could've finished that game so I could hear about all the #BlackGirlMagic that transpired. Anyway, I could go on and on and on, but you get the idea. It's clear I have a knack for determining what's trash and non-trash, and I think we can all agree that I've spent a good amount of this book thus far breaking down what belongs in the former category, so I want to switch gears and focus on what has ruled in my life.

Just being a healthy, able-bodied person who is employed, comes from a loving family, and has been in love means I've had an embarrassment of riches when it comes to non-trash. But sometimes I forget that because the curveballs life throws my way can be overwhelming or heartbreaking, not to mention that simply reading the news and digesting the current state of affairs is enough to make me want to throw up my hands in defeat. So, as a little counterprogramming, I want to pause and appreciate some of my favorite non-trash moments of my life and recharge my positivity batteries. First up . . .

Non-Trash Moment of My Life #1: Too Many White Friends—A Black Woman's Journey in Learning How to Swim

Well, the actual, full title of this non-trash moment is "Too Many White Friends: A Black Woman's Journey in Learning How to Swim with the Help of Julia Roberts, Her Übertalented Husband, Danny Moder, and Their Family After Spending a Day on the Coast of Hvar, Croatia." And yes, that is truly the Goopiest, most "my children's names are Madison and Grayson," "I'm a gentrifier descendant of WASPy Connecticut parents" sentence that I've ever written in my life, let alone experienced. Let me start at the beginning.

In 2017, I shot my first movie—more on that later—and the two-month shoot took place overseas in Belgrade, Serbia, and various other cities throughout Croatia. Serbia can be quite the culture shock for Americans, or at least it definitely was for me, but I was psyched to be making my feature film debut on Netflix. I, along with the principal cast, director, screenwriter, director of photography, and other key members of the crew, arrived in Serbs a couple of weeks before shooting commenced for typical movie duties: wardrobe fittings, rehearsals, bonding with the cast, etc. Fun times, but here is my travel warning: Do not go to Serbia in August. It was hot. Actually, it was disrespectfully hot. Ignorant, even. In fact, if temperature could be personified in ignorance, it'd be the singer Meat Loaf when he competed on *The Celebrity Apprentice* in 2011 and assumed actor and fellow contestant Gary Busey had stolen his paint supplies, so Meat cursed Gary out with the same passion Malcolm X had when delivering his "We didn't land on Plymouth Rock; the rock was landed on us" speech. It was *that* hot. *How hot was it?* It was so hot that I get why the devil leaves hell to take an Airbnb vacation to the polar ice caps and melts them because he's mad at living in such a hot-ass home. You get the point. It was hot. Moving on.

One day, after a wardrobe fitting, I was sweating like Patrick Ewing during his heyday on the Knicks and I was hanging out with Alex, the director. I mentioned I was hungry and jonesing for water. Alex said, "Oh, Danny, our DP [director of photography], has some snacks. I'll introduce you."

"Great," I responded, while dabbing my sweaty body with napkins the way bougie people dab a slice of greasy pizza.

Danny entered, and two things popped into my mind: (1) I recognized him, but couldn't quite figure out why, and (2) he's hot, like looks-wise. DaHell.No?! THERE ARE FEW THINGS WORSE THAN MEETING A HOT PERSON FOR THE FIRST TIME WHILE YOU LOOK LIKE WARMED-OVER, THREE-DAY-OLD LASAGNA. And before you object with some pump-me-up talk, yes, I know. I'm attractive. I'm cute. I'm pretty, but I'm not *hot*. Hot is next-level attractiveness that makes people trail off midsentence and forces their bodies to suffer mild and involuntary whiplash that's bad enough to war- rant a phone call to Cellino & Barnes, injury attorneys. No one is getting minor whiplash when I walk into the room. Quite the opposite. People's necks are stiff and straight like they're in the process of getting their ears pierced at Claire's. Anyway, Danny is a hottie, and after we briefly met and parted ways, it dawned on me where I knew him from. *Oprah!* In case you haven't fig- ured it out already, most things lead back to Oprah. Julia Rob- erts had appeared on an episode of *The Oprah Winfrey Show* shortly after she and Danny had married in the early aughts, and she talked about him and showed a few pictures of them together. And there he was in the flesh and in front of me.

Over the course of two months, he, the cast, and the rest of the crew were in front of each other every day, whether it was shooting the movie or grabbing a meal or swapping remedies and medicines to battle different illnesses (e.g., I had diarrhea for seven days and I talked about it to *everyone* as if I had sur- vived Dunkirk), and on occasion, folks had their significant others or various family members visit. And, yes, this, of course, included Julia and their three kids. No one in my family could come for a visit. To cure my homesickness, I jokingly not jok- ingly asked Netflix to get me a yacht for my birthday that the cast and crew could party on. Netflix very kindly said, "New phone, who dis?" and my dreams were dashed. That's until a couple of weeks prior to my thirty-third birthday, when Danny was hanging out with me and my costars (Gillian and Vanessa), and mentioned that his family was coming back to town. I should mention that Vani and I were not chill about this news. But can you blame us? We're both Midwestern gals with a penchant for forcing our friendship onto people (this just consists of a lot of smiling and telling long, meandering, yet endearing stories). This charm offensive had worked in the past as we'd hung out with Danny & Co. every time his fam came to town. So Danny was game and said, "We could rent a yacht and hang out."

Bitch, "*we*"?! Obvs, Vani and I didn't say that. I don't know a lot, but I do know this. When rich people suggest some pricey shit that y'all can do, you do one of three things: (1) Laugh uncontrollably like Vincent Price on "Thriller," pull up your checking account info on your mobile banking app, and then say, "Stop fucking around and lemme know what time you want to go to Cicis pizza tonight." (2) Toss up a Michelle Tanner thumbs-up with a chaser of "You got it, dude," while mentally going over the meth recipe Walter White came up with on *Breaking Bad* and decide then and there you're going to be a drug dealer for a few days so you can afford to hang out with said rich folk, or (3) as I like to do, just assume they know you ain't got no money and that they'll have to pay for everything.

Vanessa and Gillian ended up not being able to go, but I could, so I said, "Sign me up, Danny!" Now, normally, I'm distrustful of white people with boats (because of slavery, duh!), but I just had a feeling there was going to be hella crudités. There was no way I was passing on free prosciutto.

Cut to the day of the yacht. Julia texted to remind me to bring my passport. I thought, *Isn't this how Liam Neeson's daughter ended up in her little pickle in the movie* Taken?, but I texted back, "You got it, boo-boo!" I—alongside Danny, J. Ro, their chillrens, Alex, and Kevin, one of the movie's producers— piled onto the yacht. It was tasteful AF: There was an abundance of meats and cheeses and rosé, and more importantly, the small yacht crew was all white. This is notable for me because so often when people of color are invited to fancy things, the only other POCs there will be the waitstaff, holding a ratchet chimney sweeper broom. Oh, you have all this money and can't afford a freaking Swiffer WetJet for your employees? SortYourLifeOut.com. Anyway, a couple of rich white people paid for a bunch of other white people to wait on me as we sailed around the ocean, so clearly Julia and Danny adhered to the famous Mahatma Gandhi quote "Be the reparations you wish to see in the world."

We sailed around parts of Croat-Croat for a bit before chilling off the coast of Hvar. Throughout the day, everyone jumped off the yacht, swam around, and basically had the time of their lives in the water. I, meanwhile, kept my black behind on the yacht, sipping wine and cracking jokes because I have no idea how to swim. I know, I KNOW! Way to live up to a stereotype, right? It's just that, growing up, my parents were never swimmers, we didn't go to the beach as a family, so it never was a priority for me. I explained this to everyone on the yacht. This information was met with what I can only describe as a tsunami of positivity. I kept telling them, "No, no," yet they persisted.

Smash cut to me in the water, with a life vest on, as Julia cradled me in her arms while I screamed melodramatically,

"This is the worst day of my life!!!" She let out her signature laugh that we all love and adore, which was a fair response considering I'd been having a great time until I was confronting my fear of water. Still, she, Danny, her family, Alex, and Kevin would not let me give up. So I stuck with it. And no matter how much I tried to remain calm, the buoyance of the life vest was making it impossible to control my own body in the already buoyant and salty ocean water, so any time I attempted to move, the life vest would yank my upper body back and I'd float in a different direction than I intended. I'd call for help like a cocoa Veruca Salt, and Julia became the most glamorous Oscar-winning Oompa Loompa with fabulous windblown hair, and she would gently nudge me in the direction I'd wanted to go.

Eventually, my confidence grew and I took the life vest off, trusting the water more. Danny and his kids gave me pep talks, Alex held my hand as he taught me to do tiny jumps into the water, and Julia had me hang onto the edge of the boat and practice my kicks. All in all, it felt like the movie *The Blind Side* except I never became a professional athlete, I was not adopted into Danny and Julia's family, and no one spoke with a heavy Southern accent. Okay, so it was nothing like *The Blind Side*. And while I'm still not much of a swimmer by any stretch of the imaginaysh—doggy-paddling is my sweet spot—I can now float in water the way Denise Richards's tatas did in *Wild Things*, and honestly, this is the best anyone can wish for.

Non-Trash Moment of My Life #2: Protecting Boob Soup

This story takes places in Las Vegas, natch. A few years ago, one of my besties, Jamie, was months away from getting married and wanted to have her bachelorette party in the City of Sin so she could cut loose one last time as a single person before those teary-eyed "I do"s. See, this is what I don't understand about the concept of waiting for some "special" event such as a bachelorette party to engage in debauchery. Especially in your thirties. In your early twents, *maaaaaaybe*. You still have that new-at-adulthood flavor about you. If you were a wine, you'd probably be described as a smoky bouquet of student loans and Plan B pill residue that incorporates Cool Whip overtones and then finishes with notes of still being on a T-Mobile Friends & Family plan with your parental units. Basically, you're still trying to get it together. But in your thirts? Naw. While you're by no means a veteran at life, you've lived enough that you don't need an "excuse" to go to Vegas and act a dang fool. Plus, acting a dang fool takes on a different meaning as you age. Take me, for example. Gray hair is coming in by the strands on my temples, and each day I'm one step closer to serving Frederick Douglass realness. So, to me, going to the club and making out with a random hottie is not living on the edge. However, attending a housewarming party, being lactose-intolerant and eating two slices of gourmet pizza (because of course it is gourmet) without having taken Gas-X, and then crop-dusting the entire apartment before telling the lie, "Oh, it must be their dog," to the person I'm talking to and leaving before they can finish asking the question "Shanice and Derek have a dog?" is living on the edge. What I'm getting at is, I don't need to travel across state lines or wear uncomfortable heaux clothes to whoop it up. But it was Jamie's weekend, so I took my extremely broke behind (I put everything on a credit card; I had no idea how I was going to pay off) and newly single self to Vegas.

Despite my being a Grumpelstiltskin, I ended up having a blast on the trip. I ate amazing food, took my mind off my recent breakup, and the gals and I went to a low-budget *Magic Mike* wannabe strip club at 7:30 P.M. and left at 10 P.M. because we're in our thirties, mostly responsible AF, and armed with the knowledge that night creams don't do what they do when you're in your twenties. I need every minute of the prescribed eight hours of sleep to look as fresh as a pot of daffodils from an Anne Geddes photo shoot.

That Saturday afternoon, we headed to one of the hotel pools for some R&R and day drinking. But this pool was different because it was a private, adult pool aka topless. Yeah, no. Chilling topless in public is not something your girl Pheebs does. Despite my outgoing and somewhat foolish personality, I'm much more modest when it comes to putting my body-ody-ody on display. In fact, my boob situation is kind of like those Russian wooden stacking dolls of decreasing size that are placed inside one another, meaning there is a sweater that covers a button-down shirt that cover a bra that covers padding, and then you get to my 34A chesticles. So while all the other ladies took off their bikini tops to make tit soup, I was still rocking mine with some shorts.

The ladies and I talked about our various struggles with making career advances in stand-up comedy, discussed Jamie's upcoming wedding and honeymoon plans, and reminisced about various inside jokes we had all amassed after knowing each other for nearly a decade. Then, one by one, I noticed them growing uncomfortable and their smiles fading. At first, I assumed they were just becoming white-girl-wasted from day drinking until Giulia pointed and said, "I think that guy is staring at us."

The rest of them chimed in with their concerns: "Yeah, there's a creep over there," "Should we tell someone," "I think we should put our tops back on," "Maybe we should bounce because I feel weird now," etc.

"Hmmm, fuck that. I'm about to go cuss him out real quick," I said, and made a beeline over to that dude. As I walked, I could hear my friends protesting, but my mind was already made up. Side note: The following is a word to the wise as well as the not-so-wise. If someone's walking towards you with the urgency of an athlete trying to medal at the Summer Olympics in power walking, you're either about to get hoisted up in the air à la Rachel McAdams in *The Notebook* for a steamy makeout session or you're getting cussed out. And last I checked, I'm not Ryan Gosling!

So, about that dude. He had to at least be in his forties, so he definitely should've had the gahtdamn common sense to not stare at a bunch of women who are well within their rights to be topless in a topless situation. Now, I don't know if it's because I had a hunch that I could put him in his place without fear of retaliation or that I'd grown tired of men behaving as though the world is their oyster and they can subject women to disgraceful behavior, but I was done.

As I was nearing him, he saw the fury in my eyes and stride and quickly turned his head. I arrived at his sun-lounger chair and towered over him as he remained seated.

"What are you doing?" I demanded.

Still avoiding eye contact, he replied, "What? I'm just sitting here."

"Really? Don't lie to me. Tell me what you were just doing." Silence. And in that moment, I kicked into Black Mom Gear 5: I Coulda Been at the Stevie Wonder Concert Tonight, but I'm Talking to Your Black Ass Right Now, so Tell Me the Damn Truth, and I said, "Look, I'm not one of your little friends." When a black mom says to you, "I'm not one of your little friends," please consider your life canceled; furthermore, your afterlife has been declined like when Chase Bank is overzealous about fraud prevention and shuts down my debit card when I attempt to buy sixty dollars' worth of items from Bed Bath & Beyond.

This guy was white but had clearly been at an amusement park and seen a black kid get reamed by his mom for acting a fool because he knew what time it was and looked up at me. He started muttering out some weak excuse.

I interrupted. "I know you're ogling grown-ass women. It's disgusting. This is a topless pool where *everyone* should feel comfortable to be themselves without some creeper ruining their day. We're not over there checking out your tired ass, so knock it the fuck off."

He looked embarrassed but didn't dare say a word.

"Look at them!"

He now looked confused, but my glare told him to follow my instructions.

"Don't ever look at them again!" I snapped, and then I strutted, à la John Travolta at the beginning of *Saturday Night Fever*, back over to my girls, high-fived them, then took off my bikini top (making sure I was mostly behind my friends, of course). After a few minutes, the creeper left the pool.

Moral of the story? Not all heroes wear capes because sometimes they're topless and letting their chocolate buttons aka nipples roam free in mostly clean Las Vegas pool water.

Non-Trash Moment of My Life #3: Figuring Out the Tip at a Restaurant . . . Without the Help of a Calculator

Real talk, whenever I do that, I feel like Taraji P. Henson in *Hidden Figures* when she pulls over that giant-ass chalkboard to do genius mathematicals in front of Kevin Costner, who is quietly sipping coffee and nodding his head in approval. So, like, where's the movie about me?

Non-Trash Moment of My Life #4: Eating All the Baby Carrots That Were in My Refrigerator Crisper Before They Turned to Mush

You know when on a reality TV competition show a contestant gets sent home and signs off, "This isn't the last you've seen of me," but it's most definitely the last I will see of them because as soon as the credits roll on my television screen, my brain mentally chucks up the deuces and right-clicks + sends to trash all knowledge of said contestant? That's how I feel about buying a bag of carrots with the hopes of eating them before they spoil. Good intentions, but like that reality TV contestant, I'm only lying to myself. I can't be the only one who does this. For most of us, when we buy the bag of carrots, we know deep down that the fridge is merely a three-month pit stop before the food ends up in the trash anyway. That's why when I achieved this feat a couple of years ago, I did an Usain Bolt pose in front of my open refrigerator for twenty-seven minutes while the door alert on the fridge just beeped like, "I'm proud of you, boo."

Non-Trash Moment of My Life #5: Getting Cast in My First Movie

For people who continue to dream of acting on the big screen after years of "no thanks," "maybe . . . actually, just kidding, we're going to go with Yvette Nicole Brown,"[1] or the most common result: never hearing from the casting director again and

---

1. Yvette Nicole Brown is a talented blacktress aka black actress. She is also a little more than a decade older than me, but I have been going out for the same parts as her since I was twenty-eight. Now that I think about it, I've been asked to audition for forty-something black women since my midtwents, and I fully believe it's because all black people age at the speed of a snail trying to hail its Lyft—#TheyCantAllBeGems—and none of these white people know how old we are. They just know Blue Ivy eating chips at the Grammys and Cicely Tyson being one thousand years old and acting better than everyone else in the game. The rest of us? We're just a grab bag of coconut oil, full lips, and flawless skin who can be any age.

seeing someone else in the role, the moment you get cast in your first movie is one you'll never forget. A person might be waiting in line at the pharmacy when they get the call or might be exiting an audition they blew only to be redeemed with the good news. I was someplace far less glamorous: Manchester, Tennessee.

It was June 8, 2017, and I had flown from visiting my family in Cleveland, Ohio, to Manchester because Jessica and I were going to our *2DQ* show at the renowned Bonnaroo Music & Arts Festival (yes, this is the same Bonnaroo where I met Bono, but more on that later!!!). I was dressed like a collegiate athlete who ends up being a benchwarmer the whole season aka a blazer over athleisure, and I was tired from traveling on Southwest Airlines, which is the "fetch" of air travel. That company has been trying to make itself happen for decades, and all us broke or financially savvy folks opt to put up with their shenanigans. I was given the option of either camping on-site at Bonnaroo (www.lol.naw) or staying at a mediocre hotel forty-five minutes away. Thanks to having outdoor allergies and being too lazy to survive in the outdoors, I chose the hotel option and was driven to my destination in a van by a festival volunteer.

During the ride, I was alternating between making small talk with my driver and listening to nineties R&B when my agents over at UTA called. I answered and they tried to Carson Daly me, meaning they dragged out telling me the news by recounting my journey (even though I didn't need the recap because I lived it) and were basically like, "You've been with us for a while now. There've been some good moments, like being hired as a staff writer on a TV show, and some valleys, like when you were late on rent for about twelve thousand months in a row and your health insurance consisted of asking yourself, 'What would Meredith Grey do?,' but after much deliberation . . . you landed the role in *Ibiza*." When my agents said that I got the part, I was still in such an emotional haze from traveling on a Southwest flight—where folks were acting like they were Meghan Markle's aunties at the Royal Wedding, expecting the finest five-course meal instead of the reality, which is we were packed like sardines on an average aircraft where crinkly packages of dry-ass cashews are considered cuisine—that the exciting news almost slipped past me.

"Wait. What?!" I asked.

"You're going to be in *Ibiza*!" Ali repeated.

"YAAAAAAAAAAAAAAAAAAAAAAAAAAAAAAAAAAA AAAAAS! I have a job," I screamed, before asking for all the details. My agents told me everything and then I got off the phone, and a few minutes later, I arrived at my hotel and checked in.

Alone in my room, I did a jig and kept repeating to myself, "You have a job! You have a job!" Not "Yeah, you're about to be a movie star," or "It's about time everyone recognized how great I am and put me in a movie," or even "You're about to be rich, bitch!" Instead, it was always, "You have a job," which might sound underwhelming to the average person, but to anyone in entertainment, simply being employed is incredible.

Performing isn't like other industries, where you can prove yourself day in and day out, get a raise, get a promotion, celebrate the new job title, rinse, and repeat. Entertainment doesn't work that way. It doesn't care about the résumé you've built over the years or your potential or how you believe you deserve more than what you're getting. I know stand-up comedians and actors who have been in the game for twenty years and still haven't gotten the big break they've been painstakingly working towards. And in some cases, the big break isn't even the prize; some just want to make a living doing what they love the way folks make a living as a cook, a hairstylist, an IT support person, etc. Of course, seeing one's name in lights or having tons of fans who worship your every move is exciting, but forget all that because those are perks. To be able to support yourself without financial help from friends or family is a dream come true. Furthermore, to do that *solely* from entertainment work without supplementing income with a full-time day gig or jobs that pay horribly (fifty dollars to write a two-thousand-word article? Cooooooooool, I guess I'll enjoy an amuse-bouche of sadness with an entrée of oxygen because I, for damn sure, don't have cash to buy food) and still have money left over to afford to go to the movie theater at a reasonable hour instead of at matinee time, which is cheaper (I once watched *Dallas Buyers Club* at 10:30 A.M. #IHadToDrinkVitamin-WaterToReplenishTheElectrolytesILostFromCrying), is "making it," at least for me.

My first eight years in comedy, I routinely scraped by, but I refused to let my family know how dire things were moneywise for fear of stressing them out. I was begging to be allowed to audition for TV projects, to no avail, and more often than not, I was doing non-paying stand-up shows for audiences of twenty people and under. Simply put, it was a grind. And not the fun kind you'd want to post about on social media with the caption "#Never-GiveUp." This is the kind that chips at your self-belief and makes you wonder whether any of this is worth it. If I had given up, no one would have blamed me. I might have regretted it later, but I wouldn't have fully blamed myself for making that decision.

In any other industry, struggling for that long with the hope that it will all pan out somehow, some way, would seem like a foolish thing to do. Can you imagine a CPA grinding away on a Fortune 500 company's taxes only to be paid in free drinks and chicken wings like I was for so many years doing stand-up shows? Yeah, didn't think so. That person would be within their rights to retire their number two pencils and Casio printing calculator and go get a job elsewhere so they didn't have to piece together enough money in their checking account to pay rent, electric, and gas. Well, in my case, I'm glad I was a fool and poor for so long. Paying my share of dues was starting to pay off. Sure, I was in crappy hotel in Tennessee that didn't have room service, but my career and life had just changed. I'd booked my first movie (a lead part!) and was going to earn a salary that was more than what I made during one point when my salad days spread to a year ($40,000 before taxes, does not get you very far in NYC). And that movie was going to lead to other opportunities, which have kept me consistently employed. I am self-sufficient, and better than that, I will never again feel like the loser like I did when I was thirty years old and could not afford to buy my parents presents for their respective birthdays. No matter if people love or hate *Ibiza* or love or hate my performance in it, I am a working performer.

Non-Trash Moment of My Life #6:
When One of My Black Friends Is Ashy
and I Save the Day with Some Lotion

Not only is it unaesthetically pleasing for a black person's skin to look like the half-erased chalkboard that Bart writes on during the *Simpsons* opening credits, but dry skin feels awful, plus other black people judge you for not having your moisturizing game on lock. So it's a trifecta of suckage, and much like when someone has their zipper down in public, tons of folks are reticent to say anything because they don't want to embarrass the person by pointing out the faux pas. Well, when it comes to the appearance of dry, flaky skin on me, point away, y'all, so I can slather on some cocoa butter and be smooth like a criminal. #AnnieAreYouOkayAreYouOkayAreYouOkayAnnie. And I believe most, if not all, my melanin homies feel the same way, which is why when I spot ashiness on one of them, it's an all-hands-on-deck, DEFCON 1 situation.

It's kind like on *GOT* when Sam Tarly helped Jorah aka White Drake[2] with greyscale removal so he wouldn't die and could return to Daenerys. Remember how Sam was training to become a maester of the Citadel (aka a scholar and a healer aka

---

2. If you haven't seen *Game of Thrones*, I ain't gonna judge ya! The show had been on for six seasons before I started watching it, and I only checked it out to impress a guy, which, while not full-on trash, is def food scraps for compost that is then used in a neighborhood co-op rooftop garden. Anyway, I'm fully obsessed with *GOT* now, and one of my favorite storylines of the whole series is Jorah being the Drake to Daenerys's Rihanna. Jorah's always looking at Dany with loving eyes, and she just responds Mr. Rogers style with, "Today, we're learning about the letter *F*, which stands for 'friendship.'"

the DJ Khaled of their time) and he was forbidden by his superiors to attempt to cure Jorah because greyscale disease is so dangerous and highly contagious, so Sam had to sneak into the library, steal greyscale-removal books, and then perform a laborious and multihour scale-removal procedure in which he used pliers to take the scales off one by one, applied a topical solution, and then White Drake just chugged alcohol and bit down on a piece of leather because it was so painful? Well, my helping a friend through a bout of ashiness is just like all of that except all I do is pass the person a travel-sized bottle of shea butter lotion, they apply it themselves, hand the bottle back to me, and we carry on with brunch.

Non-Trash Moment of My Life #7: Graduating from Pratt Institute

We all know by now that college is not for everyone, and I commend those who are in tune with themselves well enough to not go, thereby avoiding wasting four years of their lives and incurring soul-crushing debt. But for me, college was where I found myself and, most importantly, where I began applying myself after years of coasting on sarcasm and passable knowledge of science, much to the chagrin of my parents, who sacrificed so much to send me to a private high school, only for me to mostly waste the opportunity.

I always wanted to live in New York City, so when I applied to college, it was half for geographical reasons and the other half because I simply didn't know what else to do. Luckily, I was smart enough to know that getting into college bought me about four more years to figure out who I wanted to be and what I wanted to do, or more accurately, to have a serviceable answer when adults asked me what I wanted to be when I grew up. This arbitrary expectation for you to have your entire life figured out while barely in your twenties is ludicrous by today's standards. Maybe a hundred years ago, when people lived until thirty-one, it made sense to be a few years into your career as a farmer by eleven and go half on a baby approximately three weeks after your balls dropped. However, we're living in an age where plenty of folks aren't passing away until their nineties. So, in case some people haven't noticed, life is operating on a bit of slow burn, so, grown-ups, enough with the full-court press about being a fully formed person by twenty-two.

Unfortunately, it would take me until my late twenties to realize I didn't need to have all the answers, but thankfully, I figured out something much sooner. And that realization happened when I arrived at Pratt Institute back in August 2002: I was no longer fine with coasting. Okay, okay, maybe that didn't dawn on me *exactly* when I arrived. I was homesick, crying off and on for the first two weeks I was on campus, and really gave it my all with my school's unofficial mandate that everyone must be super into *The Royal Tenenbaums* (I still don't get the hoopla about the movie). In short, I was preoccupied, but once I got settled in my surroundings and ignored *The Royal Ts*, I discovered something within me that I didn't know I possessed: I'm the type of person who thrives when her back is against the wall.

Despite being notified about impending due dates I'm not paying bills until fifteen minutes before they're due? Only way to live. Waiting to pack for a monthlong trip until the night before I'm supposed to leave town at 6 A.M.? Screw sleep cuz I'm staying awake all night folding sleeping bonnets! Being weeks and weeks behind yet scrambling to finish writing this very book you're reading so it can be published on time? Bring. It. On.

I thrive when there is no plan B and only a plan A, and that's exactly what moving to NYC was. I always wanted to live there, but college was an expensive debt I was undertaking. Not to mention that I had to do work-study (meaning having an on-campus job) to afford going to Pratt, so I would be a fool if I put myself into massive financial debt (fifty-five grand), only to half pay attention and get Cs. Plus, I had teachers who were used to students' nonsense and would rather fail you than deal with "the dog ate my homework" crap. Most importantly, it was fine during high school if I spent much of my free time home watching movies and TV shows, but if I wanted to have real-life friends in a brand-new city, I was going to have to stop clinging to fictional characters and get off my ass and meet some people. No matter which area of my life I examined—the financial, educational, or personal—just cranking up the charm and being laissez-faire and hoping things would work out was not going to cut it. I had to step it up or I was going to be chewed up and spit out. If I couldn't cut it at Pratt, then no way was I going to survive New York City.

Not only did I survive NYC, I thrived! I wound up being an A student, having a couple handfuls of friends, and telling people I wanted to be a writer even though I wasn't entirely sure about that, and what do you know? That worked out! My telling people I was going to be a writer and then actually doing that is kind of like when you meet someone, immediately forget their name, and are in the awkward position of introducing them to someone else, so you go, "This is . . . Steve," and Steve is like, "Haha. The only person who calls me Steve is my dad; usually, I have everyone call me Stephen. But yeah, it's Steve, Stephen." And you're like, "That's not all your dad and I have in common. We both like beer," and then you immediately walk away because words aren't your friend anymore. Jokes aside, I took a stab in the dark with the writing thing, and thanks to Pratt Institute, it has worked out better than I could have imagined, but that's not the best part about going to Pratt. It was walking across that stage on graduation day and having my parents be proud of me. Not because I went to college but because I finally committed to something, and there's nothing better than seeing someone you love figure out a part of their life, not because they were forced to but because they wanted to.

Non-Trash Moment of My Life #8: Solange Telling Me That a Copy of My First Book, *You Can't Touch My Hair: And Other Things I Still Have to Explain*, Is at Her House

That's it. She's so cool, intelligent, and wise that I feel as though Sojourner Truth's ghost visits her and *maybe* Solange puts in a good word for me to her? If not, I at least take comfort in knowing they use my book as a coaster for their container of Lorna Doone cookies as they sip tea and shit-talk Thomas Jefferson.

Non-Trash Moment of My Life #9: Driving an ATV and Not Dying

Just to be clear, I'm terrified of getting injured. I don't play sports recreationally, nor do adventure-seeking things such as rock climbing, skateboarding, or jumping—lol—but when I was on a recent girls' trip to Palm Springs, I had to take one for the team when someone suggested ATV'ing. When I think of Palm Springs, I think of unwinding in a cute AF house that I found on Airbnb, drinking tequila, and seeing old-ass white people with their Jamaican or Haitian caretakers at the grocery store. But I decided to go ATV'ing because the only thing I'm more scared of than hurting myself is FOMO. I said, "Yaaas," and went with the gang to the ATV site.

The place looked like the set of *Fear Factor* without the budget and possible accreditation. All kidding aside, it was going for a cool *Mad Max* vibe, and it kind of succeeded. We immediately were told that we had a watch an instructional video before we could do anything else. One of the owners took us into a room with a VCR, put in a VHS tape, pressed play, and then left. It was clearly a video from the eighties, and any time there was important info, the sound and image would cut out. A safety video minus the safety is just a bunch of actors who thought this was their opportunity to be the Meryl Streeps and Denzel Washingtons of instructional vids, only to be the Mr. Beans minus the fame and success. This was equal parts sad and hilarious to us, and when the video was over, we went to the next step, which was to get gear, including pads and helmets.

I asked the white guy in charge of this equipment, "Do y'all have helmets big enough for weaves?"

"What?" he responded.

And then us gang of five black women just laughed and laughed and laughed. And then he said some awkward mess about loving black women's hair. There was pause that was pregnant with triplets, and we all moved on to quickly being walked through driving an ATV. And then off we went!

Yes, I stayed in first gear the whole time I was driving. Of course, I wore a fanny pack that had three bent Band-Aids and a half-empty tube of ChapStick. Obviously, I was terrified of falling off most of the time. But I never felt like such a badass before going up and down hills and doing doughnuts in sand pits. Not only that, society is infamous for telling people of color that they don't do thrill-seeking activities. That it's just white people who are adventurous. Well, guess what? Five black women decided on a whim to do something they'd never done before. Something they've been programmed to think isn't for them and they crushed it. So, tell me again, what else aren't people of color supposed to do? I'll be there with my fanny pack full of nonhelpful first aid remedies.

Non-Trash Moment of My Life #10:
Touched by an Oprah

My first book, *You Can't Touch My Hair*, was published on Tuesday, October 4, 2016, so for the next week, I would be on edge until I found out whether I made it on the *New York Times*'s best sellers list. The best chance an author (especially an unknown one like I was) has of hitting the list is the first week of publication, and if that doesn't happen, it's nearly impossible to build momentum to get on it as new books are coming out. A couple of days after *You Can't Touch* came out, Robert, my lit agent, called me with some news. Since it was way too early to know about the list, I was surprised that there would be anything to report. So I was scared as I waited in line at JFK Airport's Shake Shack.

"I just got a phone call from Oprah's people, and she has your book. She's reading it and loves it," Robert said.

Sometimes you receive information that is so mind-boggling all you can do is roll with it because if you stopped to analyze it or let it soak in, your brain would be like the multicolored pinwheel that pops up on my laptop when I have too many tabs open on Safari. So I just responded, "Okay, sure. LOL. That's a perfectly normal sentence to say."

He laughed. "Well, the exciting news is that she has your number, so she's just going to call you directly, not go through an assistant, to talk."

At that point, I'm sure the sky turned purple, up became down, and my butthole took the express elevator to the penthouse of my body—my head—and then dove out of my ear and into the cup of nacho cheese I was holding in hand. OPRAH HAS MY BOOK, IS READING IT, LOVES IT, AND WANTS TO TALK TO ME?! Is this real life?! I was so excited . . . except I was about to get on a six-hour flight to Los Angeles and then had to go directly to the premiere of a friend's TV show. I boarded my flight and hoped that she didn't call while I was in the air.

I landed and no missed calls, so I raced to the TV premiere, changed into a presentable outfit in someone's office, and had a good time, forgetting to be on the lookout for a call. The next morning, I chatted with Robert and he asked if Oprah called. "Naw," I said as I scrolled through my missed calls, "but there is 'Unknown Caller.' Maybe that's just some rando."

"I'll be back." He hung up before I could say anything and then called me back maybe fifteen minutes later. "That was from Oprah."

Most people would have freaked out, but I just responded, "It's tight she didn't leave a voicemail. Playing hard to get. I like that. I'm sure she'll call again." Robert told me not to miss the next call, and then I got off the phone. *I'm sure she'll call again*"?!?!?! Y'all, now, I still don't know why I was so Zen about it. I must chalk it up to her not being some lame guy who hits up people he's "interested" in at odd hours of the morning. She's Oprah. She only goes after what she wants because she's serious about what she wants, and guess what? She gets what she wants. If she wants to talk to me, quite frankly, I have no choice but to talk to her. #ThePowerOfOprah.

Cut to Monday. No calls from her since the attempt that previous Thursday. But I wasn't panicking. She's a busy woman, and I was in the middle of my first book tour, anxious about book sales, and walking into a meeting with a couple of partners for a pitch meeting. Since one of my business partners was still back in NYC, we used my phone to FaceTime her into the meeting. Halfway through, the screen on my phone changed as a call was coming in. I noticed and froze. It was almost the fifteenth of the month, so I knew it was either ACS Education calling again about the $45,000 in college student loan debt that I was egregiously behind on OR it was Oprah. My phone kept buzzing while I decided. I thought to myself, *If it's Oprah, she'll probably leave a voicemail, right? But if I answer this phone in front of these white people and it's a debt collector on the other end, and I have to get my "white voice" on, they're going to know what's up, and they'll be the Whoopi Goldberg to my Demi Moore and say, "You in danger, girl."* So I let the phone ring until it stopped.

The meeting ended and there was no voicemail. Hmm. I quickly deduced that it was not my student loan people calling because in the past decade that ACS has called me, they've never *not* left me a voicemail with detailed information. For real, they're not the casual "I'm not going to leave a message and I'll just try you another time" kind of folk. No one is when you owe them money. When you owe people money, they'll leave clues like this is *National Treasure*. They'll be like, "Let's play Sudoku." And you're blowing through it because it's strangely easy and they'll stop you midgame and go, "It's easy because these are my checking account and routing numbers. Direct-deposit a bitch her money." So no voicemail when I owe Pratt Institute $45,000? Nah, the student loan people wouldn't do that. Therefore, the call had to be from Oprah! NOOOOOOO! I was crushed! Still, for some reason, I had faith.

Two days passed, and I was shooting a small part in a now-defunct TV show. Normally, I never take my phone on set, as I prefer to be present in the moment, but the previous day, I'd found out I made the best sellers list, so I wanted to have my phone nearby in case Robert had any other exciting news to share. The shoot went smoothly, and I ended up being done early. I grabbed my belongings, picked up my phone, and saw I had two missed calls from two different and strange numbers and a voicemail. I don't know what I was thinking, but I assumed the voicemail was from my parents because they like leaving me silly voicemails, so I decided I would call them back when I got to my hotel. I was very confused about these unrecognizable phone numbers, so I just called one back.

"Hello?" a man answered.

"Um, hi, someone called me from this number and didn't leave a message, so I'm trying to see who this is?"

"Excuse me. Who is this?" His energy was now less warm, and he seemed a little more guarded, as if he was not entirely thrilled that someone had *his* number.

"What do you mean 'who is this'? Who are you? You just called me and hung up. This is weird." Y'all, I have lived in New York City for far too damn long. It was so rude of me to take it from 0 to Joe Pesci in *Goodfellas*, but in my defense, all I knew was a strange man called me and wouldn't tell me who he was.

"Excuse me—"

Something told me to get off the phone, so I said, "I'm sorry. I have to check something. Bye!" And I hung up. I took a beat and then checked my voicemail. There was a message from the other number I had yet to call. I pressed play.

"Hi, it's Oprah . . . as in Winfrey—" Before I continue, I just want to go on the record: L. O. L. Look, I'm all about being humble. When someone flatters me about an outfit I'm wearing, I go, "Oh, this old thing??" when I really mean, "Oh, this extremely brand-new thing I just purchased with the express purpose of getting compliments from women and peen salutes from random dudes on the streets?" But no one has time to hear all that, so I, like everyone, act as though everything incredible I'm wearing is from a dusty-ass box from the set of *Little House on the Prairie*. But at a certain point, you can be a *smidge* less than humble. I mean, duh! "Oprah . . . as in Winfrey"? No. She is the only Oprah, no further explanation needed! At this point, if someone named their child Oprah, they're an asshole, and if the person didn't change their name when they became an adult, they, like the people who put toilet paper on the holder in the "under" position, are sadists and not allowed to procreate. They possess wasted genes and are not to be trusted. Moving on.

Queen O continued with her message, and it was beyond lovely. She let me know she had been trying to reach me but figured that I might not be picking up because her number was blocked (nope, I was just a busy dumb-dumb), so she was unblocking it. Then she got ready to leave me her cell number when she paused . . . because she didn't know her cell number and said she was going to find out what it was and text it to me! I. Want. To. Be. That. Rich! Truly, to be that rich and that busy that you need to and can afford to employ someone on staff who is getting health and dental insurance to, among other things, tell you what your own cell number is absolutely #Life-Goals and #AetnaGoals.

As soon as the message ended, I saw there was a text message from her and immediately called her cell. I'm going to be honest, I blacked out during the convo, so I only remember snippets. She called me Pheebs! Said she could relate to my black-hair journey! Stated that I'm funny and a star! I told her she's incredible and didn't say anything stupid! And just like that, the call was over. And that's normally where a story like this would end because isn't that enough? A phone call from Oprah, who just wants to let you know that she sees you? That's more than enough. It's too much. But I guess the universe knows better.

A few months ago, her team reached out to Jessica and me to ask us to do warm-up for the *SuperSoul Conversations* she was recording for OWN. Jess and I obviously said yes and were pumped that we were going to meet Oprah. To prepare for this encounter, I started a juice cleanse . . . then ended it six hours later and had mac and cheese. I decided to just be myself, so I asked HBO, which was about to release the *2 Dope Queens* comedy specials, to pay for hair and makeup people as well as a stylist. I mean, if I'm going to be myself, I'm going to be my *best* self.

The day of the taping at the Apollo in Harlem, I was beautified in a blood orange, one-shoulder, ruffled jumpsuit, and I walked around the theater, clutching her book *The Wisdom of Sundays*, hoping she would sign it. My stomach was doing flips, and no one knew what time Oprah was going to swing by the greenroom, so Jess and I just hung out there trying to be cool as we waited. I got hungry and grabbed a dry-ass carrot, didn't dip it in ranch dressing because I was trying to be healthy, and I sat in a corner, nervously nibbling with my back to the entrance of the greenroom. Then I heard the signature Oprah voice bellow: "2 Dope Queens! 2 Dope Queens!"

I immediately threw my carrot on the ground because fuck health and raced over to meet Oprah. And OMG! She hugged me! To be hugged by Oprah is to have Elton John sing "Don't Let the Sun Go Down on Me" and the sun is like, "A'ight, I'll stay up here and it'll be 2:15 P.M., all day, e'ry day." To be hugged by Ms. Winfrey is to wake up one day without Michelle Obama's bank account but with Michelle Obama arms and think, *I'm cool with that.* To be hugged by Black Jesus is to feel like Life just went onto Wikipedia and updated your story with a timeline BO (perfect because it stands for Before Oprah as well as body odor because your life pre the Oprah encounter stunk) and the new AO aka After Oprah. #RealTalk, once Ms. Oprah Gail Winfrey has placed her well-manicured hands upon you, ya done been changed.

She pointed out that I was holding her book, and I barfed out that I hoped she could sign my book, if she had time, of course. I was not cool at all, and the three of us kept chatting, she wished us good luck on opening for her, and she left to go get ready. Moments later, someone from her staff tapped me on the shoulder and said, "Oprah didn't get a chance to sign your book. Can I have it and she'll do it now?"

I passed the book along, expecting nothing more than a "Nice to meet ya! Xo Oprah," and what I got back far exceeded my expectations. It was a page-long message that I will keep private and treasure forever. I will share one thing, however. She blessed me. Wut? Oprah blessed me?!?! Is she Pope John Paul the 68th? Y'all if my wig was not pinned to my scalp when I read her lovely note, I would have ripped it off and thrown it in the Hudson River.

As you can see, since I've been alive, I've had some pretty in-credible moments that I smartly don't take for granted nor let go to my head. Instead, when I'm knocked unconscious by life's difficulties, I use these memories as smelling salts to bring me to life—#Evanescence #WhereAreTheyNow #TheyStillThe-SoundtrackForMyPeriodCramps—to remind me that not every-thing is trash. Because these days, with all that's going on in America and around the world, it's scarily easy to forget that. So it's important that for every horrible news item about a tweet from number 45 or grim update about that global warming, we lift ourselves up by remembering and feeling good about the non-trash in our lives. The major and minor victories and sweet treats we get to experience. And since I shared mine, it's now your turn.

Meeting Bono Twice Was My Reparations

And *yeeeeeeeeeeees*, I meant the word "reparations." Is that ignorant? Obvs. But does it kind of make sense if we dig into reparations a little bit? Sure, let me explain! And if you're thinking to yourself right now, *Well, I wasn't planning on taking a detour into slavery and reparations while reading this book during my bathroom break at work*, well, just know that I wasn't planning on writing about slavery and reparations while Steely Dan's "Peg" plays in the background at my apartment, yet here we are. So hear me out, please.

You know how when you buy something online from Target and for whatever reason it doesn't work out, so you take it back to the store and get in that long-ass and depressing returns line that could low-key double as the line immigrants stood in at Ellis Island back in the 1800s? Except instead of a bunch of Europeans wearing their Sunday best and saddled with holding their luggage and crying children all in the hopes of getting a fresh start in a new land, the Target line is mostly parents returning Magna Doodles their kids didn't want, thirty-somethings who OD'd on tchotchkes from Chip and Joanna Gaines' Magnolia line after spending an afternoon on Pinterest, and time-wasting heauxes who want to return a blanket without a receipt, so they turn into Annalise Keating, cross-examining the Target employee about why they're only receiving store credit. Like, really? This is Target. You honestly believe you'll *never* again find *anything* in Targs that you can spend that fifty bucks store credit on? Anyway, the returns line at Target, like this analogy, is hella long. But what's important about Target returns is that if you have your receipt, you'll get your money back, and if not, then you're on #TeamStoreCredit, which is still great because you can use it to get something you truly want. And if you really think about it, reparations kind of works in the same way. Again, hear me out, y'all!

OKAY. So, slavery ended 153 years ago, in 1865. And initially, black people who survived the unspeakable were promised forty acres and a mule as recompense for the lifetime of abuse and agony they experienced, which is akin to getting your money back . . . and also your freedom.[1] Cut to present day, 153 years (and counting) removed from slavery, which on the one hand seems like a long time, yet on the other isn't,

---

1. Btdubs, I'm fairly certain that Thurgood Marshall didn't graduate from Howard University School of Law, start a private practice, found the NAACP Legal Defense and Educational Fund, where he was the executive director, then was appointed Marshall to the United States Court of Appeals for the Second Circuit by President John F. Kennedy all before becoming the first African-American Associate Justice of the Supreme Court of the United states, a position he held for twenty-four years, all so I could half-watch three episodes of *Suits* in order to present this flimsy ass argument to y'all. But I like to think he would admire my moxie.

considering that black people, postslavery, didn't have a seam-less transition into freedom. They still had to fight for basic human rights like voting, marrying whomever they want, and not being murdered merely for looking at a white person in a way the white person perceived as disrespectful (and some would argue that those are three things black people are *still* fighting for). However, for me, I've been lucky enough that my latest trial and tribulation was being unable to afford to see Drake at Madison Square Garden and instead "suffering" the indignity of watching all these white people's Instastories of them wildin' out at the concert. Yep, I'm probably least deserv-ing of forty acres and a mule. BUT! My being black is my store credit, so meeting Bono twice it is! And in my opinion, all us black folk are walking around with store credit, and some don't know it or haven't cashed in yet. Yep, as sucky as things are right now, I truly believe that reparations are all around us. Not only that, but there's a reparations spectrum. Forty acres and a mule is at one end, and the other includes, but is not limited to, the following: winning the lottery, white people apologizing when they're wrong, being able to apply for a job that perhaps fifty years ago you wouldn't have been allowed to, Fenty Beauty existing, and when a white artist performs at the Grammys and *isn't* backed by a black choir. #BlackPeopleAreMoreThanTheSri rachaYouUseToLivenUpYourDustyAssMusic.

What I'm getting at is that all those things I listed above and more help brighten black lives, which are often riddled with macro- and microaggressions. And as I take stock of the thirty-four years I've been on this planet, I've probably had more than my fair share of reparations. Not that I'm complaining, because the world right now is practically a season two episode of *Hoarders*, so it seems like perfect timing to pause and relive the moments Bono came into my life.

Side A: When Bon-Bon Met Pheebs

Previously on *You Can't Touch My Hair: And Other Things I Still Have to Explain*—that's my previous book, in case you forgot—I not only wrote about how U2, whom I've loved since age thirteen, is my favorite band of all time but also went into detail ranking the members of U2 in order from who I want to bone the most to the least. If you are thinking that no one asked me this, you are correct. If you are also thinking that since I shared my sensual fantasies, it has now opened the doors for you to tell me who in the Commodores you want to go half on a pregnancy scare with, all I can say is if all seven slots on that list aren't dedicated to Lionel Richie, I guess you don't value a man who could rock a Jheri curl and is still making that "Brick House" money in 2018, but you know what? Eleven years ago, comedian Sherri Shepherd once said on *The View* that she was unsure if the world is round or flat, and three days ago, I drank an expired cold-pressed juice and declared to my empty apartment, "I guess this is the bougie version of *Jackass*" and high-fived myself. Clearly, we're all on journeys, most of which will lead us to the back entrance of an abandoned Blockbuster video store, but it's the effort that counts. But back to U2.

I wrote my U2 bone list, and everyone at my publishing

house was like, "This is worthy of the trees we're about to kill," and decided to share it with the world. To recap, this is how it all shook out:

1. The Edge, guitarist. He's a virtuoso who once winked in my general direction at a U2 concert and my ovaries popped out a bunch of eggs the way a confetti gun shoots out confetti at the Super Bowl.

2. Bono, lead singer. Not only does he have an incredible voice and is hella philanthropic, but like me, he has a penchant for being extra AF. Example: At the 2018 Grammys, U2 played "Get Out of Your Own Way" outside on a barge in twenty-degree weather near the Statue of Liberty (we all know this glorious nonsense was Bono's idea) just to drive home the point that they support immigrants and love the American dream narrative. Throughout the song, Bono took out a megaphone and recited a monologue that was hard to make out because *he was speaking through a megaphone during high winds.* Lmao.com/IRelateToThatWild-Behavior because I once sent a picture of me standing next to Michael B. Jordan (MBJ was unaware of my presence) to a boyfriend, then asked bae to tweak it with filters so I could post it, instead of an actual picture of the bf and I, on Instagram on Valentine's Day.

3. Adam Clayton, bassist. Because he used to date Naomi Campbell, so obviously, he has great taste in black women. I understand I am nothing like Naomi. HOWEVER! You know how when you eat dry-ass, knock-off Cheerios, and you think to yourself, *But it's still cereal tho,* and cry into your breakfast? Naomi may be a legendary supermodel, but I'm still black tho!

4. Larry Mullen Jr., drummer. He's ripped, super talented, and he now wears glasses while performing and is basically serving Clark Kent sensuality, so I'd obviously smash, but his name is Larry, so . . . that's tough.

All righty, that's a sufficient summary, although my parents read my first book, so I just spent the last page *reminding* them of information they tried to *Men in Black* from their memories. See y'all at Christmas! ✌ Anyway, the late-breaking news is that after the life events that transpired since the previous book, Bono switched places with the Edge and is now at the number one spot.

It all began with *Glamour* magazine's "controversial" decision to award Bono with their first-ever Man of the Year award at their annual Women of the Year awards ceremony back in 2016. People all over social media mocked the mag for this seemingly head-scratching decision because if there is a space that's designed to celebrate the contributions of women, why bring sauseege into it? Good question, y'all, and I answered it by getting my Alex Jones from InfoWars on during an episode of my *2 Dope Queens* podcast when Jessica was like a hot summer side-walk to my cracked egg aka roasting me—#AnalogyNotWorthIt—for Bon-Bon getting this recognition. In short, I was impassioned, was dressed like a vice principal on his day off, and my voice sounded like Macy Gray and Ted Nugent had a child. I. Was. Prepared. To. Defend. My. Man.

And defend him I did. First, I pulled out the issue of *Glamour* in which Bono was featured and I read Jessica the profile that gave an overview of Bono's contributions to society like I was Senator Kamala Harris during the Senate Intelligence Committee hearing, listing off all the trifling things Attorney General Jeff Sessions allegedly has done. Then I dug into Bono's tireless efforts for gender equality, among other causes, and that his latest endeavor, Poverty is Sexist,[2] which is what *Glamour* was recognizing him for, is another example of him using his male privilege to elicit change as opposed to leaving all the work up to women. Or, as he said during his Man of the Year acceptance speech, "Unless we address this problem, both women and men together, our world will continue down this misogynistic, violent, and impoverished path." Finally, I broke down for her how he has inspired me to be more giving and outspoken about social issues. Call me Johnnie Cochran because I just crushed my line of defense with bomb-ass exhibits. I waited for Jess, who was still looking down at the magazine. She took a beat,

---

2. One hundred thirty million girls are not in school, and it has been proven that a lack of education is directly linked to the worldwide extreme-poverty crisis, so Poverty is Sexist was created to not only raise awareness but also to encourage people to be active in eradicating gender inequality and put pressure on world leaders to fully invest in women and girls.

pointed to the picture, looked up, and asked, "Why is he stand-ing in a field?" LOL. And that was the day I quit being a lawyer. Little did I know that some of his staff at his ONE and (RED) charities listen to 2 Dope Queens and were fully aware of my obsession with U2.

Cut to a few months later. I was being pretentious at Equinox gym, drinking a green juice and writing, when a text message from Chenoa, my manager, appeared on my phone. A photo of a gorgeous bouquet of white flowers and a glass vase was fol-lowed by another. This time it was a note. I stared at both im-ages for a couple of minutes, confused. You know when you're asked to read something so unbelievable that your brain cannot possibly compute what's being communicated, so you think to yourself, *Is this written in Sanskrit? Is this a list of unintelligible "ingredients" on the back of a box of Cheez-Its? Are these aliens from the movie* Interstellar *still trying to contact Matthew McConaughey but texting me by accident?*

I immediately called Chenoa. "Is this a joke? I know it's only March, but if this is some kind of early April Fools' Day prank, I'mma take you on *Judge Judy* and sue you for emotional dis-tress and damages because my edges have been blown all the way back."[3] She laughed and reassured me this was not a joke. I immediately packed up all my belongings, told her I'd be there in fifteen minutes, and then jumped on the subway. And

---

3. You know how there's pressure on white women to keep their bathroom pantry stocked with Kiehl's at all times? All right, well, imagine that pressure times a thousand plus racism when it comes to edges. In the black community, "edges" refers to the hair around the hairline, including baby hairs, and there's a lot of pressure on black women to make sure the hair is perf lest they be judged as un-civilized people.

naturally, like the dork that I am, I started tearing up. I arrived at her office to see that what she sent me was the real deal Holyfield. Paul David Hewson aka Bono sent *me* flowers!

Phoebe and Jessica,
Heard you are giving Poverty is Sexist some airtime and helping us make serious stuff more fun...
Thank you
Your fan, locked in the studio, just trying to give Jessica some more of that music magic I KNOW she loves, deep down,
Bono (standing in for Edge)

Remember on *Sex and the City* when Charlotte and Trey were about to break up because she wanted kids and he realized he didn't, but Charlotte had that photo spread for *Town & Country* planned, so she had her apartment staged for the photo shoot? This is basically what I did when I took the Bono flowers home in order to post about it on Instagram.

Okay, well, Bono sent Jessica and me flowers, but let's be real, this is like when a guy is in da clurb and he buys a round of drinks for a group of ladies because he's trying to impress the one woman in the group he likes. So those flowers were for me (I won't hear otherwise). I don't know if any of you dear readers have had the pleasure of a childhood idol showing you some love, but "surreal" barely begins to describe it. It kind of feels like the firework of #BlackGirlMagic that explodes when Venus and Serena Williams greet each other every morning with a titty bump. Or like the pure joy that occurs when my friends and I bust out the choreography from *NSYNC's "Bye

Bye Bye" music video despite not having seen it in more than a decade. Or the hug from a parent that feels like home no matter where the two of you are when the hug is going down. Receiving such a thoughtful and lovely gift from one of my idols, on International Women's Day of all days (nice touch), was incredible, and I tucked the note away for safekeeping and let the roses remain in my apartment long after their expiration date as I was content with my place smelling like seaweed farts because I didn't want to get rid of the #BonoFlowers yet.

Months later and about a week and a half before Jessica and I headed to Bonnaroo, we were invited to the (RED) Supper, a charity dinner organized by (RED) and ONE, the organizations which Bono cofounded. We, of course, said yes and scrabbled outfits together for this meal because there was a rumor that Bon-Bon might swing by to address everyone at the event before going to the band's sound check. Jessica was serving Lisa Bonet realness aka cool yet chic bohemian vibes; meanwhile, I decided this was going to be the moment to shoot my shot,[4] so I went the tasteful THOT route.[5] Meaning I wore a body-con dress that a Love & Hip Hop castmate would rock at a christening because appropriateness is for fools. I looked like a babe, in my opinion, and Jess and I headed to this dinner.

Cue a record scratch because Jess and I arrived to the dinner

---

4. You know when someone is singing the nash anth when they barely have the skill set to get through the "O say can you see" part? That's what "shooting your shot" is. It's you telling your ego and inner doubt, "I got this," and going after something or someone you have no business going after.

5. "THOT" is a loving acronym created by a dude that means "that ho over there." Ugh, but also lol. Btdubs, "Ugh, but also lol" will go on my tombstone.

and (1) we had to walk across muddy *Jumanji* grass that jacked up my stiletto shoes, (2) the attire of most of the dinner attendees could be best described as upscale NASCAR aka pale white men showing off their pale white arms and legs via overpriced tank tops and shorts they were wearing, and (3) Bono couldn't make it to the dinner. That's the problem with dressing like a THOT, because life will come through with the record scratch to bring you back down to reality. Imagine if Angelina Jolie got all hot looking to go mack on Brad Pitt at craft services during the shooting of *Mr. & Mrs. Smith*, but in Brad's place was a dude named Gerald from accounts receivable. Her whole life could've been different; she'd be married to a dude named Gerald and would have two kids instead of the seventeen she has. J/K. She'd just wait until she was on set with Brad and flirt. Back to me. Wasting a heaux outfit sucks and always makes me go, "I shaved above my knees for this?"

There I was at the (RED) dinner with my legs feeling smooth like dolphin skin for no damn reason, but the food was good and the company was even better. Everyone there was smart and working to improve other people's lives either as their day job with (RED) or on the side when they aren't in the nine-to-five grind. Shan, who used to do artist management for U2, came over and introduced herself and said that everyone was working together to ensure that Bono and I met at the festival (Wut? People are actually spending their working hours trying to fulfill the teenage dreams of a grown adult?), so in the interim, she would like to invite me to U2's sound check, which was going on that night and is notoriously private.

"Are you serious George?" I asked. Note: Even when emotionally overwhelmed by information, I still have the presence of mind to slip in a pun. #AlwaysBePunning.

Shan let me know this was 1000 percent a real offer, I said "Yes" immediately, started crying at the table, and Jessica went about the business of canceling the *Wonder Woman* movie tickets she had bought us. And yes, I know that canceling an empowering lady date because four dudes in a band are playing and fine with you hanging around is basically putting feminism on read receipt after it texts you about attending a meeting for an upcoming rally, but this is my troof, not truth, but *troof* because I'm ignorant, so the movie would be seen another time.

Now for anyone who hasn't been to a sound check, only the essentials such as sound and tech folks, etc., are in attendance, and the rest of the venue is completely empty. For nonessentials like me, you're seated in an area far away from where the musicians can see you; otherwise, it's slightly college-student-losing-her-virginity-on-*Party-of-Five* awkward to be sung at in such an intimate setting. So Jess and I (I'm still in my heaux outfit) chilled in the back while U2 ran through the set list for the concert, which was going to be the following night. It was amazing to see a group, forty years in, practicing the way I imagined they did when they started out: just full of passion and leaving it all on the stage. I was in heaven, and even Jessica, who never listens to U2, got into it.

The clock struck 9 P.M., Jess and I were still drunk from the dinner and tired, so we hitched a ride from one of the festival drivers back to the hotel. During the ride, I sent Shan a thank-you text, and she replied:

9:00 PM

Bono says he wants a pic of you in your dress! I told him you dressed up for him

9:07 PM

He wants to meet tomorrow before their show!!!!

Let's get a couple of things straight:

1. If you think that upon reading those messages, I screamed as if I just finished the *New York Times* Sunday crossroad puzzle—a'ight, fine, as if I just finished *People* magazine's Sunday crossword puzzle—you are correct.

2. Bono is not a creep and this is not the start of a story about a trifling extramarital affair between myself and a rock star. GROSS! It's just that, as Bono later told Shan, it's only fair that he saw what fancy outfit I was wearing since he sent me flowers. THE MAN RE-MEMBERED SENDING ME FLOWERS! Sometimes I'll forget to brush my teeth before I leave home in the morning and ruin several people's breakfasts with my yuck mouth, yet this man is remembering the one time he sent flowers to someone he'd yet to meet.

Back to the story. Jess and I arrived at the hotel and drunkenly did a photo shoot in the lobby. All my poses were senior-year-of-high-school basic, Jess mostly had the camera out of focus, but among the turds, there were three good pictures, so I fired them off to Shan and went to bed.

The next day was B Day. Jess and I spent the day doing comedy shows in hot-as-a-microwave-bowl-of-Velveeta-mac-and-cheese heat. We were both rocking breathable outfits, she in a jumpsuit, me sporting baggy, horizontal-striped overalls and a paper-thin cotton crop top and Nike Cortezes. I hit that sweet spot in the Venn diagram of "dressing to help a friend move apartments" and "tomboy sexy on the cover of a R&B girl group's debut album before they realize that showing lots of skin is what will move records." In short, I could lift a box of books, yet be ready to, in a moment's notice, drop them on the ground to body-roll to Fifth Harmony #RIP. Despite being satisfied with my look, I knew the outfit lacked that extra oomph. So *I THREW ON A VINTAGE 1980S CALVIN KLEIN JEAN JACKET THAT HAD THE COVER OF U2'S FIRST ALBUM HAND-PAINTED ON THE BACK, WHICH I HAD PURCHASED OFF ETSY AFTER LEARNING I WAS GOING TO BONNAROO.* Ummmmmm . . .

I know, y'all, I know. The fact that I'm just *now* remembering this purchase as I'm telling this story means I've spent the past sixteen months suppressing this embarrassing memory to the nether regions of my brain alongside everything I learned from high school Spanish class, instructions on how to use my Sonos speaker, and lyrics to "Gangnam Style." Plus, even though I'm #TeamDontHateOnChildlessPeople, spending money on a semiexpensive jacket warrants me being paraded around a

Mommy & Me with Unella from *Game of Thrones* saying, "Shame," and ringing a bell behind me. Anyway, I was in full dork mode, so Jess, Chenoa, and I headed over to the band's trailers backstage before the show kicked off at 9 P.M.

We were escorted inside one of the trailers, which was jam-packed with people. I was simultaneously relieved and crushed. On the one hand, this was going to be a drive-by meeting because there were so many other folks he was going to have talk to, meaning the less time I had with him, the less likely it was that I would say something stupid. On the other, my dreams of this magical hang session with Bono were dashed. I quickly felt silly because the fact that he had asked to meet me should be enough, so I returned to alternating between feeling nauseated and threatening to leave due to nerves.

Just then, someone on his staff came over to me and whispered, "Be quiet, grab my hand, and follow me."

"Huh?" I said in the voice of a woman in a horror movie who wastes time questioning everything, causing delays that get people killed.

"Shhh and c'mon."

So I did. I shut my mouth and grabbed this nice British woman's hand, and Jessica and Chenoa followed us outside. Chance the Rapper stood a few feet away from us, and farther down, there was a little group of people eagerly waiting. After what felt like the first seventeen hours of *Star Wars: The Last Jedi*, as more pockets of people started to populate the area, I saw a door open at the farthest trailer away from me and out popped a small tuft of grayish-white hair, and I was excited as if I went into Sephora, picked out five beauty products, and the total didn't come to the cost of Tina Turner's evening wig collection.

I gasped, "OMG! It's Adam. Everyone be cool." Everyone else was already cool.

He quickly breezed past folks, doling out friendly nods, and when I greeted him with a "Hello," he responded: "Lovely day, isn't it?" and started heading into the trailer I was standing in front of.

"Who's that?" Jess asked within earshot.

"*That's Adam Clayton. He's the bassist. Don't fuck this up for me!!*" I yhisphered aka yell-whispered.

We all laughed at how serious I was taking this, and then we saw the Edge come out, chat and take pictures with Chance the Rapper, and mingle with other folks outside. (Not pertinent to the story, but Edge is very cute and I did not get a chance to meet him. I have to believe that will happen another time.)

Anyway, after a few more minutes, I saw him. BONO! He exited the band trailer, and it was like when former president Barack Obama would enter the House Chamber to deliver his State of the Union addresses and was greeting everyone, shaking hands, having mini convos about brunch plans that will absolutely never materialize. Point is, when someone is that magnetic, you can just feel the molecules in the air change; there's a buzz of excitement and a palpable sense of him drawing everyone's positive energy towards him, only to amplify it and send it back out to us. It was unreal, unlike anything I had witnessed before, and I was at peak nervousness, but camouflaged it well. Then he was pointed in my direction.

Dressed in all black, Bono sauntered over the way rock stars do and playfully did an MMA bob and weave before wrapping me up in a warm embrace. He proceeded to tell me he was so happy to finally meet me and dropped to his knees and wrapped himself around my legs. On the outside, I was cool as a cuke aka cucumber, yet on the inside, I Crip Walked real quick to the *Black Panther* Wakanda afterlife because I died, went to heaven, and then remembered that I needed to be alive to finish this encounter with Bon-Bon, so I Crip Walked myself back down to planet Earth and said, "I'm so happy to be meeting you right now."

He stood up, and I turned around to show off the denim jacket. He seemed impressed and said it was dope like me. Again, on the outside, I'm the coolest cuke at Trader Joe's. Inside, I'm twerking.

I ripped off the jacket because a gal knows that a photo op is coming up, but Bono had something else in mind: "I have a present for you."

Me on the outside: "Oh, really? That's so thoughtful of you."

Me on the inside, singing: *I love, love free shit! Gimme dat T-shirt, I'mma wear it when I do laundry.*

He reached for a giant iPad and went, "I made you a painting."

Me on the outside: "Wait. Wut?"

Me on the inside: My deceased hymen makes contact, says, "This is what we've always wanted. I'm proud of you, boo-boo," and then started playing Vitamin C's "Graduation (Friends Forever)."

Y'all, the dude straight up took one of the pictures I sent him and did a mixed-media painting that included him respectfully

AF drawing within and around my Afro to accentuate my black excellence and writing out lyrics to a soon-to-be-released song because he thought they would resonate with me. Attention to famous dudes I meet in the future: This is what you're required to do if you ever ask for a picture from me. Don't look at the photo and then J off onto some three-hundred-count bedding. You team up with Black History Month and say, "We about to fuck up her June, too," and turn me into a Basquiat painting that looks like it could sell for $2.2 mil.

In all seriousness, I was completely floored because no one has ever turned me into artwork. Bono promised he would send it to me (he did), and I, surprisingly, kept my composure, telling him how much his music and philanthropy have meant to me over the years. He said some lovely compliments back about my work, blah blah blah, and we posed for a picture side by side, like bros on a guys' night out. While awesome, I felt like I was too stiff and asked if he would be down to take some fun photos.

"Sure! What do you want to do?" Bon-Bon asked.

Uhhhhhhh, I thought. "Uhhhhh," I said.

He started taking off his scarf and said, "I like me at your feet." Then, he bent the knee Jon Snow style—yaaaaaaaaaaaaaaaaaaas!— and directed another mini photo shoot, which resulted in the following picture that will be used for my future wedding invitations, pregnancy announcements, evites to my annual Oscar parties, mug shots if I were ever smart enough to learn about stocks and then be arrested for insider trading, and at my funeral:

This is the cover to the erotic U2 fan fiction
I'm writing entitled *Uno, Dos, Tres, Clitorce.*

A'ight, so Broadway musicals like *Hamilton* have intermis-
sions so the performers can rest their voices, and the audience
can stretch their legs, buy T-shirt merch they'll never wear but
give as a last-minute office Secret Santa gift, and use the restroom. Well, while my recount of how I met one of my heroes is
nothing like a Tony-Award-winning musical that changed pop
culture, mainly because the people in *Ham* had to dance, sing,
and act for two and a half hours whereas I'm telling you about
Bono while I'm sans pants and wrapped in a comforter on my
couch, I still do feel as though I'm *Hamilton* adjacent and thus
worthy of taking a breather. Please note: I'm only *Hamilton* adjacent in terms of existing in the space-time continuum as the

musical. This is, at best, very, very circumstantial evidence that would get me cussed out by *The People's Court* judge, followed by a ruling against my favor, in which I would have to pay Lin-Manuel Miranda & Co. for emotional distress and wasting three and a half minutes of their lunch break for this case to be tried in court. Welp, after writing this out, I guess we can all agree I haven't really earned an intermish, so I should, as the Brits say, "crack on," and tell you about the *other* time I got to chill with Bono.

Side B: Bon-Bon and I Are Totally Friends (Lol, We're Not)

But wouldn't it be cute if he and I were? Like some of my other friends and I, we could grab meals, have inside jokes, and get our hair done together. But because he's white, his hair appointment would be about twenty minutes while mine would last the entirety of a Presidents' Day weekend mattress sale at Macy's. Anyway! This story takes place a few days before the Fourth of July in Cleveland, Ohio, where all my family still lives.

As per usual, I had been working nonstop but wanted to spend some quality time with the fam and, yes, my vacation to Da Cleve just so happened to coincide with when U2 was coming to town last year. LOL. Who am I kidding? Flying home to see U2 in Cleveland was intentional as hell. In fact, when I was getting ready to buy tickets months prior to the show, I made the rounds, asking everyone in my family if they wanted to go.

My parents immediately yet politely declined. They're not concert people, and I don't think they *quite* understand my love of the band. I mean, they get that I'm ride-or-die for them, but they don't understand *how* it happened. You know how a person can be born with red hair even though no one else in the immediate family is a redhead and it's all because the red-hair gene can skip a generaysh? Well, it's not like Grandma Bertha Robinson (not her real name, obvs) stopped leading choir rehearsal of "Lift Every Voice and Sing" aka the Black National Anthem to blast U2's post-punk debut album, *Boy*. No one in my family listens to U2, and none of the friends I had growing up did either. Yet my parents support me spending my hard-earned and leftover cashola on harmless activities such as U2 concerts.

As for my brother? He finds my dorky love of the band comical, but not enough to part ways with *his* hard-earned cash just to watch me sing along to Bono for two-plus hours. That left my sister-in-law, Liz, and she was down! She digs a few of their albums and had always wanted to see them live. But between you and me, she was going to be seven months preggers with her second child at the time of the concert, so I think she also viewed it as one of her last times to "turn up" before Baby #2 arrived. I mean, if Cardi B could proudly dance her behind off during her Coachella performance while being around six months pregnant, then there was no stopping Liz from doing the Tootsie Roll during "Beautiful Day." Plus, I'd already seen them five times during *The Joshua Tree* tour, so it was kind of nice to end my run with U2 at home in Cleveland with a family member. Aww!

But also I need some responsibilities or to start a soup

kitchen so I'm not spending my free time and money following around a band and being the most hands-off groupie.

Normally, groupies follow around bands or solo acts in hopes of smashing or getting autographs, but I'm content with just showing up, wearing a tasteful sweetheart-neckline tank top from Madewell, drinking sparkling water, and giving thumbs-ups to divorced dads in the audience who also know the lyrics to U2's deep-cut tracks. Sensual seductress I am not. But that doesn't matter to me. I had that fateful and once-in-a-lifetime meeting with Bono at Bonnaroo a month before the Cleveland concert, so in the words of Kenny Rogers, "You gotta know when to fold 'em," which I did and moved on with my life. The Cleveland show was just to be some sister time, and thankfully, unlike the New Jersey debacle with Michelle (more on that later), the trip Liz and I took to FirstEnergy Stadium was uneventful.

No heavy traffic. No circling a parking lot forever just to find a spot. We simply left my parents' and got downtown shockingly early, so we killed some time at the Rock & Roll Hall of Fame. If you've never been, it's kind of like when someone was a high school star athlete in their hometown and they kept all their memorabilia at their house in order to relive their glory days with whoever visits. It's like that except it's a beautifully constructed museum, containing artifacts from legends, and not an upstairs attic with exposed fiberglass and broken dreams. #OopsThatGotSad.

After chilling at the museum for a bit, Liz and I went over to the stadium, got our passes, and chilled in the VIP lounge (Liz and I were on the "Friends and Family of U2" list), snacking away and having girl talk. About fifteen minutes later, I received a text from someone on #TeamU2:

> Hey Phoebe, Sophie from team U2. The guys would love to say a quick hello before the show tonight. Can I meet you and bring you backstage?

Woooooooooooooooooooooooooooooooooooooooooooooow. Y'all, I highly recommend hanging out with a family member while receiving word that a world-famous celebrity wants to say "Whaddup" to you. Sure, this is almost impossible to plan, but if you can make it happen, you'll seem really cool in the eyes of the family member. More importantly, this feat allows you to go back in time and undo past embarrassing moments, like when you were at a sporting event and tried to high-five the person, who was celebrating with other people and ended up leaving you hanging; that one time you stuffed Kleenex in your armpits to help with your sweating and then when you hugged your crush, the tissue fell out the shirt and to the ground (just me?); and all the times you accidentally said, "You, too," in response to a waiter telling you to enjoy your meal. Of course, a celeb wanting to show you love can't undo all that, but it sure feels like it.

Sophie scooped us up and took us backstage. As expected, it was much less hectic than the backstage area at Bonnaroo, and the other folks waiting for the band were Team I Had Adult Acne When *The Joshua Tree* Originally Came Out, meaning Liz and I were, by far, the youngest people there. Everyone in the room was cute, eagerly waiting and talking U2. After a short while, the Edge entered and chatted up a foursome, and moments later, Bono walked in. And this time, I got to witness how great he is to his fans.

He talked to one group for at least ten minutes as they laughed over inside jokes; to another set of fans, he caught up on their lives and then gave them a handwritten letter for their friend who was in the hospital and couldn't make it to the show; then he'd go over to Edge and tag him out and take over talking to some fans. No matter who he was with, he made sure each person felt special and was fully engaged, listening to every word people were saying to him, and he was generous with his time in a way that many folks, myself included, aren't sometimes. After making the rounds, Bono headed over to Liz and me, who were the last people he had to greet.

Even though he had asked to see me, I was still surprised that he knew me. We chatted a bit, I introduced him to Liz, he wished her best of luck with her pregnancy, and then he agreed to take some pictures with me.

"Bono," I started, "the lighting is bad. And I'm black. No one's gonna to see my face."

He laughed and said, "This is just like Bonnaroo when I directed our pictures," and then positioned me so the lights were serving me dramatic Hitchcockian eleganza. #WhosThere-Hunty #IDontKnow #ImJustAScaredWhiteLady.

Aaaaah!!! He remembered! We took a few photos (including one I took of him and Liz), but the cutest part of our whole exchange? Midconvo, he saw Ali, his wife, and beaming with pride, he brought her over to introduce her to me. It was obvious how in love he is with her. She complimented my blue-green hair, and the four of us talked about the tour. Eventually, his assistant told him he had to go get ready for the show. He said, "Okay," and then kept talking to Liz and me as if he didn't have to entertain sixty thousand people for two hours. I knew he had to go, and in that moment, I kicked myself because I hadn't brought him anything to sign. Then I looked down at my purse from & Other Stories and asked him to sign it.

Concerned, Ali was like, "But it's such a beautiful bag."

I shrugged. "It's all I have."

Bono took the purse despite his assistant telling him he had to go and, with a Sharpie, quickly sketched a cowboy on it with the caption "B 🖤 P."

"All right, you really have to go," the assistant politely reminded him.

"Wait," he said. He flipped over the purse and drew a quick portrait of me. Y'all, I don't know what it is about me, but I must be giving off some Kate Winslet "Draw me like one of your French girls" vibes because the man is always inspired to do some art when I'm around.

Bono handed the purse back to me, and then he and Ali walked out of the room holding hands. #CoupleGoals.

And just when I thought things couldn't get any better, the next day, I went on U2.com (because of course I did) and saw that the pic of Bon-Bon and me that I had posted on Instagram was screenshot and placed on the website:

Not going to lie, this picture of Zaddy B and me ending up on U2.com filled me with the same amount of pride as the *Washington Post* organization must've had when they reported the Watergate scandal. #Ig.

Listen, boo-boos, I don't know how else to explain either Bonarios aka Bono scenarios other than that they have to be my reparations for the annoyances I've had to put up with as a black person. So now it's your turn to take stock of your life and look back on all the reparations you've received. Except if you're white. If you're white, maybe don't call it reparations. Call it "living your best Meryl Streep life when she and Steve Martin made chocolate [obnoxious French accent] *croissants* in *It's Complicated.*" Or "Tuesday." Yeah, call it "Tuesday."

Money Is a Trifling Heaux
and Also Your BFF

~⌒~

I know name-calling isn't cool, but I spelled "ho" the French way to make it classier, kind of like when I take something ignorant (unbuttoning my pants halfway through dinner at an Italian restaurant) and make it slightly less ig (bringing up net neutrality during dessert) to distract from the fact that my underwear is making a cameo. But in my defense, (1) carbs bloat me out, making my stomach look like Dizzy Gillespie's cheeks when he played the trumpet,[1] and (2) I only undo my pants while dining out because I've mistakenly worn my standing jeans instead of my sitting ones. You know what I'm talking about. Standing jeans are gorgeous, skintight, hug every curve perfectly, and are compliment magnets because they have you looking like a

---

1. This reference is for those old enough to remember back in the day when they had to call the movie theater for movie times, when they knew people's phone numbers by heart aka BCPC aka Before Cell Phone Contacts, and when playing Fred Astaire's "Puttin' on the Ritz" was a signal some hanky-panky was about to go down.

delicious Fiber One snack. #HeartHealthy. Sitting jeans, on the other hand, are what you wear for all the things you can't do in standing ones: eat, breathe, live, have the trash posture of the Hunchback of Notre Dame but the joy of Rudy when he played for Notre Dame. For real, take notice the next time you're at da clurb or some other "hip" place. Most of the women there in booty-hugging bottoms aren't "chilling out, maxing, relaxing all cool." Instead, they're stiffly standing upright in first position like a bunch of low-budget Black Swans. ANYWAY! I should stop stalling and just get on with the essay.

But I'm nervous! I'm talking frazzled like in ninth grade when the teacher called on me to read the next passage in the *Odyssey*, but I wasn't paying attention because I was daydreaming about Kevin from Backstreet Boys,[2] so I panicked, said "Life's an odyssey" Deepak Chopra style, and then mic-dropped like I blew some minds. But I didn't. Everyone stared at me, so I asked what page we were on and read aloud.

All kidding aside, I'm anxious because this essay is about cabbage, loot, ducats, moolah, scratch, "dolla, dolla bills, y'all," coins, cheddar, Benjamins, dough, cake, greenbacks, M to the O to the N to the E to the Y, money. And as we all know, talking about money can be weird.

It's awkward if you're lacking cash yet people assume you have some. It's worse when e'rybody knows your pockets are like my Afro after a night out on the town: full of lint,

---

2. While most girls my age were all about Brian Littrell or Nick Carter, my young ass had designs on Kevin, who I think we all can admit was older-looking and seemed like he was spending his off-hours clipping coupons for Back to School sales because he's all about getting his kids what they want while being frugal as hell. What can I say? I like guys who have #IPayMyChildSupportOnTime face.

down-pillow feathers, cracked M&M's, and not much money. And if people know you have plenty of money? You best believe they're looking at you like, "I left the milk and cookies out, St. Nick. Where's my shit?" and expecting you to start paying for things.

However, it's not just financial status; it's also about how we *display* our real and/or imagined financial statuses. Some are dressed head to toe in the latest designer fashions despite being in massive amounts of debt, while others are serving affordable camp-counselor realness, yet they're hella rich (ahem, Mark Zuckerberg). But except for an outlier like him, whose portfolio is public knowledge, there is a whole lot of keeping mum about money. I mean, a girlfriend will sooner tell me the deets of her sex life than reveal what's in her bank account, and that's because sharing sexcapades can now be considered a charming party trick while it's still thought to be impolite or gauche to talk about money. Well, as the *Citizen Kane* of our time, MTV's *The Real World*, taught us: It's time to "stop being polite and start getting real. *The Real World.*" Well, in the real world, money (or lack thereof) partially determines our self-worth and dictates how we live. And I should know because I used to be one of those people who would avoid talking about money openly and honestly.

I mean, sure, most of us grew up on either *Lifestyles of the Rich and Famous* or *MTV Cribs,* where celebrities would show off their glamorous abodes and allow us to ogle over all the expensive and mostly unnecessary things they own, but the average person? I don't know about y'all, but I don't want HD cameras to see that my not-having-central-air-conditioning behind put ugly-beige-air-conditioner covers on my ACs that I sloppily slap blue painter's tape around to seal out the cold air the way I used to wrap my friends' presents in newspaper and pieces of Scotch tape that already had clothes fuzz stuck to it while saying, "'Reduce, reuse, recycle' is how I live my life," when I knew damn well I wasn't trying to be the Scottie Pippen to Captain Planet's Michael Jordan. I just forgot my poor homie's b-day. What I'm getting at is that if you're a wealthy celeb, it might be cool to show how much you're balling out of control. But for the average person, money is simply too painful a thing to discuss as it often leads to feelings of not measuring up to family, friends, and even strangers. Then there's the added pressure from financial experts who tell us about the unrealistic standards we're supposed to meet (e.g., Fidelity Investments stating that by age thirty-five, one should have twice their salary saved). It's all too much. But just because we're not saying *everything* about our financial sitchy-ations doesn't mean our lips are sealed.

Plenty of people, myself included, will in that "everyone who has a decent-paying job" way say, "I'm strapped for cash," and then order a thirty-dollar lunch from Grubhub. This, of course, is pure bullshit, performance art in which a lot of us play the role of Pretend Broke Person, because actual, *truly* broke people are not ordering takeout lunch five times a week. That is classic PBP nonsense. They'll go on and on about being low on funds yet will go to concerts regularly, decorate their apartments, enjoy small shopping sprees, buy expensive phones to keep up with the latest technology, and so on. To be clear, it doesn't mean PBPs are playacting like they're Oliver Twist when they're rolling in the dough. They aren't. This fake "bro-keness" performance is the result of societal grooming. The phrase "keeping up with the Joneses" ring a bell? Consumer-ism reigns supreme in Murrica, so having spare cash to indulge in small luxuries like ordering takeout or enjoying nights out on the town is a must. However, having *too* much money and splurging on niceties without giving it a second thought? That's just trifling. And thanks to good old conditioning, one might feel a twinge of guilt and worry that those less well-off will resent and want to *Single White Female* them, so it's in everyone's best interest to downplay being flush with cash.

Quite the "damned if you do, damned if you don't" scenario, isn't it? But that explains why, when money comes up, most people behave like Taylor Swift when she wins at an award show, just all "Oh, wow" and "Golly gee." It's like, bitch, you make fifty-five thou a year, but when the server at Chipotle says guacamole is extra, you're gonna act like the character of Abuela Who Only Says "Ay Dios Mio" and Does the Sign of the Cross on a telenovela? Listen, Pretend Broke Person: Ya ain't poor, and you're holding up the gahtdamn line. So get the guac, then make it rain next door at McDonald's and buy all the sauces they have but none of the nuggets because, guess what? You can *afford* to be this ridiculous, ig, and reckless with your coins. Now Truly Broke People, on the other hand? Nope. They don't have the scratch or the time for that foolery. I should know, because for a seven-year stretch during my first decade in com-edy (2009–2016), I left behind the PBP world and ended up be-ing a TBP. Here's a snapshot of what my life was like:

- I brought one of two packed lunches to work every day: (1) a small handful of Dole premade salad and a sad sandwich with one thin piece of lunch meat folded into many layers like a Chinese fan to give myself the illusion that this was going to fill me up or (2) a Boca brand meatless Chik'n patty,[3] with a side of ketchup and steamed broccoli. I, of course, explained to coworkers that this was my diet to go along with working out at the gym, but in actuality, I had secretly canceled my gym membership long ago because I couldn't afford it.

- I only went out if it was to a comedy club whose bouncer knew me and would let me, for free, watch national headliners perform. The comic discount for food allowed me to buy a meal, which consisted of seltzer water and a basket of fries. #DinnerOfChampionsForPeopleWhoWatchTLCInTheHopesOfNotLearningAnything.

- For my birthday I asked for money from my parents and used it to pay bills. Meanwhile, my brother and sister-in-law were on H&M gift card duty, and I treated the GC like it was a black Amex card, except instead of renting private jets and getting flashy

---

3. Look, vegetarians and vegans, I love y'all, but I'mma need you to stop trying to make nonmeat "cool" with absurd street spellings. That's like when record execs have rappers do a guest verse on a Tim McGraw song as if that's going to make Tim McGreezy more enticing to black listeners. It doesn't. It just makes them go, "Aaah, I guess that rapper wanted some extra cash to go on vacation and I can't even judge. I've sold Tummy Tea on Instagram so I could chill at a Sandals resort for four days."

watches, I was living my best damn BOGO life (aka buy one, get one free), buying padded tank tops and sensible cardigans.

- Vacations? Never.

- Still new in comedy, I performed stand-up out of town either for free or for very little, but thanks to some life hacks, I was able to not lose as much money as I could've. For instance, I'd purchase a ticket from BoltBus or Megabus during one of their one-dollar trip sales or I'd travel at odd times so I could get a cheaper seat. As for hotels? Hotels, schmotels. I just slept on the couch of a comic in the city I was visiting. If I had to fly to a gig, I only took the job if the pay was enough to cover my plane ticket, and then the leftover money would be used for food and for getting to and from the venue.

- Even though I was fortunate enough to be able to afford to live by myself (a small one-bedroom), my living situation was a hot mess. I was saving up to buy a couple of ACs, so I MacGyver'd a solution for the summer to keep cool. My sleep routine consisted of turning on a tiny oscillating fan, taking off all my clothes except my undies, and putting ice-cold white towels on myself. The towels kind of looked like a bootleg version of Milla Jovovich's iconic white bandage costume from *The Fifth Element*. Okay, that actually sounds kind of cute, but you know what wasn't? Half the ceiling in my bathroom collapsing due to a massive mold problem my super was too lazy to fix. The building controlled the heat, and the only two settings were: (1) Barely on During the Winter, So Unfortch, You Have to Serve Swarovski Realness aka Have Icicles Grow on Your Nips and (2) Hot as the Devil's Taint After He Did the White-Nonsense Version of Yoga aka An Hour-Long Yoga Class Where Dashboard Confessional Plays in the Background. And last, but not least, the occasional cockroaches popping by, unannounced, like an annoying in-law on *Everybody Loves Raymond*. In fact, I got so used to them that one time while cooking, I realized a cockroach was crawling up my thigh, nonchalantly brushed it away, and then resumed cooking. What in Orkin Man hell?! THIS IS HOW YOU KNOW YOU'VE LIVED IN NEW YORK CITY FOR TOO LONG. WHEN YOU CASUALLY SWEEP AWAY A COCKROACH WITH THE FLICK OF YOUR HAND THE WAY A FEY KING DISMISSES A COURT JESTER FROM HIS PRESENCE, IT'S TIME TO LEAVE NEW YORK CITY FOR A SECOND AND REALIZE YOU SHOULDN'T BE SO GRIZZLED THAT IT DOESN'T BOTHER YOU THAT HALF THE CAST OF *A BUG'S LIFE* IS STRAIGHT UP AIRBNB'ING IN YOUR CUPBOARDS.

Moral of the story? I was too broke to live elsewhere. So, for many years, I stayed. Heck, there were a few dicey months when I was too broke to even live in *that* apartment. When deep financial distress like that occurs, one of two things happens. The world sticks out its hand, says, "I got you, boo," in the form of a loan from a loved one, a small jackpot from the lottery, or a tax return deposit just as you're running out of funds. Other times, the universe cackles like a cartoon villain at your checking account's soundtrack being the sad parts of *Les Miz* (which is *all* the parts of *Les Miz*) and goes, "Ya been served, bitch!" And in my case, the universe served me a no-expenses-paid trip to housing court. Quick time-out.

Mom, Dad, sorry for not telling you about this until right now as I reveal it very publicly in a book. Admittedly it's kind of a trash move, like at a wedding when the minister basically goes, "If you think this union is a steaming pile of doo-doo, then totes feel free to stand up and give everyone your Amazon one-star review of the couple's relationship."

First of all, Minister, why are you being a messy little bitch? People put on nice underwear, used Schick Mach 5 razors to get the smoothest shave, dressed in tacky bridesmaid dresses and goofy-ass Colonel Sanders beige suits, paid for flights and hotel rooms, both the bride and groom/bride and bride/groom and groom went through the painful process of cutting certain folks from the guest list, and the wedding band had to learn both Journey's *and* Earth, Wind & Fire's entire oeuvre, and *now* you want to take the temperature of the room? Unless your name is Al Roker and you're paid a million dollars to *maybe* sometimes guess correctly about the weather, you need to shut the fuck up.

Second, to the fool who stands up to air their grievances: Please sit your ass down. I've already purchased a Cuisinart four-slice toaster, so I'mma need this nuptial to happen so that in three weeks' time, the married couple will send me a nice thank-you card from Papyrus. Now, if they send me some generic Hallmark card garbage with a boo-boo illustration of a tulip on the front, then, wedding interrupter, *and only then* will I join you in doing a sit-in on the couple's front lawn to recite the spoken-word poetry classic "Y'all Ain't Shit and Y'all Ain't Never Gonna Be Shit."

Point is, just like it's kind of ridic to wait until the final moment to publicly express that you don't think a marriage should go down, so is my choosing to belatedly publicly inform Ma and Pa Robinson about the crippling financial strife that almost resulted in me being evicted. So why has it taken me so long to spill the beans?

The day I got the housing court summons, I was heartbroken, terrified, and full of shame. I was supposed to be "good" at money. My parents taught my brother and me about the value of saving and living within your means and shared their own financial struggles with me. I was not supposed to screw up like this. Plus, they'd been very supportive about my move to New York City for school and my decision to pursue comedy as a career, so I didn't want to disappoint them or cause them to worry. Plus, I knew that saying, "I'm about to be four months behind on rent," to the parental units, who had their own finances to deal with, would've made this nightmare scenario unavoidably *real*. So I said nothing to them. Or anyone. I took the housing court notice and went inside my apartment.

Long story short, housing court is a soul-crushing, demoralizing cesspool containing good-intentioned, hardworking people who are, for one reason or another, struggling. Despite this cold reality, there were small breaks from the despair. Couples nervously and sweetly held hands, and little kids, oblivious to the severity of the situation, used the holding room like a jungle gym. But outside of that? Housing court makes you feel like a loser and an embarrassment, so how did I end up there in 2009?

I could blame it on circumstances being out of my control, like the 2008 recession or the fact that pursuing stand-up comedy mostly bled funds rather than adding to them, or I could even blame it on the rain—#MilliVanilliTruthForever[4]—but the truth is that the housing court clusterfuck was partially my fault.

In 2008, I was an executive assistant at an independent movie company and making decent money. Sixty thousand dollars, to be exact, but because it was not the career I wanted and I was working around the clock with some difficult personalities, I was weary. Like "just came home from a long travel day, took my bra off, and discovered that I'm out of LaCroix and all the supermarkets are closed" weary. But I got through having a crummy job like most of us do: listening to pump-up music; taking extra-long poop breaks in the bathroom to the point

---

4. We need to pause for a sec because back in 1989, Milli Vanilli got busted for lip-syncing during a performance of "Girl You Know It's True," when the recording jammed and kept repeating the line "Girl, you know it's . . ." and people reacted to this betrayal like they did in the nineties when Olestra, a fat substitute used in WOW! chips, was revealed to cause anal leakage and result in folks having soggy bottoms—#TheGreatBritishBakeOff—in their underwear. WOW! chips were eventually canceled, and so was Milli Vanilli. But cut to 2018, where lip-syncing isn't a career killer anymore. I mean, Britney Spears practically walks around onstage like she's looking for an available outlet to charge her phone and lazily lip-syncing the way I did at my old day job when we'd have to sing "Happy Birthday" to some dude named Darrell when all I wanted was to go back to my cubicle and watch *Pretty Little Liars* when I should have been autosumming data in Microsoft Excel. And she sells out every. Single. Concert.

where the automatic light goes off and you comfort yourself by singing "One is the loneliest number"; and, finally, spending all day with a Katie Holmes barely there "can someone get me outta Scientology" smile plastered on my face. But the biggest way I coped was by telling myself the money was worth the misery and then buying dumb shit to distract from my soul-sucking job, which is, unfortunately, typically American. But for the most part, I was pretty good with money, I was paying off my credit cards in full, being prudent with my spending, etc. That is until October 2008, right in the middle of the nation's recession, when the indie film company folded and I was given a severance package.

Fuck severance packages, y'all. Actually, severance packages are great and necessary so people can support themselves and/ or their families when unforeseen hiccups happen. So what I should say is: Fuck being a twenty-four-year-old who was given a severance package in the ballpark of $15,000 and was arrogant enough to believe that even though the *entire* country was struggling to find work, I, somehow, was exempt from the recession, so I thought, *Why be sensible with this influx of cash? I'm easily going to get another $60,000 job (and, yes, I'll settle for $55,000 to $58,000 because I'm reasonable and generous), so this severance package is less a safety net to help me survive and more like when you get "bag fries" aka when the server at a fast-food restaurant puts too many French fries in the container, so some of them spill out at the bottom of the bag. In closing: You're rich, bitch! So go 'head and hella live that billionaire Jay Gatsby life with your bonus money.*

LOL.com/BitchIsYouSerious. That line of reasoning was dumb for several reasons. One, when a recession hits an entire naysh, it doesn't just duck, duck, goose its way around the middle class, picking a select few; everyone is goose, so everyone is chosen by the economy to be fucked. Second, I love how my willingness to take a $2,000-to-$5,000 pay decrease was a sign of generosity. That'd be like a dude saying, "Instead of seven blow jobs a week, I'll settle for six and a half. The half being a handy where you can tug at my sauseege indifferently like a tired housewife tugging at the dinner-bell rope to call farmhands in for supper." And finally, there's no such thing as bonus money! There's just money, and it's either spent responsibly or irresponsibly. And lemme tell you, I was running-with-scissors irresponsible.

I put none of that severance package money toward the FORTY-SIX THOUSAND DOLLARS' WORTH OF STUDENT LOAN DEBT I had. Instead, I acted like I was pulling a fast one on my student loans by deferring them with a "woe is me," "BRB, me have no money" excuse. I didn't even set aside some of the cash for rent (mine was $1,150 a month); I just proceeded to blow the money on concert tickets, West Elm furniture, trips to Macy's and Banana Republic, both of which I opened store cards with, and full-price bus tickets to all my out-of-town comedy shows. Eventually, I started racking up debt on my other preexisting cards after maxing out the Macy's and West Elm cards.

Lol. Wut?!?! How the hell did I max out the Macy's card? The West Elm one I understand because they'll have a 20-percent-off sale once a decade, yet the discount is immediately erased because of their astronomical shipping costs. Seriously, one time I ordered a coffee table and a couple of vases and was like,

Phoebe Robinson

"Am I decorating my apartment, or did I unknowingly invest in a Silicon Valley start-up?" Point is, it's easy to max out a card with Dub Elm, but Macy's? Not so much. They practically give everything away because they have sales all. Da. Damn. Time. They'll go, "Hey, y'all, it's Flag Day. Do you want this Samsonite suitcase, a couple of memory foam pillows, and the entire Tommy Hilfiger department? Oh, you don't have any coupons? No worries! Our employees will ring up thirty coupons so that you can buy everything for forty-eight dollars. Come back tomorrow!" You see, Macy's seems like a great friend, but don't be fooled. It's the Blue Magic of stores, getting everyone hooked on deals to the point that you're compulsively buying from them. And *that's* how I ended up maxing out the Macy's card. But the saddest part? I couldn't even (and still can't) remember half the garbage I charged on any of these cards. All I knew was I had no idea how I was going to erase the debt, and as you've probably guessed by now, I was having a hard time getting a new day job.

By spring of 2009, my severance package had completely dried up, I wasn't earning enough from my meager unemployment checks or the low paying temp jobs I took (packing boxes full of makeup to be shipped overseas for Fashion Week or manning the reception desk at ad agencies), and I performed on nonpaying stand-up shows around New York City. Before long, all the chickens from Sallie Mae, Macy's, West Elm, and both my RadioShack and Bank of America credit cards began coming home to roost.

I started dodging phone calls. As I hunted for work during the day, humiliation repeatedly washed over me for believing that there would be no consequences for my poor choices. Once I got home, I paced my apartment like a conspiracy theorist until the wee hours of the morning, calculating how I would divvy up the upcoming month's money in the hopes that I'd have maybe a couple of hundred dollars left over so I could buy groceries and pay for public transportation. I told absolutely no one, not my friends and especially not my family, about any of this. I acted as though everything was okay and my struggle was just the charming first act on an episode of *E! True Holly-wood Story*.

Summer was just around the corner, and a recurring theme was emerging during interviews for full-time jobs: My $60,000 salary as an assistant was more than a lot of places were willing to pay, so I was routinely offered a little more than half that. Other employers told me that I was overqualified or questioned my passion for administrative-assistant work. Listen, I under-stand companies wanting employees to like their jobs because spending forty hours a week around peeps who behave as though they're saddled with a perma-wedgie is undesirable. However, we can cut the shit at a certain point. No one has a passion for an entry-level admin position; they have a passion for not living in their parents' basement like a bridge troll in the children's tale *Three Billy Goats Gruff*. Thankfully, after nine months of searching and being a couple of months behind on rent, I was offered an executive-assistant position at IAC, an internet company. Yaaaaas! But the salary was only $40,000, which was one-third less than my last full-time job. Naaaas aka nooooooo!!! #TheyCantAllBeGems.

Don't get me wrong, I was thrilled to be employed again;

however, I was screwed. A 33 percent pay cut meant that it would be nearly impossible to pay rent and basic living bills, make monthly student loan payments, and knock down my debt all the while continuing to hemorrhage money on a comedy career that was in its infancy. Hell, making $40,000 meant that being able to afford the apartment *and* cover the necessities (heat, electricity, internet, and public transpo) was going to be a Herculean task. And I failed. Every thirty days, I was strategically paying some bills over others or opting out of paying rent if I was short one month because I didn't have enough to pay for that *and* keep the lights on and food in my fridge. And that's how I ended up in housing court.

So, the morning of my appointment, I emailed my boss and told him I was coming in late due to an emergency water leak, which was not a far-fetched lie as he had been brought up to speed about all the deficiencies of my home. Then I put on my most professional-looking outfit and took a thirty-minute subway ride, alone, to the Brooklyn housing court.

As I sat watching the concerned couples, the playing children, and the smattering of folks who appeared to be single like myself, I became depressed. In that space, so acutely aware of the sound of the ticking hands on the clock as I waited for my number to be called, the potential for the outcome to not go in my favor was oppressive. Granted, seeing the sadness wash over everyone's faces as they also contemplated their fates helped me feel a little less alone, but not much. I knew it was impossible for everyone there to leave with a happy ending. Still, I held a sliver of hope that my speech-and-debate years of high school were going to aid me in convincing a judge to give me time to come up with the $4,600 in back rent that I owed. So as I waited, my mind raced.

I wished I had someone I could have talked to about this, but even in that moment, with my cell phone in hand, I couldn't bring myself to call anyone and let them know how the recession and my own idiotic spending had led me to this point. I feared being judged for my financial stupidity, and that my current situation would define me in the eyes of whomever I told, my parents included, who, by the way, are not judgy. Okay. That's a lie. They are, but they're like, black-people judgy. Meaning, it's not personal; it's just that their baseline emotion hovers somewhere between demanding I take a shower before dinner after leaving the house for 0.0000000068925 seconds because, as they say, I "smell like outside" and wrinkling their noses at seeing white girls put their dirty feet on dashboards. But ultimately, they have their kids' backs about big-picture stuff. However, I was too afraid to say anything, and also I was *pissed*. Not at them but at money.

I blamed the existence of the severance package, which had seduced me into wanting a taste of how I thought some people lived. I was furious that I couldn't make more money being an assistant. I was livid that comedy wasn't paying much of anything. I was upset that money was seemingly punishing me for wanting to have a little bit of fun. Why did *I* have to be laid off when I finally had a good paying job? Money was an asshole, and this was all its fault. If I just had more of it, I wouldn't be in the mess. Deep down, I knew that wasn't true. If I had more of it, I'd be in an even *bigger* mess. But I needed to put the responsibility on something else, so I kept repeating this script in my head until it was my turn to save my own hide.

I may not be Johnnie Cochran "if the glove don't fit, you must acquit" good when arguing a case, but when my back is against the wall, I'm def Ally McBeal level, meaning I've used a unisex bathroom before. Nebulous lawyer skills aside, I, at least, was skilled enough to quickly weigh my options and figure out a plan of attack before I spoke. There's the crying route, though judges are, for the most part, impartial, so I couldn't risk dehydration, only to have his eyes glaze over the way mine do when my Kindle app sends me a long-ass notice outlining their updated terms and conditions. Deflecting and complaining about the things my landlord or super hadn't done to make my apartment perfectly livable was an aggressive approach, but the "Oh yeah? Well, what about you?" technique tends to backfire once you're out of grade school. So I tried honesty. I explained that I was trying to get back on my feet during the recession, but unemployment and student loan debt made for a bad combo, like Michael Jackson and Eddie Murphy collaborating on the 1993 song "Whatzupwitu."[5] A'ight, I didn't say that last part, but

---

5. Lmao forever. Remember this hot mess? First of all, the spelling of the song title is disrespectful to the entire history of language, all the way from hieroglyphics down to Wingdings. Second, it's pointless for MJ to wear nice tailored clothes in the music video if he's just going to stand in front of a green screen displaying Microsoft Windows '91 blue sky, which will make the video look like it had a budget of five dollars. Third, MJ and Eddie had the Harlem Boys Choir sign permission slips to miss school, delay eating their Dunkaroos, and put off their tetherball tourney all so they could dance and sing around animated clip art of music notes and peace signs. Fourth, I do not, I REPEAT, I do not want a friend who believes in me the way MJ believed in Eddie. Instead of being like, "Listen, dawg, this song is hot trash; I'm not collaborating with you on it," MJ was in the corner, warming up with some "may, me, my, mo, moo"s so he could deliver "Whatzupwitu" with some gravitas.

I made it clear that I was in the process of overcoming this temporary setback by getting another day job and working nights as a comedian.

I don't know if the judge simply took pity on me, or if he was having a good day and wanted to be generous, or if maybe, at one point in his life, he had been where I was standing, desperate to stay in a city that was backbreakingly expensive. But he and my landlord agreed to not kick me out of my apartment and gave me a couple of months to catch up on the nearly $5,000 that I owed.

And that's exactly what I did. I depleted most of my 401(k) account from the indie movie job and lived lean and mean for the next two months to get current. That meant taking the subway home instead of taxis if I had a super late night out performing stand-up, eating two meals max a day (IAC provided breakfast and tons of snacks, so I only had to worry about making those sad lunches), and not spending money unless it was necessary. The two months passed, my rent debt was settled, so I bodysurfed into the sunset, right? Wrong.

I dealt with varying levels of stress-inducing financial debt for the next seven years, ranging from Sweet Baby Jesus, It's Beans and Rice Again for the Second Week in a Row (paying the bare minimum on my student loans was still too much for my broke behind) to Fuuuuuuuuuuuuuuuuuuck (buying a plane ticket home for Christmas left me strapped for cash for weeks) to I'mma Have to Do My Heaux Stroll Down the Werther's Original Aisle and Snag Me Old Sauseege to Be My Sugar Daddy (defaulting on one of my student loans *and* getting oh-so-close to creditors garnishing my wages). No matter how much I tried to stand on my own two feet financially, I got Dikembe Mutombo'd back down to the ground.

For instance, by 2013, I was freelance writing for a couple of pop culture blogs, including Glamour.com (earning about seventy-five to one hundred dollars a post), consistently making student loan payments (granted, they were so small that I was really only paying off the interest, but it was the effort that counted), and in good enough financial standing with my landlord that *I* was now threatening to not pay rent and take *them* to housing court if the super didn't make repairs in a timely fashion. In short, I felt how Cardi B must feel whenever she stops and remembers *she's* Cardi B. During this high, a friend asked me to write on her television pilot for VH1. There were just a couple of caveats: I had to quit my day job, and there was absolutely no guarantee that the show was going to be a series, which meant that after working on the pilot episode for three weeks, I would be relying solely on blogging to pay the bills unless the network gave us the green light. Damn.

On the one hand, I'd been dreaming every single day about quitting my day job and pursuing comedy full-time. On the other hand, my debt was a loud-ass rooster crowing and waking me up at dawn like, "Bitch better have my money!" I was like, "How did you get into my Rihanna Spotify playlist?" and then the rooster disappeared. The point is, I wasn't sure if it was wise to leave IAC, but I had been waiting five years for a moment like this—#KellyClarkson—so I quit, took the pilot job, had the time of my life, and . . . early in 2009, the verdict was in: The show would not go to series. Ugh, but luckily there was some good news.

Glamour.com was digging my writing. It didn't matter that I wasn't rolling in the dough; I was just impressed that I had successfully negotiated my first raise by outlining how I go above and beyond in all my posts (my posts would easily be two and three times the length of the average ones on their website). Besides, if you would've said to twelve-year-old TV-obsessed Pheebs, "In about fifteen years, you'll have a job where you get to be home, pantless à la Jane Fonda in her eighties workout-video heyday, while watching your favorite TV shows and writing blog posts, including one about how *Scandal*'s President Fitz is a bowl of expired refried beans, which will be the Gettysburg Address of your career," twelve-year-old Pheebs probably would've worried less if boys thought she was cute after getting her hair cut into Civil Rights bangs. This was a win! Then, a few months later, Glam-Glam had to revert back to my old wages, so to supplement my income, I shopped my wares around and was, at one point, writing for six or seven different websites with an income ranging from $50 to $150. Once again, I was barely making ends meet, but I was doing it.

This up-and-down pattern continued. I was hired to be a warm-up comic for a now-defunct late-night talk show, only to be fired a month later because they didn't think I was a good fit. For the first time, I was an opener on tour for a semifamous comedian who offered to pay for my travel and accommodations when I mentioned how poor I was. Not gonna lie, I felt like Blac Chyna when Rob Kardashian paid for her plastic surgery and she showed off her new body on Instagram. I was like, "Ooooo, I gots me a man to take care of me!" As per usual, my joy was short-lived because a member of my team never explained that actually, I would have to pay for my hotel and travel first and *then* be reimbursed, and then she took the credit card of mine that she had on file (which, by the way, was the only one I had that wasn't a mess) and proceeded to charge *all* the flight and hotels and maxed it out. And to make matters worse, it took her seven months to get the reimbursement from the comic's manager. Then there was the time I got hired to write on a television show for Fuse at the end of 2014 (hell yes!) and it was canceled by spring of 2015 (hell no!). Y'all, my career was up and down like a premenopausal woman's body temperature. But the absolute worst moment in my money life was August 2015.

At the beginning of that year, I was thirty years old and had just moved in with a boyfriend whom I thought I was going to marry. Despite having some reservations about the relationship not being right, I followed my heart and was down with the cohabitaysh. And . . . and . . . okay, fine. What I'm about to write is gross as hell, but I fell in love with the idea of my rent being significantly cheaper, and I could finally leave my shit hole of an apartment. Aaaah! I know, I KNOW! That was Janet, Ms. Jackson if ya nasty of me, but, moving in with a significant other for less-than-noble reasons is a common phenomenon in New York City. And in my defense, the city is too expensive, and I had been living on my own, supporting myself for the past six years. I had been auditioning for on-camera work for two years and hadn't booked one part. I was tired. Sure, I was in love with my ex, but y'all, I was *tired*. I may have been a youthful thirty on the outside, but on the inside, I was one hundred and twelve and doing the backing vocals on the DJ Khaled remix to "Wade in the Water." I was exhausted as hell and wanted a break!

So the boyfriend, who was also struggling with money, and I moved in together, and almost immediately, our relationship fell apart. Every single incompatibility was clear as day, and eventually I broke up with him and we agreed that since I ended the relaysh, I would move out. But I ain't have no money, y'all—despite getting an advance for my first book and soon-to-be bestseller, *You Can't Touch My Hair*. "How can that be?" one might ask. "I thought authors were rich?" Ummmm, the lucky few like J. K. Rowling and Stephen King are. But lil ole me, an unproven author who will probably only be able to afford to shop at Forever 21 when I'm sixty-one? No. "But not even with your book advance?" Again, no. You see, advances are divided into installments: You get a chunk when you sign the contract, more cashola rolls in when you turn in the completed manuscript, and the final third arrives to your bank account shortly after publication. My advance for #YouCantTouch was $25,000 before taxes and before my manager's and lit agent's commissions. So when all was said and done, what I received from my advance was somewhere in the ballpark of $18,000 . . . spread out over twenty-two months. Yeeeeeeah, you know when you get a box of decadent cookies and the serving size on the back reads, "Excavate one chocolate chip from one cookie like Indiana Jones unearthing an artifact, grind that chip down to a fine powder, and then whisper, 'Sssh, it'll be over soon,' and vacuum up the powder with a Dyson"? That's how it felt to have this paltry advance divvied up.

Since the Fuse show was over, I was auditioning for on-camera work and applying for writing jobs, so I used up the first $6,000 to stay afloat. I explained to my publisher my dire situation. They put a rush job on depositing the next batch of money to me and I used it *all*. Most of it went towards securing my new apartment (the three months' rent worth), so I opened another credit card, and combined with the last of that 6K, I hired movers, bought plates and an air conditioner (that UPS subsequently lost and never replaced) and a bed frame and a terrible mattress that eventually jacked up my back. Turns out getting rid of all my possessions to move in with ex-bae was not such a good idea, but thank Jesus, aka Janelle Monae, I got to take one thing with me, the couch I bought for us, because in my new place, it's what I slept on for two months while I waited for my bed from CB2 to be delivered.

So there I was. Almost thirty-one, heartbroken, making $150, if I was lucky, per blog post, with the most debt I'd ever had in my life: $46,000 in student loans and $19,000 in credit cards. And all I could think was, "How did I get here again?" I mean, the same financial troubles that were dogging me in 2009 were still knockin' at my door in 2015. But this time, they were worse.

I remember one night, when I was going over the mountain of bills a few months before my book came out in October 2016, I said aloud, in my empty apartment, "Who do you think you're dealing with? I'm not one of your nappy-headed friends." And I gotta tell ya, talking to money the way some black parents reprimand their kids may feel good in the moment, but it didn't change my situation. I was scraping money together, taking horrible stand-up gigs at colleges, accepting tiny loans from a couple of friends, relying on the kindness of strangers such as hotel employees when I'd ask them not to charge me for incidentals because I didn't have enough in my bank account for that and to pay for a taxi to get me to the airport the next day. I felt horrible. And I certainly couldn't tell my parents at this point. I was too embarrassed and, more importantly, I was livid.

I believed money had it out for me and was the enemy who was always getting the best of me no matter how hard I tried to outsmart it. And you best believe I was trying. Yet I was failing every single time to get ahead. Why me? Every single day, I would ask why. Why am I going through this financial situation when other people I know aren't? Why can I never get ahead of this debt? Why am I struggling in New York City, eight years into a career that still isn't paying off? Why will no one hire me? Why does no one believe in me? I don't deserve this, so why is this happening to me? Why can't I have money? Why does money hate me? Why is money a stupid heaux? And then, on a particularly low day when I was doing pre-book-release press with a smile on my face even though I was stressed AF, something in my brain took over and I asked the following question: What am I supposed to learn from this?! Pause.

What am I supposed to learn from this? Whoa. What. Am. I. Supposed. To. Learn. From. This. Huh. How did that question get in there? I mean, in the seven-year-debt saga, I must have asked myself a million questions, and this was the *first* time I ever asked myself a question in which I wasn't the victim. It wasn't about money having power over me, or about distracting myself by worrying about my friends' bank accounts, or about my comedy career being nothing but fits and starts. It was about me. So what the hell was the lesson? I mean, yes, obviously, don't blow your severance package. Be conservative with money during trying times. The real way debt gets ya is the interest, so only charge what you can pay off in full; otherwise, it ain't worth the headache of having. Those are all wonderful lessons. But the real point: Money isn't the enemy, and if I'm going to spend my whole life fighting it or being mad at it or fearing it, then it's going to rule me.

Money rules some folks by making them believe they have to spend all the time. It makes others be so cheap that they can never take a time-out to treat themselves every once in a while. But for me, I tried to pull a fast one on it, thinking I was cute and could get away with taking from an unknowable heaux, and I got caught. And instead of accepting the consequences, I got mad, and the debt became all I thought about, all I thought I would ever know, so I never truly tried to change my ways. I was going to be saddled with this dictator, so I might as well accept it. I might as well hide this part of my life, hide this shame and accept my fate. But what if I didn't anymore? What if I decided to think about money differently?

So, fine. Maybe money is a heaux, but in a good way. It's that thing I call on for a good time, but like a BFF, it will also show me tough love, and usually that tough love was in the form of an overdraft fee for overdrawing my account or high interest rates for abusing my credit card. And perhaps money is just like everyone and everything else in the world: If I stop being a reckless fool and accept responsibility for the choices I make, it'll roll with me. After all, I didn't have to pursue comedy. That was a choice I made. I didn't have to quit my day job with a flimsy-ass backup plan because the alternative—staying in a job and never really going after what I want—is one I've seen too many people take. Again, that was a choice. I don't get to have everything on my terms just because I want it my way, and that includes money. So accept it, Pheebs. Accept the good and the bad that comes with my approach to money. So I did.

One night before my book came out, I called the friend who I had borrowed money from to pay my rent, thanked her for the loan, Venmo'd her back, and told her, "Um, I'm nineteen grand in the hole." And guess what? She didn't judge me. She just listened. I told another friend and still another friend. Again and again, no one judged me. They just were there for me emotionally. Still, I didn't tell too many people. I didn't want everyone in my grill—lol—and that everyone included my parents. I wasn't quite ready for Ma and Pa Robinson knowing what I got myself into. I was just content that I could say my truth to anyone, and what I feared—ridicule, shame, disappointment—never came. I could talk openly about money and it wasn't going to be the end of the world or make people talk bad about me or gossip about me to others. Sure, there are people who will make a feast out of talking about other people's finanacial woes, but you know what? You can't control that, so who the fuck cares? Life is too hard and we're all trying to stay afloat financially to let what others *might* think matter just as much, if not more, as having enough money in the bank to live. And if we all just decided to not be so secretive about money, maybe we'd all feel better? I know that once I stopped hiding, I did. So with relief and the empowered energy coursing through my veins, I returned my focus to fixing my financial future.

In fact, I made a deal with myself: You are paying off all your debt in the next two years. I would say this to myself every single day. You *are* paying off all your debt in the next two years. Yeah, *you*. No excuses. You can do this. As I started gaining momentum, I amended that statement: You are paying off all your debt in the next two years and then, and only then, can you tell your parents. Having them, not the eradication of the debt, as the final, ultimate goal made me more determined than ever. They became my North Star in a way, and I repeated this goal to myself at some point almost every single day. . . . Wait a minute . . .

Holy fuck. Time-out. This is not for show. I am truly freaking out right now! HOLY. FUCK! Okay, you're probably like, "Pheebs, what the hell is going on?" Okay, okay. Sorry. This is just wild. So October 2016, I made that promise to myself. With the last of the book advance and the determination to live extremely tight and take every single freelance gig I could get, I paid off all my credit card debt by the beginning of 2017. In the spring of 2017, *2 Dope Queens* the podcast was blowing up in popularity. So much so that Jessica and I had Carrie Brownstein of *Portlandia* and Sleater-Kinney fame as a guest. A week later, I was asked if I wanted to write on the show; I said yes. By the beginning of the summer, that writing gig was over, but I had earned just enough money to pay off the entirety of my student loan debt. Cut to right now. This book is being published in October 2018, almost exactly *two years* after I made the promise to myself to tell my parents what I'd gone through. A promise that I literally just remembered right now as I'm freaking writing this essay that my parents are reading. Woooooooooooooooow!

If you're reading this and never believed in *The Secret*, I don't see how you can deny its power any longer. Practically everything in my life these past two years was about making money so I could climb out of debt but, more importantly, so I could talk to my parents about it. All righty, I got a phone call to make.

You're Not Curing Cancer (Unless You Are—Then Carry On, My Workaholic Son)

To kick this essay off right, I'm taking a page out of Alcoholics Anonymous meetings. Actually, the AA meetings I've seen in movies and TV shows. I have no idea what the *real* ones are like, but this is what I've gathered from Hollywood: (1) Chairs are arranged in a circle like you're having a session with the Long Island Medium, (2) there are boxes and boxes of doughnuts, and (3) people stand at a podium, giving their one-sentence summary about themselves: "I'm Ethan and I'm an alcoholic." Well, I'm typing this while seated on my couch because, for the past three weeks, my office chair has had a pile of clean laundry on it,[1] I'm drinking a green juice, pretending it

---

1. A'ight, I need to get all the way real with you. Every chair in my home is a mess. Like I stated, the office one holds clothes, the chair by the entryway that's supposed to be where I sit to put on my shoes is currently occupied by a stack of Target plates I want to donate to charity and for some inexplicable reason there's a drawstring gym bag lying on top, one of the dining chairs has a couple of my couch's throw pillows on it, and the other dining chair is a catchall that includes a hanger, a letter from Hillary Clinton I've been meaning to get framed for the past year, a fanny pack

tastes as good as a doughnut, and I'm saying aloud, to no one, "My name is Phoebe Robinson and I'm a workaholic."

I'm not suggesting being a workaholic and alcoholic are exactly the same. However, there should be some middle ground in the kind of support alcoholics receive (meetings, sponsors, twelve-step programs, empathy from some friends and family members) and the support workaholics get. Workaholics Anonymous exists, but when was the last time a person was asked, "Have you tried WA?" Exactly. What usually goes down is a drive-by comment of "Just work less!" from people on their way to free bagels in the break room. Well, duh, bitch, that's an obvious solution! But telling someone that, as if the notion never crossed their mind, is like when I'm troubleshooting with Spectrum about my DVR not working correctly and I'm asked, "Did you try turning it off and then back on?" I always want to respond with, "Nope! I suspected pressing the on/off button twice on my DVR could easily fix this, but I opted for the relaxing process of troubleshooting while you pretend to care that I can't watch the Cooking Channel right now. And yes, I'm aware the Cooking Channel is the poor man's version of the Food Network, but sometimes it's nice to come back to your trash roots and enjoy things that are less good, like Red Vines, Katherine Heigl movies, and not reading.'"[2] Point is, suggesting I

from H&M's Coachella collection (lol for the rest of my life), a tape dispenser, a half-empty box of Downy dryer sheets, and used nipple covers. Okay, fine, I'm a bit of a slob; however, isn't *everyone* like this? Who the hell is using the chairs in their home for actual sitting?! I feel like whenever I'm at someone's house and all their chair real estate is available, I think, *Oh, this is a person who can put together a Dexter-esque kill room and tidy it up routinely like they're doing a showing for an open house.*

2. I probably shouldn't bring up how sometimes I love not reading while you are kind enough to be reading my writing. But I must stand in my truth, and if I'm

work less is unhelpful and a waste of the oxygen you just exhaled (although photosynthesis thanks you for your contribution).

I daydream about taking it easier every single day of my life, about sending one fewer email, not always answering my phone when it rings, occasionally saying no when asked to attend a meeting/do a press thing/work a gig that will stretch me thin and prevent me from relaxing for a moment. Unfortunately, I'm not there yet. That doesn't mean I'm giving up. A few months ago, I took a look at the woman in the mirror— #MakeThatChange—to deal with this problem. And that's where I fucked up.

I hit up Google (don't worry, this isn't like the David Bowie fiasco I told you about at the beginning of this book), looking for some "guidance." You know when you want to change, but only if the change is surface-level? Like, one time, I had a friend tell me how a coworker is revamping his eating habits. This piqued my interest since I knew my questionable eating habits were partially responsible for why I was feeling run-down. "What's he doing?" I asked. "Maybe I can copy him and see results."

She responded, "He's vegan in the mornings."

OBVS, THE TWO PEOPLE IN THIS STORY ARE WHITE; HENCE THIS IS SOME GRADE-A, *BILLBOARD*-MAGAZINE-CROWNING-JOSS-STONE-REGGAE-ARTIST-OF-THE-YEAR-IN-2015, WHITE-FORMER-NAACP-LEADER-RACHEL-

---

going to own up to being garbage, then I can't pretend that I'm at home reading *The Catcher in the Rye*. I did try though, y'all. I got fifty pages in and was like, "Too long," and then stopped to watch old clips of *So You Think You Can Dance* on YouTube.

DOLEZAL-WHO-PRETENDED-TO-BE-BLACK-FOR-YEARS-
CHANGING-HER-NAME-TO-THE-WEST-AFRICAN-NAME-
NKECHI-AMARE-DIALLO-MEANING-"GIFT-OF-GOD"
NONSENSE DE BLANCO. "Vegan in the mornings" ain't a
thing. Not eating meat in the morning doesn't mean you're
veegs; that just means you're eating apples and other fiber-rich
foods because you don't want your bootyhole backed up like a
freeway during rush hour. Moving on. Basically, I was lazy as
hell in my attempt to find a cure for my workaholism. I mean,
all I typed into the search window was:

> What is a workaholic?

Haha. I already knew the definition, but pretended I was
making an effort and learning breaking news. Anyway, one of
the first results that popped up was an article by *Psychology
Today*, so I clicked on the link and this was the opening para-
graph:

> Workaholism is a soul-destroying addiction that changes
> people's personality and the values they live by. It dis-
> torts the reality of each family member, threatens family
> security and often leads to family break-up. Tragically,
> workaholics eventually suffer the loss of personal and
> professional integrity.

Gahtdamn, *Psychology Today*! This is how you open?!?! You're
at a twelve (my Lyft driver blasting Metallica at 11:45 P.M. in his
compact Toyota Corolla), and I need you to be at a two (the

volume my music is at when I'm at the checkout counter and have to spend five minutes correcting the cashier's spelling of my first name). In all seriousness, while the picture that *Psychology Today* painted is accurate for plenty of workaholics, it wasn't for me. My family was not on the verge of falling apart because I was juggling two podcasts, nor had my professional integrity been compromised, leading to my committing a white-collar crime. So I just laughed at the doom and gloom of that opening para and went back to working. Eventually, the consequences of being a workaholic became too big to ignore or laugh off.

Before the publication of *You Can't Touch My Hair*, I was cast in a recurring role on a now-defunct television series (the same show I mentioned in a previous essay). For a newbie actor, this was career-changing news! There was just one thing: The show wanted me to cancel my book tour so that I could be on standby for them; however, they would not guarantee the number of episodes I would appear in (they just said, "You'll be in it a bunch"), nor did they agree to pay me more. Yikes.gov /MidtermElections for a couple of reasons. The reality is most books don't sell, hence why most publishers don't waste the money touring writers. Therefore, when a publisher *does* want a tour, they believe the book will not only sell but also has a shot at the best sellers list. And as you guessed by now, doing press and touring is integral to getting on the list. Besides, I had alerted the producers months in advance about the impending tour and they had assured me it was no problem, so their change of heart, coupled with the new options they presented, all of which adversely affected me, was not only shocking but also straight-up doo-doo.

Look, I don't have an MBA, nor have I read many financial books, but I know the following from experience: (1) If the VH1 *Behind the Music* narrator's voice pops in your head with a "And that's when things took a turn for the worse" right before you make a financial decision, you're about to fuck your life up, and (2) be about your money because no one else will and more often than not, folks will try to pull a fast one over you. And that's how this scenario of "give up everything for maybe a whole lotta nothing" felt. All I could do in the moment was quote the unreleased poem from the legendary poet Langston Hughes:

What Am I?

Bitch, I'm not the one.

Jokes aside, my team and I pushed back, and eventually, an agreement was reached. I kept my tour (only canceling one date that conflicted with the shooting schedule), and I got to stay a part of the show where, when all was said and done, I ended up being a glorified extra. Not complaining. It was my first semi-regular television role, so I was thrilled to be acting, but based on how little screen time I had, it certainly would've been a mistake if, for the sake of that role, I didn't do the tour, which ended up being a great success and helped me get on the *New York Times* best sellers list. So yaaas to everything working out perfectly. Except it didn't.

A few weeks prior to book publication at the end of 2016, I

had been flying all over the country, bouncing between the tour, the TV show, the other gigs, last-minute meetings as a result of the book, and my podcasts back in NYC. Except for Thanksgiving, when I took the day off, I was either working or traveling or sometimes both. And I was doing this typically on five hours of sleep or less. I was concerned about how tired I was and how it was taking longer than usual to recover from being sick, but plenty of folks would've killed to be in my position, so I chalked up the tiredness, illness, and eating my feelings as nothing more than paying the cost to be the boss. Until early December.

By that point, I felt the way some of Picasso's iconic portrait paintings look: kind of a scrambled mess. All right, all right. Before any of you art heads start cussing me out, this isn't shade, okay? I enjoy a lot of his work, and even the stuff I don't quite understand, I'll still be in the museum, doing the obligatory "stand in front of the artwork for the length of time it takes me to mentally recite 'My name is Kiiiiiiiiiiiiiiiiiiiiiiiiiid! KID ROCK!'[3] from that song 'Bawitdaba' before doing a head-nod like two black dudes who spot each other in a sea of Caucasia aka a bunch of white people." This head-nod is, of course, the dude equivalent of the Celie-and-Nettie patty-cake from *The Color Purple*. Point is, I respect the man's artistry, but

---

3. Listen, heauxes, don't be over there judging me for referencing Kid Rock. First of all, I only ever listen to that intro of "Bawitdaba" before turning the song off because duh. Secondly, there's no denying that this minute-fifteen-second intro is equal to the drama eleganza of an award-winning BBC miniseries starring Dame Judi Dench and Benny Cumbs aka Benedict Cumberbatch, and you cannot convince me otherwise.

Picas-cas has been dead for forty-five years. Isn't it now safe enough for me to admit that some of his work is ugly-ish and not in a cool, artsy way but more like a "Quit Ludovico-techniquing my eyeballs with this bullshit right now" kind of way? Honestly, if I was gifted one of his ugly paintings, I would fully regift that shit the way I do when someone gives me a bottle of Victoria's Secret perfume. Whew! I feel so much better for getting that off my chest. What I was talking about? Oh, yes, December 2016.

My body clock was jacked up due to constantly switching time zones. Some days I woke up not knowing what city I was in. Other days I worked nonstop, returned to my hotel room, ordered two meals' worth of food, and scarfed it down prior to passing out. So I was looking forward to being back home in New York for a few days in my old routine. Sure, I was going to be working most of the time, but at least I would be in my home and could sleep in my own bed with my own sheets. Except I couldn't sleep, which was strange because I was *exhausted*. I yawned frequently; my short-term memory was shot; I asked people to repeat themselves because I couldn't focus; my eyes alternated between stinging and twitching, which were signals that I had been staring at my laptop screen too much. Despite all this, my body refused to power down until it was 5 A.M., and it automatically woke me up at 8:30 A.M. The same thing happened the next night despite my having taken Advil PM to make me drowsy. On the third night, after a long day of work, insomnia reared its ugly head once more, and I tried everything to tire myself out. I watched a bunch of TV in hopes that would make me sleepy. Nada. I lay down in the dark.

Nope, my mind still raced. I tried reading, a go-to for helping my mind slow down, to no avail. I tidied up around my apartment, and all I ended up with was a very organized vinyl collection and a floor smooth enough for the US Olympic curling team to practice on. Nothing. Was. Working. The clock struck 4 A.M., and I returned to my living room, plopped down on my couch, and cried.

And I'm not talking that pretty-cry crap singers do in music videos where a single tear falls down their perfectly contoured faces. I mean, Carrie Underwood even has a song called "Cry Pretty," and in the vid, her "tears" are strategically and artfully placed glitter and she's rocking a sequin minidress while serving *Pretty Woman* thigh-high-boots realness. That, my friends, is not the crying I was doing. Actually, I wasn't even crying. I was sobbing. Snot bubbles, inhaling big gulps of air, asking myself, "Why is this happening to me?," the whole works. It was the kind of sobbing my niece does until she starts coughing, then momentarily forgets why she's upset but feels like she should still be mad, so she resumes bawling. I was sobbing like I was doing the community-theater version of the "It's not your fault" scene from *Good Will Hunting* and I was playing both Robin Williams's and Matt Damon's parts. I was sobbing like old black church ladies at a church event when someone brings a healthy version of collard greens aka collard greens without the bacon or ham hock. Yeah, it was *that* bad. I eventually fell asleep, knowing exactly why this was happening to me.

I woke up the next day and hit the ground running with work, but I decided something, *anything*, had to change. Obviously, I would never shoot a television show and do a book tour at the same time again. That's an easy fix, but the poor sleeping? Well, that continued for a little while longer before getting better, and even when it did, I rarely went to bed before two or three o'clock in the morning. Want to know what I was doing? Nothing fun like playing video games, watching classic movies, or spinning on the ones and twos (read: self-loving on my vajeen). I was answering emails, working on my never-ending to-do list, or brainstorming on "big picture" projects and ideas. Ay-yi-yi! Even after that scary bout with insomnia, I was still staying up all kinds of crazy hours. This is not to say night owls aren't more productive once the sun sets and the moon is chilling in the sky like an on-duty Dunkin' Donuts employee does at the counter. Sometimes they can be. But c'mon!!! It's 3 A.M. If, at that ungodly hour, you're not making the beat drop on your bangers and mash—#PenisAndBalls—or the OG Goop Chute—#Vagina #SorryGwynethPaltrow #SorryMomAnd Dad—then why the hell are you awake?!

In all seriousness, Hollywood had gone dark, and somehow I managed to overstuff my schedule and ended up working until the morning of Christmas Eve, when I flew home to visit family. I was, as usual, very present when visiting family. And then, as soon as everyone went to bed, I would stay up until the wee hours of the morning, mapping out my one-year, three-year, five-year plans. Yeeeeeah. Four out of five planners would agree that trying to figure out the next year of my life at 1:45 in the morning on December 27 is ig AF. That's when I finally had to admit that what was going on was beyond being passionate about my career. I was consumed, and I was finally ready to get insight into why I was doing what I was doing.

Everything's Trash, But It's Okay

Since December 2016, I've read quite a bit about being a workaholic, but the following excerpt from the article Harry Bradford penned for HuffPost.com, entitled "Why Being a Workaholic Is Awful for You AND Everyone Around You," is not only enlightening but sums me up in a lot of ways. Bradford writes:

> According to a new study published in the *Journal of Management*, there is a significant difference between being engaged at work and being addicted to it. While the former is characterized by hard work because the worker is passionate about the job, the latter is often motivated by negative feelings like guilt and compulsion.
>
> The problem is, workaholism is the rare mental health issue that can often have positive rewards in the short term—namely, the praise of a happy boss. That's one reason psychologist Bryan Robinson once called workaholism "the best-dressed mental health problem."

And not to be a contrarian, in Jordan Weissmann's article for the *Atlantic* entitled "Is There Really Such a Thing as a 'Workaholic'?" he questioned whether workaholism is an addiction or more of "a condition [that] may well have a certain social cachet." At the very least, he is skeptical that everyone who claims to be a workaholic is actually one. It's kind of like how people are constantly proclaiming how busy they are even though a lot of times we're goofing off on social media or looking up our potential compatibility with someone based on our zodiac signs. Oh, right. I forgot. I'm the *only* person who has done this.

Riiiiiiiiiiight. Look, whether you wanna fess up or not, I know a lot of you mofos are click-clackin' on your laptops like you're the court stenographer during the Bernie Madoff trial, all so you can see if it's in the stars for you to splurge the extra five dollars to get you and your future boo's names embroidered on his and hers towels from Bed Bath & Beyond. But you know what I'm talking about. In America, we pride ourselves on being busy and grinding all the time. But perhaps more importantly, we pride ourselves on *documenting* how busy we are, no matter how true that is or isn't for us. Just look at sosh meeds.

The hashtag #NoDaysOff is omnipresent. For every vacation post that exists, there's one in which someone is bragging about not vacationing due to working so hard. People post Instagram videos of themselves working out with some variation of the following caption: "I got up today at 4 a.m., worked out, made a smoothie, and then went to work an eleven-hour day. What are you doing?" Old me would've been inspired, but the new me? By the way, new me started like three seconds ago, lol, but new me is like: SLEEP, MOTHAFUCKA. I. AM. SLEEP. ING. #JeSuisSleep. Hashtag that, bitch. For real, we place such a premium on sacrificing everything to get ahead because we are *rewarded* for going above and beyond what is necessary to get ahead. Whether the reward is money, respect, being exalted as an example others should follow, or simply the quick fix of a like on Facebook or da 'Gram, there's a rush that comes along with living the #NoDaysOff lifestyle. And who doesn't want to feel good or be admired or get a nice bump in the cashola department? But the issue is there's danger in a sort of Pavlovian response to building your world around work because not only are you chasing the high of approval, you're get addicted to the concept of being productive, which can turn into just doing . . . anything.

Now, make no mistake, at the root of all of this, I *love* comedy and entertainment. Creating from scratch is one of my happy zones. I get joy out of coming up with a new stand-up joke or riffing with Jessica on *2 Dope Queens* or with my producer Jo-anna on *Sooo Many White Guys*. It's thrilling to make someone laugh or write a killer sentence. And I always, as Oprah would say, "set my intention," so I was never willy-nilly just working on any old thing. However, it was clear that over my ten years in comedy, my intention was morphing like the people in Mi-chael Jackson's "Black or White" music video.

First, I worked hard because I loved comedy and wanted to get better at it. Then, when I was digging myself out of my fi-nancial quagmire, my intention was just "take almost any and every job so you don't end up on the *skreets*." Next, it was about building the foundation of, hopefully, a decades-long career. Then, it was falling in love with seeing the fruits of my labor. As a results-oriented, idea-executing person, I got into the groove of doing things and crossing them off a list, which, to be honest, was never-ending because there can always be more to do. *2DQ* was fascinating to create, but what if I started my *own* podcast where I interviewed people, which would then require me to do research? Let's go! Why publish one book in the span of two years when I could pub *two*? Only doing one book is for slackers, so write away! Should I choose between being a stand-up comic, actor, author, podcaster, and producer? Hell naw, do all five, Pheebs! And most importantly, why take a second and stop to enjoy what I just accomplished before moving on to the next thing? EXACTLY! And that's what began happening. Rarely did I take a step back and live in any of these moments; a part of me was always focused on the next goal or things that were unfinished or what I could have done better. Not that I was being negative about any of my successes; however, having a "there's always more work to be done" mentality prevented me from fully enjoying anything I achieved, and moreover, my sleep problems continued into the next year.

By then, I was aware of the side effects of insomnia—fatigue, daytime sleepiness, irritability, diabetes, cardiovascular diseases, obesity, increase in work-time injuries, mental illness such as depression, and so on—and some of them were applicable to me. I was taking Lyfts to meetings just so I could squeeze in a midday nap, and as I've documented throughout this book, I was packing on the weight, which I didn't mind all too much except for the fact that none of it went to my boobs and instead migrated south to my stomach, hips, butt, and thighs the way New York Jews move to Florida during the latter years of their lives. And as a lifelong member of the 34A club, I could have used some of that extra fat in the tatas department. I don't mean anything spectacular like upgrading to a C cup. I just would've liked . . . Look, here's the deal. My boobs don't move. Not when I run, not when I dance, not when I'm startled. Nothing. There's no jiggle to be found. My chesticles just remain still, standing at attention like the Queen's Guard outside Buckingham Palace. Meanwhile, my newly expanded lower half was just jiggling and sliding all over the place like the cast of *Star Trek* whenever the USS *Enterprise* would get struck by enemy forces. It wasn't fair, y'all, but those were the cards I was dealt! Anyway, the point is, I gained weight, was working around the clock and running on fumes with the occasional nap sprinkled in to help me through the day. Still, because I wasn't sleepless like I had been in 2016, I convinced myself that my workaholism was cured (despite making zero real changes because that's the American way) and I was now getting around seven and a half hours of sleep a night.

Natch, this estimate was way off base, and I soon learned that when I, out of sheer curiosity and to solve this exhaustion mystery, downloaded a sleep app and used it for a couple of weeks. Now, yawning nonstop and constantly saying, "I'm sleepy," should've been all the evidence needed during the ongoing case of *Robinson v. Her Tired-Ass Body That Is Slowly Morphing into the "Before" in a Shaun T Fitness Infomercial*. But ever since cell phone apps were invented, I've put my brain on low-battery mode and have not allowed it to process the simplest information without the help of the trial version of an app that runs a *Final Fantasy VIII* ad every ten seconds because I'm not about that "pay full price for an app" life. Hence, needing an app to show me how little sleep I got. The results came in. Turns out I was only sleeping, on average, four and a half hours a night. What in the Serta-Counting-Sheep-jumping-over-a-wooden-fence hell?!?! Four and a half hours? You can't even get the veggies for a beef stew all the way soft in a slow cooker in that amount of time, yet I was carrying on as though four and a half hours was all the fuel I needed to function out in the real world. It made zero sense.

What did make sense, however, is that my feelings of exhaustion were now accompanied by feelings of unhappiness. And this was kind of a new-ish scenario for me.

Of course I was bummed when I didn't book an audition or had a bad stand-up set, but that sadness was fleeting, and even during the salad days of my career, I'd maybe be down for a week or two. What I was going through now was much more in line with what Spence and Robbins wrote about in a groundbreaking 1992 paper for the *Journal of Personality Assessment* called "Workaholism: Definition, Measurement, and Preliminary Results." In it, they argued that people who are workaholics work not only compulsively but also without enjoyment. Ding, ding, ding! That was it! I was in the zone of creating and doing, but I had lost that loving feeling a little bit, and in its place was a stench of "meh" funking up the work. You know when you go in a public restroom, and there's a general pee smell, but also you're thinking, *Yeeeeeeeeeah, but someone doubled down on the asparagus,* and now that scent is overpowering everything? That's what many of my jobs felt like. Wait. No. That's not right. I don't mean to say that my career was basically like urine accented by a cloud of asparagus-pee odor. Ya know what? When you've been writing a lengthy book, this can happen. The analogies start out like . . . and then by the time you're elbow-deep in the process, the analogies end up like . . . See?! #TheyCantAll-BeGems #TheyCantEvenAllBeCostumeJewelry #Sometimes-TheyAreDentedEarringsFromClairesWithTheBacksMissingBut-70PercentOffAndWhoAreYouToPassUpADeal.

Anyway, the bigger point that I'm attempting to make here

is that my workaholism had become a joyless exercise. I'd go out of town for stand-up gigs and only leave my hotel room to perform and not to explore whatever city I was in. My to-do list became so backed up that I would go from one project to another, but more often, I was working on multiple projects at once. And then there was the social aspect. I wasn't calling home as much, always putting it off because I was swamped and saving the phone calls for another day. I was constantly canceling plans with friends. Stating that I had no time to date because there were more important things on my plate. I was burying myself in a mountain of tasks and wasn't particularly excited about any of them. So how the hell did I get there?

It's not something I learned from my parental units. Sure, they have a great work ethic, but for every memory I have of them working their tails off to provide for their chillrens, I also distinctly recall them being physically and emotionally present for my brother and me, whether it was helping us with a school project, reading to us, or teaching us how to cook and do laundry. They absolutely put family first. And like I explained earlier, I was a high school slacker, and even in college, when I got my act together, I fully enjoyed each and every one of my weekends. Trust and believe that I routinely spent my Friday-to-Sundays reclining on my twin bed with one hand down my pants, Al Bundy style, channel surfing premium cable. You could've called me Philippe Petit of *Man on Wire* fame because I was nailing the work-life balance. However, once I graduated and made the leap into stand-up comedy, everything kind of changed.

To even pursue it as a career meant that I had to have a nine-to-five and then routinely stay out until 11 P.M. and midnight performing on unpaid shows. So, in my defense, becoming a workaholic then was a necessity. And even though it was a grind, having that kind of around-the-clock schedule at twenty-four was no biggie. Other advantages to being twenty-four (or in your twents, for that matter), in case you're in that bracket and need the reminder or beyond that age but want to take a trip down memory lane:

- No hangovers! Or, if you do have a hangover, you really had to drink a *lot* to earn the *Guitar Hero* drum solo that's going off in your head. At thirty-four, I legit will have two glasses of wine and not enough quinoa and grains for dinner, and the next day, I'm crying out, "Jesus be a fainting couch from a Jane Austen novel because I can't stand no mo'."

- You'll be invited to a white party and excitedly prep for it by dipping your sneakers in Crest HD whitening mouthwash or whatever to make sure you're on theme; meanwhile, when you're in your thirties and beyond, you'll show up in your "I'm wearing what I'm wearing because it's clean" outfit, and no one will be mad at you because you brought Stacy's Pita Chips.

- Dewy skin! Seriously, I once interviewed Zoë Kravitz on my *Sooo Many White Guys* podcast, and she has a lovely, warm, and inviting dewy glow, while my skin looks like the smudged lenses on a pair of Oakley sunglasses one might purchase at an ExxonMobil gas station.

- Up until twenty-five, you can be on your parents' insurance, which is tight AF and sort of feels like when you played the *Teenage Mutant Ninja Turtles* video game and you'd start a level by grabbing a pizza that gave you a bonus life.

- You can eat a massive amount of food, take a dump, and your stomach could possibly revert back to a six-pack.

Clearly, being in your twenties is awesome, and sleep is something you can go without much of for stretches at a time and it's all good, hence the whole doing stand-up in the evenings after putting in an eight-hour day at the office. And while I can argue that developing my workaholic tendencies during this phase of my life was virtually inescapable, I'll also have to concede that the times I've been single gave me the opportunity to devote myself more fully to my career.

And I hate, *hate* writing that because it makes me sound like the tired trope of a professional woman we so often see in movies and TV shows and magazine profiles who is presented to us, in part, as a warning: "See, ladies, you can be successful, but you won't be happy." That lie is used to keep us in check and make sure being in a relationship is a high priority, but here is the thing. Finding something you love to do so deeply that also can pay the bills is rare and fucking dope. That may not be the most elegant thing to say, but it's fact. Some folks spend their whole lives stuck in jobs that are a means to an end but don't inspire, surprise, move, challenge, excite, or fulfill them.

Well, I've been extremely lucky to have found my calling, and the fact is that being single simply allows me to focus as much energy as possible on my career, and as positive results like being a stronger stand-up comedian or writer become evident, not only does it feel damn good, but it's hard to pump the brakes. Who wants to slow down when the fruits of their labor are ripening? It's not like LeBron James ever says, "You know, I ought to chill on all the days and nights in the gym because the result is my teammates and I are winning a lot of games lately." Obvs, I'm not saying I am LeBron James, but I gotta be the LeBron James of something. Like I'm the LeBron James of Taking My Jeans Off Literally Fifteen Seconds After Arriving Home. Nailed it! And on the first try, which is a very LeBron James thing to do. All kidding aside, making strides due to my hard work felt damn good. What didn't were instances like with one of my exes, who felt neglected at times during our relationship because Duty booty-called at all hours of the night. Our union, as all others, ended for many reasons, but my working all the time certainly didn't help. So, naturally, once I was out of that particular relationship and could just be all in with work without fear of hurting a significant other's feelings or even having to check in for the little things like what time I'd be home for dinner, my career completely took off, which was all the reinforcement I needed to remain a workaholic. But all of this takes a back seat to what I believe is the truest reason for why I'm always on my grind.

A year ago, I was hanging out at WNYC after I finished taping an episode of one of my podcasts. A host of another show and I were chatting, and she said she was interested in how people work and achieve the things they do and was curious about my process. Normally with these kinds of queries, I, like many people, would launch into prepared sound bites: "Oh, you know, I turn my Wi-Fi off when I work" or "If I've been sitting for too long, I'll go for a nice twenty-minute walk to get my creative juices flowing" or, one of my favorites, "I just really love what I do and that pushes me when times get tough." Like a pop star using Auto-Tune, that sounds good, but it's not the entire truth. But they are perfect surface-level answers that people want to hear and I want to deliver so I can conserve my brainpower for actually working. However, maybe because this WNYC host caught me after I had been recording for a couple of hours, so I was in full stream-of-consciousness mode, I said something I've never, ever, *ever* said aloud.

"Ya know, I work so hard because I'm trying to outrun death."

I wasn't necessarily shocked that I said this—plenty of people feel this way—I was just surprised that I said it so casually and nakedly in conversation. Usually, this might be the sort of thing you admit after a few drinks or in a therapy session, but I was stone-cold sober and I could have been flipping through a magazine with the same intonation I have when I go, "Hmm, those jeans are cute." It was just so matter-of-fact and accurate.

"Ya know, I work so hard because I'm trying to outrun death."

There's nowhere to hide in that sentence. No joke to diffuse the honesty. To my core, this is how I feel, which is partially why I loved the musical *Hamilton* so much outside of its blatant genius. It resonated with me in such a real way because Alexander Hamilton was also a workaholic, and while his work was far more intense than mine (he founded America's financial system; I make jokes), the way the show presented his story made me feel like a mirror was being held up to my face. At one point in the show, there's a lyric the other characters sing about him that goes, "Why do you write like you're running out of time / You write day and night like you're running out of time."

That is so me! I'm agnostic, and I deeply fear death because I don't know if there is an afterlife. All I have is the now, and I'm terrified of running out of time and not getting a chance to do all the things that I want to do. So I work and work and work, because when I look back before I die, if I'm so lucky to have the opportunity to do so, I don't want to regret anything in my career. So I'll stay up until 5 A.M. if it means I can figure the wording perfectly on a new joke. The only problem was I wasn't happy.

Because I had no life, only work, the fear of dying became my main motivator instead of just *one* of them, and isn't that depressing? Life is this big, beautiful, messy, complicated buffet, and I kept coming back to it, empty plate in hand, just loading up the same pasta I get every single time. Well, I got tired of pasta. I wanted to see what chicken parm would taste like. How yummy the salmon is. You get my point. I no longer wanted work to be the only thing, and I knew that it couldn't be the only thing or it was going to kill me dead long before I exhaled my last breath. I needed to do something not related to my career. So I organized a girls' trip.

Remember that Palm Springs excursion where I ATV'd? This is the trip I'm referring to. Last year, I took my second ever vacation in my adult life (my first one being a vacay with an ex-boyfriend in 2013). Since I was organzing the vacation, I wanted to arrive in the morning before everyone else got there that evening so I could make sure the house wasn't doo-doo and also take care of my host duties by stocking the fridge and planning activities.

Once all that was done, I was so . . . antsy. I had no idea what to do. No meetings to go to. No phone calls to make. I went for a walk. I checked my emails. There was nothing to do but sit. So I did. I sat. At first, anxiously. Looking around, feeling as though something was wrong or that there was a serial killer hiding in a closet somewhere. Like, lol . . . but also, for real. Arming myself with a big metal spoon, I checked the house. Everything was fine. *Yay*, I weakly thought, and then my mind chimed in, *Don't worry. Just get through these five days and you can get back to working.*

"Oh, well, fuck this," I said aloud. I'm not going to crumble literally two hours into a vacation.

So I decided to explore the house in a real way instead of looking for the boogeyman. I went outside and saw the hot tub/pool combo. *Cool! I'm not about to get my weave wet, but I can get clavicle deep in the h-tub and feel like a* Girls Gone Wild *lady minus the white-girl-wasted vibes.* I ran inside, changed into a bathing suit, grabbed a magazine, maybe a cocktail, and then got into the hot tub. Again, my mind started drifting, but before I could let it formulate a thought, I stopped it. I closed my eyes as if to say, "Bitch, if you don't shut up."

After a minute of cussing myself out, I opened my eyes and noticed the palm trees. How insanely green the grass was. How the outdoors didn't have the stinky mist that New York City has in the summers. How it was nice to take the slowest of sips of my drink instead of downing it so I could get back to working. Then I smiled. Like a big, goofy grin. And then I started laughing and truly believed that everything was okay despite my not working. I'm not running out of time; I'm making the most of it, and it changed my outlook.

Listen, there's no perfect button I can put on this because workaholism will probably be the great struggle of my life. It has continued to get better since that trip. I'm always trying to figure out that balance. And sometimes I get it right. For instance, as the deadline for this book loomed, I might have worked around the clock to complete it—a'ight, I kind of did—but I took a weekend off from writing so that I could fly home and see my dad on his birthday and spend some quality time with him. I wouldn't have done that a year ago. I would have succumbed to the pressure of work and stayed in New York. I would have sat in my apartment that entire weekend, writing and talking to no one except for a half-assed phone call to my pops on his birthday. I would have done all that instead of remembering, *Hmm, my dad is also going to die one day. It's not just you, Pheebs. Everyone you know and love will die, and do you want your memories of them to be tainted with hints of regret that you blew them off or put off seeing them until next time? There may not be a next time.* So I got it right that time, enjoyed hanging with my dad and the rest of the family. And the icing on the cake?

When I returned to the book, I wasn't stressed out. I wasn't all doom and gloom about how I was going to get it done. I was actually pretty psyched about diving back in and finishing it. I was looking forward to seeing if I could make myself laugh with a crazy joke instead of keeping one eye on the word count at the bottom of Microsoft Word. And I wrote from a place of joy and it felt amazing. I've gotten the pure, unbridled happy back, so if it's all right with you, I'd like to get back to work, so I can finish this bad boy and take another vacation.

How to Be Alone and Only Mildly Hate and Lukewarm Love It

⌒

Y'all, I hope you're reading this last essay the way I assume we all want our lives to end: alone. I mean, right? Dying alone ensures some weird-ass Heaven's Gate cult bullshit didn't pop off. Now, I know some of you want to die surrounded by loved ones, but in my opinion, that's low-key rude as hell. That's just like when my family and I took my mom to see the movie *Precious* on her birthday and then we #JoyStruggled the rest of the day to have fun and celebrate my mom's life. Suffice it to say, it was extremely awkward. And that's why we now just watch *The Voice* and *An American Tail: Fievel Goes West* on Mama Robinson's birthday. Jokes aside, even though I'm 90 percent #TeamDieAlone, that last 10 percent is down to die mid-O with the hottest possible dude. Imagine, for a second, film/TV director Cary Fukunaga (Google him ASAP if you don't know what he looks like) putting his illustrious career on pause because he was going to have the honor of smashing me. It would be artistic, sensual,

273

and wild—#ReeseWitherspoon—and, ultimately, too much for my body to handle, so I'm pretty sure my orgasm would just be me holding up two peace signs, telling him, "Thanks, dawg," and then floating out of my body the way that trash bag floated in the wind in *American Beauty*. Side note: While writing out this scenario, I went from "lol" to "but for real though" status, so someone get on this, please! Look, I'm no fool. I know death by orgasm is highly unlikely, so I'll settle for Electric Sliding into the afterlife solo. Now that we have my demise moistly figured out (leaving the typo because it's clearly a gift from the Kwanzaa gods), let's gather around because I want to tell you about a time where I wasn't about being alone. In fact, it made me almost lose my gahtdamn mind in a way I hadn't done since the summer of 2015. But first, here's the tea about that summer.

After three years and eight months together, my then boyfriend and I sat down in the living room and had a sad conversaysh where I informed him that we were currently experiencing the series finale of *This Is Us*. Initiating the breakup was anxiety-inducing for me for many reasons, one of which is that I'd never dumped anyone before. Well, I take that back. I had done my fair share of chucking up the deuces to incompatible dudes after a few bad dates, but never had I canceled a significant relationship, let alone one in which both families were on board with the union, where marriage seemed to be on the horizon, and where the breakup would involve someone moving out.

You know when there's inclement weather and meteorologists call it "Snowpocalypse" or some other melodramatic name to scare us into buying provisions? Well, as soon as I ended the relationship, I did a "Crymageddon" all over Brooklyn and Manhattan. It was a lovely little tour on which I sobbed on the street, in a cab to a friend's apartment, and after I left that friend and hopped into an Uber, I cried some more, then met with a different homie for dinner in which I burst into tears as soon I sat down; then after the meal, I sobbed and snotted in a Duane Reade, while standing on a subway platform, throughout the duration of the subway ride home, and finally back at the apartment, I cried myself to sleep on the West Elm couch I'd bought mere months ago when the ex and I had been so hopeful about us a couple. And as for Crymageddon provisions? Instead of canned soups and flashlights, I rewatched the entire *Sex and the City* series and blew through boxes of Kleenex. Once the initial shock of the breakup subsided, I had to contend with a five-layer dip of emotions that most people deal with in situations like this.

First, your brain pumps out the National Anthem of Failure because, according to society, marriage is the end result; otherwise, why bother dating? Then, like an annoying mailing list you got placed on without your permission that you try to leave but it asks you seventeen times if you're sure you don't want to continue getting updates to a one-man show about being a foosball fan, regret chimes in to second-guess you following your gut instinct. This, of course, is followed by sadness aka an "In Memoriam" of all the happier times during the relationship that plays in your mind and the montage is backed by Gotye's "Somebody That I Used to Know."

Next is something that you might feel guilty about, but we would all be lying if we didn't cop to being relieved once the bad relationship is over. Not just for the two people in it but also for both sets of their friends. Much like when my niece, Olivia, made me watch *The Lion King* with her five times in five days, yet every time we watched it, she'd constantly ask me what was happening in the movie like she didn't already know, I spent *months* prior to my ending the relationship talking ad nauseum to my friends about every problem we had, only to—on the next phone call with those very same friends—be dumbfounded as to what was going on in my dusty-ass relationship.

Finally, there's shame, a feeling we're all too familiar with. I shamed myself into thinking I was a quitter the way that my dad shamed me for watching *The Real Housewives of Atlanta*. Not only did he believe it was bad television, but he felt the need to list some of the important figures in black women's history, how they fought for their lives and for equality, and how showing black women yelling at each other over nonsense is setting the movement back. To which I responded, "Well, now that you brought Sojourner Truth into this . . ." Pro tip: If you ever start a sentence by mentioning a notable person from your race like Sojourner or Tito Puente or Malala, then the takeaway is that you need to get your *CSI* on and examine your life. Moving on. Over time, I began to heal.

Besides leaning on my parents and close friends, a major facet of the healing process was the decision to not date for a year. A few peeps told me I was a bowl of Froot Loops for having this rule, but I had seen too many people immediately Plinko their way down onto new D/into new vajeen and start up an oft ill-advised relationship, thus making the baggage they carry the responsibility of the new partner. It's kind of like when you give a friend your old cell phone without wiping it clean and they're like, "Thanks . . . but there's no storage left because you've kept a record of all your text messages like you're a stenographer for the most boring recurring court case about brunch places that are cash only."

So I remained single for a year. That year then turned into fifteen months, and before I knew it, a year and a half had passed. As I wrote earlier, I dipped my big toe into the dating pool via dating apps such as Tinder with no success. I was frustrated and incredibly lonely. I know. The dreaded *L* word; it's something we're not supposed to utter aloud.

Owning up to being alone? That's fine because folks hearing this will often go into Build-A-Bear Hospital mode and try to fix you. Meaning they'll fix you up (whether you asked to be or not) with wack choices that make you go, "Oh, you think this is a damn episode of *Storage Wars*, and I like to spend my time and money gambling on trash and seeing if I can make this person better." Simply put, it seems that sometimes, to people in relationships, being alone is a curable disease for folks sans baes. But loneliness? That doesn't feel hopeful. It reminds us that we, generally speaking, come into this world solo, walk through life as individuals, and will most likely die solo. Not fun stuff to think about, let alone talk about, which is why loneliness is basically the dentist appointment of life: something to be avoided at all costs.

But for me, I didn't necessarily want to *avoid* loneliness. I just wanted less of it. My career took off shortly after my breakup, which ate up some of my alone time, as did catching up with family and friends and working on myself, but there are only so many places to go or activities I could do or freelance jobs I could take on. Eventually, I'd have to go home, alone. I'd have to sleep in a bed by myself. I couldn't ignore the pangs of sadness I felt from not having a partner in crime. This is not to say I didn't enjoy being an independent woman who wasn't defined by who I was with—I did. However, I missed being a girlfriend, and the moments where being single and alone felt like literally the worst thing on the planet were becoming more frequent. I imagine a huge part of my sadness was due to societal conditioning.

It's no secret that single women and men are treated and viewed differently. Single dudes are encouraged to be like the Greenpeace folks who stand on the street with clipboards, spreading cheer, but instead of asking passersby to help save the whales, single men are asking to pass their sauseege around like peanut brittle samples at Sam's Club. Meanwhile, unattached women, especially once they reach a certain age, are jokingly referred to as "cat ladies," "spinsters," "old maids," and are understood to be as thirsty as Gollum was about that damn ring in *The Lord of the Rings*. Only for women is being someone's partner considered an achievement, a key part of their identity, and the cure-all for loneliness. Sure, I know you can be alone as hell *in* a relationship, but I still hoped that finding a boyfriend would help keep some of the judgments or pity from other people at bay. And it's not just friends and strangers who sometimes weigh in with the doom and gloom.

There are endless studies and countless experts warning us about how detrimental loneliness and being by yourself is. In an interview with *Fortune* magazine, John Cacioppo, the coauthor of *Loneliness: Human Nature and the Need for Social Connection*, concluded that being lonely has a negative physical and psychological effect on people's health and offered up this Debbie Downer of a nugget: "Well-being goes down, depressive symptoms go up, your likelihood of developing mental and affective disorders increases." Great! Why don't I just call up Marina Abramović so we can collabo on an art installation piece at the Museum of Modern Art entitled *Sad Bitch*, which is just me sobbing in a dark corner and listening to Tori Amos while froyo dribbles out of my mouth? Okay, okay. Maybe I'm overreacting. There's gotta be more layers to this whole loneliness thing. So let's keep digging, shall we?

The 125th Annual Convention of the American Psychological Association went down last year, and research was presented showing a connection between loneliness and premature death. What the hell?!?! This is worse than what that John mofo said! Anyway, at this convention, Julianne Holt-Lunstad, a professor of psychology at Brigham Young University, basically offered up an entrée of sadness served two ways. She did two meta-analyses on how one's health is affected by connection or lack thereof with people. In the first one, she looked at 148 studies that comprised more than three hundred thousand people. The big discovery? People with good social connections (both platonic and romantic) had a *50 percent* lower risk of dying early compared to those who don't. As for the second analysis of seventy studies, she found that loneliness, isolation, and living alone all had a significant effect on a person's risk for early death. So, in summary, if you're rolling solo through life, you're on the fast track to be clanging on the cowbell while the Angel of Death sings "(Don't Fear) The Reaper" in the afterlife. But it's not like anyone is taking this damning data to heart, right? Wrong.

Everyday Health conducted their own survey of three thousand women in the US and discovered that a *third* of them are more afraid of loneliness than a cancer diagnosis. That's insane and goes to show just how scientific research and societal pressure make women, in particular, believe that singledom is a worst-case scenario. While I wasn't in that camp, a year and a half of not dating was enough for me to take another stab at hunting for a boo and I joined Bumble.

A few weeks later, a friend of mine named Michelle Buteau, who is gorgeous and hilarious, has tons of freckles, and is happily married, was in Vancouver shooting a television show, and she invited me and our friend Amy, another talented black woman in Hollywood who was fresh off a breakup of her own, to the Couv (no one calls it that) for an impromptu girls' weekend. Amy is based in LA, and I was working in LA at the time, so we figured a quick trip to Canada would be fun and that the Canuck Bumble pool might be better than the LA one.

Long story short, it wasn't. Amy found a cutie to flirt and make out with; I, however, ended up with bubkes. Seriously, the most viable option I had was a divorced dad who had his kids for the weekend but was open to going on an early-morning hike before getting back on dad duty. I was like, "Cool, cool, cool. Is *Dateline* running low on the broads who are too trusting and get killed by strange men who want to squeeze in killing somebody before racing back home to give their kids some Go-GURT? Hard pass." So no fun dates for me that weekend, but as I was boarding my flight back to LA, I got a message on Bumble from a guy who seemed normal. I let him know I was leaving town. He seemed bummed, and I figured that, at the very least, we would text for a little bit and it'd be a nice distraction. It turned into more as we talked on the phone every day, and he eventually decided he was going to come to LA to visit me. Not going to lie, I was pretty excited since I hadn't really liked or sparked with anyone since my last relationship. The next day, we had slightly less contact than usual, which was fine by me because I was swamped with work. Then, the next day, I didn't hear from him at all. The following day, he sent me a long message about being broken, that he couldn't do this but thinks I'm amazing—blah, blah, blah, you can fill in the rest. I was devastated. Way more than I should have been for someone I had only chatted with for a couple of weeks. I'm talking being livid, hashing this out with friends, crying, the whole works. And deep down, even I knew this reaction was melodramatic, and that's when I had a lightbulb moment that life coaches always talk about.

The entire time I had been single following the breakup, I was working on myself . . . but only kind of. During that time, I acknowledged that I can be an enabler, a fixer, and allow my partner to lean on me in instances when he should stand on his own two feet. I accepted that sometimes there are no bad guys in a relationship. Sometimes you love hard, fight for the relationship, and it just comes down to it not being right. There's no one to blame, no one to be angry at, just a matter of people growing and changing, and the best you can do is just try to grow together, have fun, and work on yourself. And, finally, I grew to believe that a relationship isn't a complete waste of time just because it doesn't result in marriage. All of this is fine and dandy and important to realize. However, it's all in relation to someone else and doesn't have anything to do with *me.* Furthermore, none of it gave me insight into why my reaction to a nonstarter situation with a Bumble rando was almost the same as to my four-year relationship ending. And that's when I had to face this truth: On some level, I viewed being single and feeling lonely every once in a while as a death sentence.

I never did the work to learn how to be fine with loneliness, to be comfortable with myself. This is not to say that I'm a serial dater. Far from it. My dating history has two extremes: I'm either in a relationship or single for a very long stretch of time. And during the times when I'm single, I'm busy being a workaholic or chilling with friends and family. Plus, as I have done ever since I was a teen who never got the guy, I'd spend a lot time in my head, fantasizing about having a boyfriend, hoping some guy was going to love me. Never once did I fantasize about me loving me or even me liking me. Not once did I ever sit still and enjoy myself for all that I am. So that night after the Bumble rando blew me off and I was emotionally ravaged, practically kneeling on the ground, arms out in the Scott Stapp/ Jesus position à la Andy Dufresne on the poster for *The Shawshank Redemption*, I thought to myself, *Am I going to fall the fuck apart every single time some guy I meet doesn't end up being the one?* Not only is that dumb, but it's a sign that, unlike everyone who appears on *The Bachelor* and *The Bachelorette*, I was not there and dating for the right reasons. LOL.

I knew I had to change. My joy couldn't be rooted in the possibility of getting a man. It had to be rooted in who I am. I should be happy because I can enjoy my own company and be confident in my capability to build a full life. I should be content with being alone sans distractions and daydreams. After all, the longest and most important relationship I'm ever going to have is with myself. And based on my track record, I've been spending most of my life neglecting it.

For the first time, in my early thirties, I truly got to know me and do things I'd never done before (travel overseas solo) and take better care of myself (exercising not because I wanted to look like a Hollywood starlet but because the hit of endorphins I'd get postworkout had me higher than Tinker Bell in the sky). I read more. Laughed more. *Cried* more. Worried less. Stopped monopolizing convos with friends by griping about dating. Thought about other people. Started doing charity work. Became more creative. And, thankfully, became happier as a person. To be clear, there are days when I'm jonesing a little bit for a partner, when I wish I had someone to help zip me into an outfit or run an errand for me because I'm busy or give me the perfect kind of hug that instantly destresses me. In those instances, loneliness comes and with it all my bad habits of falling into despair. The only difference now is that I treat those feelings like they're Jehovah's Witnesses ringing my doorbell on Saturday morning. I ain't going to open the door. Ain't going to look through the peephole to see who's there. Ain't going to turn my TV down so I can clearly hear what is being said. I'm just going to get up, stand about three feet from the door, and go, "Now, I've told you about coming here on my Saturday mornings . . ." And that's all I need to say. Because JWs and feelings of despair, like everyone and everything else, understand that when someone who has zero damns to give reminds you about the times they told you about the shit they don't have time for, that is your first and last warning that you're about to get dragged like Bernie's dead body in *Weekend at Bernie's*. #ThatTookATurn.

The point is, I have my good days and my bad days. Scratch that. I just have one day and then another and another. And I refuse any longer to assign a negative connotation to being alone and feeling lonely. It's not bad. It just is, and it's merely one of thousands upon thousands of emotions I'll feel in my lifetime. I don't have to be over the moon about being alone, but damn it, I'm not going to waste my energy hating it anymore.

Aww, well, isn't that special? Writing all that, much of which I've never said to anyone before, has me feeling free and warm and fuzzy all over. I think I want to stay here for a moment. Mmm. Wait. Where are you going? This essay isn't over. I gots more I want to say, and I want you to hear it, especially if you're not in a relaysh. Welcome to . . .

#TEAMBEBYYOURSELF: A Starter Guide/ Refresher for People Who Don't Have a Plus-One to Kid 'n Play Their Way Through Life With

Hey, boo-boos! Welcome to the single-and-ready-to-mingle, single-and-down-to-pop-a-Pringle, and single-and-I-ain't-got-time-to-see-nobody's-dingle-or-vajingle life. Now, some of you might've had no choice in your current dating status (ya got dumped or a tough tragedy happened, in which case, my condolences), while others made the call to throw your relaysh in the garbage like it was expired 2 percent milk, and finally, some of you simply needed to take a breather from the Snagging Some Strange Olympics and be on your own for a bit. Whatever the case may be, we have to feel good about our single statuses. Not necessarily all the time (no one is asking you to Stepford Wife your emotions), which is where I come in because I'm using all my (French accent) experience in singledom to give y'all some handy tips and reminders on how to be alone and only mildly hate and lukewarm love it.

1. **Money! You'll have more of it!**

    For real, being single is the best Cialis for one's bank account. When you're in a relationship, there are dinners, concerts, trips, birthdays, holidays, anniversaries. In short, you're constantly spending money on someone else. It's like love is a small-time gangster shaking you down every week for all that you got, and as you scrounge up all your cash, love goes, "Don't make me come down here again just for these wack-ass Jacksons and Lincolns." But when you're single, you can do whatever the hell you want with the money. Wanna not spend it on activities without worrying about being called cheap? Go for it.

Feeling a little rich and wanna pull a Michael Phelps and backstroke your behind through a pile of it? Well, don't do that. Money is dirty AF. And. It's. All. Yours.

2. **You can watch a TV show whenever the hell you want without fear that you're committing an act of treason to the Nation of Bae.**

Here are few simple truths once you're in a relationship: You can't bone other people (unless you're in an open relaysh), compromise and communication are a couple of keys to the union lasting, and once you start watching a television series together, you cannot ever, under any circumstances, watch an episode of the show without the other person. I know, I know. You and your boo ain't in the military, but when you're in a relationship, watching a television series turns into a Band of Brothers situation in which you're not allowed to leave a man behind. I don't know how or when it happened, but watching an episode of a show solo when it's you and your boo's show is a rule you don't break. And as a TV junkie, I take this decree very seriously, which is why I've never broken it . . . Okay. One time, I slipped.

A few years ago, I got into a fight with an ex and, out of spite, I watched an episode of *Breaking Bad* without him. And I'm not talking early seasons; I mean only three episodes left in the final season. Yeah, I was a coldhearted sssssssnake—#PaulaAbdul-Forever—but, in my defense, much like those folks who murder a loved one, my watching *BB* without my ex was a crime of passion. He had upset me so much that all I saw was red, and I started quoting Harpo from *The Color Purple*—"All my life I had to fight"—and decided to take back my life. Mind you, ex-bae and I were having the age-old champagne problem most noncohabiting couples have in which one partner rarely wants to go to the other's home. The night #BreakingBadGate went down, he and I had been a little over two and half years into our coupledom and I was sick of packing an overnight bag to stay at his place. He conveniently was tired twenty minutes before *Breaking Bad* was supposed to air and no longer felt like coming over to my place to watch the show even though that was the plan. Instead, he wanted me to travel thirty-five to forty minutes via subway to him. After arguing for a bit, I was like, "Okay, cool. Set your DVR up. We can watch *Breaking Bad* when I get to you." He agreed. And then I stayed my black-ass in bed and

watched the episode without him. How Petty Lu-
Pone of me. But like I wrote earlier, it was a crime
of passion, and as soon as the show was over, I
thought, *Holy shit. That was an incredible hour of TV
and I'm an asshole.* I gathered my things, got to his
place, and was so racked with guilt that I immediately admitted the betrayal. He was a little annoyed
but laughed it off because I didn't even have the
strength to enjoy the triflingness I'd just done. We
then watched the episode together and everything
was fine. And while this moment of indiscretion
didn't lead to a huge blowup between us, I learned
an important lesson: If spitefully watching Bryan
Cranston cuss a mofo out without my boyfriend by
my side is too emotionally draining, there's no way
in hell I'm capable of committing a real crime.

3. **"No More Drama" isn't just a Mary J. Blige song;
it's a new way of life.**

Word to the wise, when you're one of the people
in a couple who are arguing in public, you look like
an early-aughts music video where Usher is singing
and you're fighting in slo-mo. And trust that every
person who is walking past you and hearing snippets of the fight is for damn sure picking sides, making rulings about who's right, and before you know
it, a bunch of unqualified heauxes are Iyanla Van-
zanting the hell out of your relationship. So enjoy
your single status, where you and a significant other

aren't out in these streets reenacting only the sad parts of *Fences.*

4. **You have so much free time now to CrossFit your mind.**

I know, I know. We all go to the gym, especially after a breakup, in the hopes of getting bodies like a Pilates teacher to celebrities, but if you're anything like me, having a pricey gym membership, particularly one that allows you to go to any of their locations in the city you live in, like I do with Equinox gym, quickly devolves from exercising five times a week to just having expensive places where you can take dumps while running errands in the city. Convenient? Yes. Cost-effective? No. That's why I think it's great to also focus on the mental and get your mind in shape. I don't know about y'all, but having a significant other can sometimes make it difficult to do that. There are vacations, work events, date nights, mundanities of relationships, mingling with each other's families, not to mention your own solo shit like the day job and recharging your batteries. So sometimes it can seem like there's not much time to read a book or the news, but guess what?! Now that you're single, you're getting hours and hours of your life back to beef up the old noggin. Think about it! Breaking up with my last ex freed me up to do things like learn how to pronounce the word "Worcestershire" because there was no one distracting me by poking his erect penis in my back.

5. **The days of hiding your shopping purchases the way Ray Liotta hid guns throughout his house in *Goodfellas* are over.**

Look, we can all pretend that we're on point financially and never buy ish we don't need, but our lives are 93.8 percent about buying unessential crap. Sometimes it's because we've saved up money to treat ourselves with a little sumthin'-sumthin' nice, and what do ya know, other times, marketing really fucking works. Case in point: I went to Sephora to get a cheap knockoff brush to apply blush with and ended up buying a seventy-dollar editorial eye shadow palette containing twenty-eight colors (read: this is for professional makeup artists) because the display looked dope as hell. Last I checked, I'm not an unpaid intern hired to assist Michelangelo as he painted the Sistine Chapel. I'm just a basic B with minimal makeup skills: Every time I go to apply eye shadow, I deliberate for a long time like I'm a jury member in *12 Angry Men*, only to, yet again, use the *one* sparkling gold color in the palette, leaving the rest of the colors untouched. So why in the hell do I need a *twenty-eight-color* eye shadow palette when not only do I just use one color, but I also already have a bunch of mostly unused eye shadows at home? *Exactly.* I don't need it. This was absolutely a waste of my money, but I did it, and guess wut? If I were boo'd up, I would've left

Sephora, immediately stuffed the receipt in my mouth and swallowed it as if I were a drug mule, then gone to Walgreens and bought toilet paper and paper towels, hidden the small Sephora bag *inside* the Walgreens bag, and then, when I arrived home, I would have breezed past my boyfriend and hidden the eye shadow in the one room in the house bae is not allowed to go in like the Jenningses did to their kids on *The Americans*. But because I'm single, I rolled into my crib, put the receipt on the fridge like it was a hand turkey I made out of construction paper for my parents in elementary school, and I have the palette sitting out in plain sight like it's a family crest at a country club. Y'all, I am living life out in the open and it feels damn good—expensive, but damn good.

6. **Not having to wait for your significant other, who decided right as you're about to walk out the door that he needed to take a dump, which undoubtedly will make the two of you late to the event you're about to attend.**

Y'all, I don't wanna get into the specifics, but this has happened to me more times than I care to discuss, so I want to go on record and state that I don't necessarily run on CPT aka Colored People's Time; more often than not, my exes have had poor boo-boo time-management skills. Seriously, like, dude, if you know we're about to go out to a party, maybe don't

eat seventy-two different kinds of lettuce and aru-
gula because that mess is going to run right through
you and now we're going to miss our train because
you needed to drop the kids off at the pool.

7. **Glory be to the internet Gods aka social media
and Wi-Fi because when you're feeling hornier
than all the bulls who participate in the Running
of the Bulls, you can go on Twitter or Instagram
and write a thirst post about a hot celebrity.**

There are folks who channel their unused sensual energy into doing philanthropic work or picking up a hobby or binge-watching TV. That's cool,
but sometimes you want to be ignorant. In those
moments, do what I do and hop onto Instagram and
write an ode to a piece of A you have no chance in
hell of fraternizing with. And be sure to make this
ode so good that Walt Whitman will come back
from the dead and be like, "I spent all my life drinking and writing poems about trees when I could've
been sober and ignorantly writing bon mots about
dreaming of macking on Ulysses S. Grant."

Seriously, being single means I can devote time to
researching hot peen with the vigor of a Politico
.com fact-checker. I can get my scroll on by going
through my social media feeds and take notice of
cuties whose looks, for some reason, never really
registered with me in the past (Hugh Jackman,

Chadwick Boseman, and Riz Ahmed, just to name a few). Then there are some folks whom I recently discovered exist and their hotness has made me sign up for a lifetime subscription to *Fap Magazine:* peeps like *The Walking Dead*'s Steven Yeun (never seen the show, but saw pics of him on sosh meeds) and country singer Luke Bryan (never listened to his music, but I watched the *American Idol* reboot because I'm a grandma at heart). And finally, there are the tried-and-true personal faves who have done something recently to remind me to bow down at the altar of their good looks. Take, for instance, legendary tennis player Rafael Nadal.

Tennis is one of my favorite sports to watch, and I've been #TeamRafa since he came on the professional tennis circuit back in 2002. He is, hands down, one of the best to ever play the game, and the fact that he is a person of color who has dominated a predominantly white sport is dope as hell. But let's also be real: Homie is a hot and very in-shape Spaniard, who, in his spare time, does ads for Calvin Klein while glistening like your grandma's finest polished silver, which is something that hot people tend to naturally do.

As I am every year, I was all about his journey to winning the US Open Grand Slam Championship in 2017, especially because he had been having some injury troubles in the latter part of his career. So

when he won last year, I used my #Throwback-
Thursday post on Instagram not to highlight a
dorky picture of me from high school or a fun goal
I achieved in my career. Instead, I honored Rafa by
writing a #TBT to a video I found of him on Insta
that was from one of his earlier matches during the
2017 US Open tourney where he was running back
and forth, hitting the tennis ball and grunting
loudly:

> Somebody change "Seasons of Love" to "Seasons of
> Chub" because it's gon take 525,600 mins to get over
> this (with a lisp) sessy ass vid. Today's #TBT is @
> rafaelnadal being hella Zaddy-ish on the road to be-
> coming this year's @usopen champ. I mean, this
> mess right here about to be my ringtone, the outgo-
> ing message on mine and CeCe Winans's voicemail
> (#Lol. #Wut. She has nothing to do with this), and
> will be the In Memoriam clip they play at The Os-
> cars when I die because me watching this ish is
> straight up better than any film work I will ever do.
> If Helen of Troy's face launched 1000 ships, then
> Rafa's badonk made 1000 eggs military crawl their
> way to uteruses like they're doing a Tough Mudder
> challenge. If Martin Luther got so mad that he
> nailed 95 Theses to the door of the Wittenberg Cas-
> tle church, then Rafa's angry tennis grunts made 95
> peens stand at attention like the people in Billy
> Blanks's Boot Camp DVDs. #DatingMyself. And if

The Proclaimers would walk 500 miles to get to some vajeen in that song "I'm Gonna Be," then I would use my JetBlue points and fly 500 miles to be the almond butter Rafa spreads on his rice cake. IDK what that means either. The point let's give thanks to Rafa Nadal for being one of the greatest tennis champions of all time as well as one of the hottest dudes of all time. #YQY #YaaasKingYaaas #PeenHistory #IgButNecessary

#IgButNecessary indeed, but after I wrote this post and watched the clip a few more times, I moved on with my day of doing whatever the eff I wanna do because I'm single, which leads into . . .

8. **Casual dating!**

It's a thing, or so I've heard. Look. I've never been able to casually date. I'm either so not into the person that I cannot envision wanting to meet up again to split a side of broccoli rabe, so I cut things off from the jump,[1] or I'm pretty much all in and have figured out what our portmanteau is (e.g., Brad Pitt

---

1. Most people would say, "I can't imagine falling in love with you," or "I cannot imagine you getting along with my family," or even "Hanging out with you at a baseball game would suck," but my barometer for whether I see even a temporary future with someone is if I can handle eating a basic-ass vegetable dish with them. Probably explains why I've been single two years because my standards make as much sense as an IKEA instruction manual. It's kind of like when I told Ilana that people who want to cut meat out of their lives should just do the following: Everytime they want to eat steak, just swap it out for applesauce. To which, she responded, "No one has ever gone to a restaurant and asked to substitute a cup of unsweetened applesauce for filet mignon." Good. Point.

and Angelina Jolie were known as Brangelina) and how we can use it as a hashtag on Instagram. Clearly, there is no in between for me, but please, go forth, put your feels on low-power battery mode so you can enjoy meeting and making out with new peeps, having fun, and just remember that I'm going to be all up in your grill like a TMZ cameraperson, trying to get all the scandalous deets, then segue ungracefully into asking your thoughts on Lindsay Lohan. IDK why, but the TMZ dudes always want to know how everyone feels about LiLo.

9. **Sure, learning to love yourself can help you in the long run if and when you want a life partner, but more importantly, being your own biggest fan is only going to make you happier and have a better quality of life.**

As the legendary RuPaul states at the end of every episode of *RuPaul's Drag Race*: "If you can't love yourself, then how in the hell are you going to love somebody else? Can I get an amen up in here?" Well, I'm only going to focus on the first part of Ru's statement. Learn to love yourself, because if you can't do it, life is going to be a bumpy-ass rollercoaster ride like the one I took where the safety bar went perfectly across the dude I was with, but because he was bigger than me, there was a decent-sized gap of space between myself and the bar, so I spent the two-and-a-half-minute-long ride writing,

in my head, a spoken-word poem entitled "Ain't
This a Goofy-Ass Activity That White People Find a
Way to Die From or at the Very Least Get Hit in the
Face by a Flying Bird Like Fabio Did in 1999?"

Well, #TeamBeByYourself, that's it! A quality starter/refresher
pack for your journey with singledom. I hope it helps, but if
you're ever in a pinch and loneliness gets ya down and upset,
just freakin' go for it and cry. It's good for your soul.

Addendum: I Have a Boyfriend Now . . . Well, I Had a BF at the Time I Turned This Book in to My Editor—J/K, We're Still Together

~~~

[In *Office Space* Bill Lumbergh voice] Yeeeeeeeeeeah. A couple of things. One, I only learned that what I'm currently writing is called an addendum after I looked it up. In the past, I loosely referred to it as "When the reader is done with the book, but the author is like 'Naw, dawg,'" but I knew that was too ridiculous, so I typed into Google, "What if the book you're writing is over, but you still have some things that may be mildly amusing to 17 percent of the people who bothered to read it in the first place?" To which Googs responded with, "DaFuq.What?" Good point. In the end, I spent twenty minutes fumbling around on the internet until I found what I was looking for. Thanks, Googs, for having the patience of Stanley Tucci making over Anne Hathaway in *The Devil Wears Prada* and putting up with my nonsense.

Two, I recognize that it's awkward that I'm like, "Btdubs, I gots me a man," after I *just* wrote an entire essay about how being alone is not awful and can be as cool as the schadenfreude I feel when on *Bar Rescue*, Nightclub Hall of Fame inductee[1] and bar rehabilitator Jon Taffer trains an ill-equipped bar staff for seventeen minutes on how to undo every incorrect thing they've done for years and then throws a "stress test" aka floods the establishment with patrons, which, by the way, will be 1000 percent more people than will ever, ever, *ever* show up to this place in the future, so the staff fails miserably and cusses each other out like they're on *Jerry Springer*. Y'all, I totes didn't mean to get a bae after I had given up on dating and learned to (mostly) enjoy being on my own, nor did I plan on meeting someone after I started writing this book. But as we all know, life doesn't give a damn about our plans and will throw in a surprise or two to keep us on our toes. Sometimes the surprise is a pregnancy. Or an unexpected, wild, and once-in-a-lifetime kind of night. Other times it's new overdraft fees from Bank of America. Hey, I didn't say they were going to all be good surprises, but in the case of my relationship status, it's hella good. #NoDoubt. With that said, before I begin, I have one disclaimer: My boyfriend, due to his job as a tour manager, wants to retain his anonymity, so instead, we will use the nickname #BritishBaekoff because he's British and loves *The Great British Bake Off*. Good? Good. Now lemme tell you the story of how we got boo'd up.

---

1. Lol. I know! I didn't realize that hall of fame is a real thing either, but Jon always leads with that info the way a college football player will intro himself as attending "*THE* Ohio State University" even though no one says "the" before OSU's name. Let's just be supportive like a stage mom and go with it, shall we?

Bae and I met at a U2 concert. YES, I KNOW HOW ABSURD AND PERFECT THIS IS, AND THAT IF WE STAY TO-GETHER, WE WILL GIFT THE BAND *ONE* AMAZON ECHO (TO SHARE) THAT WE BOUGHT DURING A CYBER MON-DAY SALE BECAUSE WE DON'T HAVE MONEY LIKE THAT TO BUY FOUR, AND BECAUSE BONO & CO. ARE NOT ASS-HOLES, THEY WILL PRETEND THAT THEY WILL USE IT. So, yes, I met #BB at a U2 concert, which is the universe's way of saying, "If you can't get physical with anyone in the band, the least I can do is send some other pasty and more *age-appropriate* foreigner with an accent your way." A little blunt and judgy, but, hey, that doesn't make it any less accurate.

So last year, as some of you may know, U2 toured in celebra-tion of the thirtieth anniversary of *The Joshua Tree* album, and one of the stops was a two-night stint at MetLife Stadium in New Jersey. When the tour was announced, I made it my life goal to see them as much as possible, but even I knew that go-ing back-to-back nights might be too stalkerish, so I purchased tickets for just the first night and then sat alone in my apart-ment wearing a U2 T-shirt and melodramatically staring at my laptop while muttering to myself, "Yeah . . . yeah. No, yeah, I made the right call. I made the right call. I mean . . . yeah." Basi-cally, I was like Miss Havisham at the end of *Great Expectations*. However, despite feeling early-onset FOMO, I knew that finan-cially and sanity-wise, I had made a sound decision and carried on living my life until an angel in a maxi dress hit me up a couple of weeks before the NJ concerts.

Neyla, cellist and vocalist from the Lumineers, sent my manager an email stating that she loved *2 Dope Queens* and wanted to invite me to a U2 concert because the Loom-Looms were opening for them. For the uninitiated, the Lumineers are an Americana folk music band featuring the occasional banjo minus the "lemme make a sharp left because 'my kind' is not welcome in this neighborhood" vibe. In short, they are white, but not "h-white." Before I continue, I should probably explain what exactly the difference is between the two.

White and "h-white" both concern white people, but the former category is run-of-the-mill stuff that is silly and sometimes annoying but usually harmless, while the latter category is screwed-up trash that makes you wanna do a drive-by at 23andMe.com to make sure you're not related to the white nonsense you're witnessing. Some examples include:

- White is Gwyneth Paltrow, in one of her Goop newsletters, intentionally referring to Billy Joel as William Joel for no gahtdamn reason; "h-white" is an AP reporter calling black child actress Quvenzhané Wallis by the name Annie because it's "easier."

- White is when, in 2015, the *New York Times* decided that the traditional Mexican dish guacamole needed some zhooshing and published their recipe, which included green peas; "h-white" is racist white nationalists using tiki torches, which have Polynesian origins, to protest people of color being in America.

- White is Mel Gibson when he had a feathered mullet, stonewashed jeans, and crazy eyes in *Lethal*

Weapon; "h-white" is Mel Gibson just Mel Gibsoning it up in his day-to-day. Full stop. Period.

Thankfully, the Looms are white, not "h-white," so I listen to them. In fact, I turn on "Ho Hey" when I wanna feel like a white girl who is artistically yet unnecessarily barefoot all the time (read: Joss Stone). Therefore, when I was presented with a two-for-one situation—meeting Neyla's band as well as seeing U2 again for free—I obvs had to say yes, so she connected me with the band's tour manager (soon to be known as #British-Baekoff) and then I set about convincing one of my friends to come with me to the concert.

That friend is trusty ole Michelle. Even though she's not a U2 fan, she's always down for a good time. Plus, she's black, so we def upped the "black people at a U2 concert who are not venue staff members" from zero to two. #ThisIsMyDiversityInitiative #SoNotWhatTheACLUIsReferringToWhenTheyTalkAboutDiversityInitiatives.

On the day of the show, I met Mishy at her house at 5 P.M. so we could drive to Jersey and get there early to hang out in the VIP guest lounge until the show started at 8 P.M. Fast-forward to us being stuck in the worst traffic of our lives with every shortcut we tried to take being blocked off by the city. So there we were among the limos, convertibles, and other concertgoers as well as folks heading home from a long day at work. Ruh-roh! Michelle only agreed to go to this concert because of the promise of the VIP lounge aka free alcohol, and the arrival time on the GPS kept getting pushed later and later: 6 P.M., 6:15, 6:28, 6:45, and so on and so on. While I panicked internally, a welcome external distraction came.

Pointing to the window, I said to Michelle, "Look at these white people," a comment that all black people (especially Maxine Waters and Danny Glover) usually utter when they see standard-issue white nonsense like being barefoot in public spaces or playing a slowed-down acoustic version of a Migos or Cardi B rap song and getting 17,000,000 views on YouTube. Well, thankfully, what I was pointing at was charming ignorance, which is the foundation of my soul, so I was into it. There were two white people power walking/soft jogging across the damn highway towards the entrance of Lincoln Tunnel.

"I bet they're trying to get to the U2 concert," I said.

"How do you know that?" Michelle asked.

Was it presumptive to assume these strangers were going to see my favorite band, especially in a place like New York City/New Jersey, where there is a litany of options for night-time entertainment? Maybe, but, y'all, I was confident that my hunch was correct based off the following exhibits: (A) These peeps are white, (B) they were walking across a freeway while dressed in clothing that implied they summer in Vermont, and (C) the last time I was at a concert, it was at a festival in Boston and I saw hundreds and hundreds of white people run as fast as they could at the faint sound of Mumford & Sons tang-a-langin' on a banjo, which signaled the beginning of their performance. It was like a Black Friday sale at Net-a-Porter. It was like that scene in *Braveheart* with soldiers running up that hill if those soldiers were fighting not for their freedom but instead for the right to brag about *not* owning a TV and to continually host writers' workshops. It was Tom Cruise running in every movie ever: perfectly upright posture and with a purpose. And even when some of them tripped and fell, it was like when I play Luigi on *Mario Kart* and his turtle-shell car drives over a banana peel, spins out for a few seconds, and self-corrects. The M&S fans were not deterred and got the heck back up and kept running. So, in closing, while my definition of running or moving at a swift clip is basically me skipping to my Lou, my darling, like I'm doing runway for dELiA*s Fashion Week (a thing I wish truly existed), these Mumford & Sons fans were risking personal injury to see their favorite band. So, seeing two white people walking across a freeway during rush hour traffic, which is a dangerous thing to do, seemed par for course.

I rolled down the passenger-side window and asked these strangers, "Are you trying to get to the U2 concert?"

"Yeah," the guy yelled back. "How did you know?"

Y'all, if I had a mic, I would've dropped it; if I had on a heaux-ish miniskirt that exposed my vajeen, I would have popped it. But I didn't, so I just told them it was a guess. Then Michelle and I waved them over, and the dude and his lady friend got into the car.

As we inched along in traffic, we quickly got to know each other—where they're from, friends we had in common—and it turned out that the two of them had seen Michelle and me do stand-up before. Then Mishy pulled out a bunch of CDs and turned on some Jimmy Buffett, and the three of them rocked the hell out while I pulled a Jim from *The Office* and blank-stared at the camera that wasn't there. Eventually, the clock struck 8 P.M. and not only was it officially *three hours* since we'd left Brooklyn, but we also missed the VIP lounge experience. Fuck! But the good news was we finally got to MetLife Stadium. Halleloo! Our car buddies jumped out to look for their friends while we went about finding a place to park and kept encountering a bunch of Sam Elliott–looking mofos who gave zero damns about the clusterfuck that was the parking situation. And I get it. Dealing with 65,000 demanding concertgoers is like eating an omelet made entirely out of eggshells. #Wut #WhoWouldEatThat #WhoWouldMakeThat #ImNotGoodAt-Analogies #IveWrittenABookBefore #How.

Anyway, I was now on the verge of tears because not only had I promised Michelle a VIP experience, but the Loom-Looms were onstage, I was missing my new friend Neyla perform, and I kept texting #BritishBaekoff (who, among hundreds of other tasks, had to oversee escorting Mishy and me inside the venue) false alarms about our parking situation. Michelle reassured me she was fine, but like any normal human being, she was tired and kind of ready to go home. And even I was starting to think none of this was worth the headache, and just when I was ready to throw in the towel after sixty minutes of driving around the parking lot, we finally saw an available spot and freaked out. We parked, our spirits lifted, and I texted the #BritishBaekoff to see when U2 was going on.

"I don't know. Maybe five or seven minutes," he responded.

I immediately start booking it. Michelle, who was in heels, did her best to keep up, but I had focus like Forrest Gump. I was *determined*. I rounded the corner of the stadium and eventually saw a white guy in a suit, whom I assumed was #BB, and I kept running towards him.

He stuck out his hand, and I detected a British accent. "Hi. I'm [name redacted].[2] Nice to meet you."

"No, no, no. I've been in a car for the past four hours. You're giving me a hug." And then I ran into his arms and hugged him. Michelle finally caught up, I introduced them, and then I immediately returned my focus to U2.

Once inside MetLife, I gathered my bearings and felt I was pleasant enough to #BritishBaekoff while trying to move the proceedings along to get to the concert. Like I thought I was as nice as the average person is when they're at a restaurant and the waiter wants to tell them about all twenty-six specials, so they smile politely, waiting for the monologue of elaborate dishes to be over, so they can just order basic-ass grilled chicken and veggies. That's what I thought I was like. Apparently, I was not. I later learned that I was—cringe alert—rude. For instance, #BB gave me the tickets in an envelope, an envelope that he later told me he'd especially decorated for me because I was a U2 superfan (I didn't notice the 'lope). He wanted to show us around the VIP lounge, but I didn't care and interrupted the tour to go to the bathroom. I came out of the restroom, and when he took us outside to a sea of people in the general admission section (aka nonseated but close to the stage), I said, "I need to find my friends," and left him without saying thank you for anything he had done for Michelle and me. About ten minutes later, I realized I'd misplaced my tickets and sent him

---

2. Lol. I'm trash for that "name redacted" mess. This isn't Watergate.

a text asking him what my seat numbers were in case Michelle and I got tired and wanted to sit in the stands for part of the concert. In short, I was a hot mess who was so concerned with the U2 of it all that I completely put my manners on snooze.

Michelle and I left #BB, found my homies, U2 put on a bomb-ass show, all us ladies sang along, and I inappropriately twerked to "Sunday Bloody Sunday." It was a good-ass night, and towards the end of the concert, Neyla brought Michelle and me backstage since we hadn't had a chance to eat any dinner, and there was #BB. The four of us chatted (I was much nicer and more charming as Michelle and I shoved food in our faces), and then Neyla asked, "Do you and Michelle want to go to the U2 after-party?"

Do I want to go to the U2 after-party? Do *I* want to *go* to the U2 . . . *after* . . . *party?!?!* Yaaaaaaas!

To be clear, I'm not an after-party person. After-parties are insanely loud, full of people getting sloppy drunk, and, especially in the case of industry get-togethers, so many of the attendees are just looking around you while in conversation *with you* in hopes of finding someone richer, more attractive, or more famous than you to hobnob with. Barf. I'm much more of a home-by-10:25-P.M.-and-watching-Nancy-Meyers-movies kind of person. So, as you've probably assumed at this point, I've typically abstained from the after-party life. However, this was U2, so I sniffed my armpits, in which the all-natch deodorant had worn off exactly twelve minutes after I left my apartment, and told Neyla and #BB that Michelle and I were game and we were going to drive to the party, which was in Manhattan, and meet them there. #BritishBaekoff told me to text him if we had any problems getting into the party, and then Michelle and I left.

As we drove back to the city, I looked down at my phone at incoming text messages from #BB. "Michelle, why does he keep texting me? There's literally nothing to talk about. He got me into the concert. End of transaction. We good."

"Oh, my God, you idiot. He likes you."

Y'all, I can be a real Oblivia Pope. #MomJoke. All kidding aside, I processed what Michelle said and responded with an "Oooooooooooooooooooooooooooooooooooooo."

She laughed.

"Yeah . . . he is kind of cute."

Then I immediately texted Neyla: "What's the deal with your tour manager? He's cute. Is he single and straight?"

She wrote back: "Yes and yes." And I was pumped up.

Lmao forever. A mere five minutes ago, I was basically negative 17 percent interested in someone whose face I 3 percent remembered—#AndForThoseReasonsImOut #SharkTank—and then I find out #BritishBaekoff is available and immediately I become 2000 percent invested in him like I'm Lori Greiner trying to close on a business venture by talking about QVC deals. But truth be told, my reaction to #BB is typical trash that all current and former single people have been guilty of doing from time to time. Sometimes the reaction is because you think you might get a good story out of fraternizing with a fellow single person; sometimes it's because you just want to get a little attention from/kill a little bit of time with a good-looking person; or sometimes you simply decide to not overthink things and just be open. I was probably a combination of all three that night, so with the confidence and slight BO of a hippie yoga teacher, I headed into the party with Michelle.

The party was surprisingly low-key. Don't get me wrong, there were quite a few celebrities there, but it wasn't an extremely crowded, bottle-popping, wild shindig. Instead, it felt like a laid-back and spontaneous barbecue that happened to take place indoors. Famous people milled about, reconnecting and laughing with each other; there was a reasonably sized buffet table covered with crudités, snacks, sliders, salads, and dessert; there was also an open bar, and Questlove was DJ'ing the best set I've ever heard a DJ do. Cool-people factor aside, it was a pretty calm affair.

And so was I. In the past, I might have been the UN representative of Desperation Nation, but at that point, I had been single for two years partially because I was so focused on my career, but also, I wanted to try to enjoy singledom for a change. Meaning *not* being single and secretly hoping to meet "the One" while running errands or outwardly bitching about my relationship status/cracking jokes to hide the fact that I'm miserable or initiating girls' night outs with the hidden agenda of meeting a cute guy. Instead, I wanted to be single, get to know myself, and spend time with my girlfriends (where the topic of conversation is not just about dudes and dating) because I love them and genuinely care what's going on in their lives. So that night I was, instead, the UN representative of Wearing Very Comfortable and Loose (Because the Elastic Has Died) Undies Because I Just Wanna Party with My Girlfriends Nation.

Still, despite making my girls my number one priority and

#BritishBaekoff still being on the clock for the Loom-Looms, he and I kept gravitating towards each other throughout the night. He was definitely key-oot aka *cute*, charming, funny, a bit on the shy side, and I learned he lived in Portland, Oregon. Again, due to my chilling in the Alone Zone, I figured we would probably make out and then never see each other again as he went off traveling the world with a band and I kept on splitting my time between New York and Los Angeles for work.

With this game plan in mind, I moseyed back over to Neyla (Mishy had gone home by this point) to hang some more. That's when a drunk black woman came up to me, slightly slurring, "You're Phoebe Roberson!"

"It's Robinson, but sure."

"It's all the same. Whatever. Shut up! I knew it! I was hoping you were going to be here!" And then she punched me in my shoulder. I believe she was aiming for a "way to go, kiddo" punch, but it landed *hard* and made me stumble backwards a little.

Immediately, out of my periphery, I saw #BritishBaekoff stand up, surveying the situation. Neyla whispered to me, while the drunk woman was talking at me, that if at any point I was too uncomfortable, she would have #BB remove me from the situation. I nodded but didn't want to cause a scene, and more importantly, I knew this woman was just an inebriated fan, so I carried on the conversation as if I hadn't been hit. #BritishBaekoff, sensing my growing discomfort as this woman kept invading my space and speaking way too loud, walked over, grabbed my hand, and pulled me away. I thought, *Oooh, he's like the Kevin Costner in* The Bodyguard *to my Whitney Houston. Yaaaaas!*[3]

But nothing romantical happened, y'all! No kiss or tender hug! #BritishBaekoff and I just kept talking/flirting until I tried to get him on the dance floor to no avail. So I left him and joined Neyla on the dance floor, and later that night, I got a text message from #BB explaining that he had to leave to help one of the Loom-Looms get back to his hotel, but he had a great time with me and if I'm ever in Portland, I should look him up.

When I read that text, all I could think was, *Yeah, bitch, no. Ya had your chance, bro.* I love how when I'm over a guy, I instantly sound like a *Jersey Shore* cast member. But for real, I had (and still do have) a busy schedule, no plans to go to the Northwest, and if I did have to go there for work, I was certainly not going to carve out time to see some dude I had a few flirtatious moments with who is just as swamped as I am with work. So I chalked up this text message to him politely blowing me off and I enjoyed the rest of my night.

The next day, Neyla hit me up and let me know the entire band roasted him like peppers in fajitas for not making a move

---

3. Remember when K. Cos and Whitney go on their date and end up at his crib, and their foreplay is her swinging his samurai sword around (#NotAMetaphor), and then he takes off her silk scarf, throws it up in the air, and it falls across the blade and is sliced in half because the sword is so sharp? And you can tell she is now hella turned on? L. O. L. Can movies chill out with trying to reinvent the wheel when it comes to foreplay? I don't need my expensive silk scarf that I got on sale at Bloomingdale's, which I will TELL EVERY DAMN PERSON I MEET THAT I GOT IT ON SALE AS A BADGE OF HONOR, destroyed by a weapon. Just tell me I'm pretty, make sure your breath doesn't smell like the cauliflower you had for dinner, kiss me softly, and rub on my butt cheeks like they're dice and you're trying to roll snake eyes at a Las Vegas casino. I'll eventually be ready to go.

on me. She then suggested it could be a TBC aka a to-be-continued kind of situation. I tepidly agreed and went about living my life until a week later when I was talking about the U2 concert with Jessica (she did not ask about it) and I mentioned I met #British-Baekoff. She asked what he looked like.

"Well, he's white and British. Wears glasses . . . facial hair." I couldn't really recall what he looked like, but I was certain that he was a hottie. I felt like I was back in school and had an exam on Joan of Arc. I knew I read all about her achievements, but all I could write down is, "She sliced off her titty like it was a piece of turkey she was serving it up at Thanksgiving." Basically, my description of #BritishBaekoff was garbage and vague as hell. So I decided to find him on Instagram, but his account is private[4]—#EyeRollEmoji—and I had to request him. He accepted my request and I found one picture of him (many of his photos are scenic from his travels), which turned out to be a group photo where everyone was lined up in two rows like class picture day in elementary school and he was in the back row. All we could see of him was his bearded face, but it was enough for her to agree that he was a cutie.

Later that night, he slid into my DMs while I was about to see a play with my friend Alison. #BB and I chatted for a bit. It

---

4. Nope on nope on nope. Enough with private accounts on social media, y'all! People will explain that it's because they only want friends and family to see what they post. Bitch, the definition of living your life is literally your friends and family witnessing it in real time and silently supporting and/or judging you. Why involve Fios internet technology and waste the hours some folk spend learning how to code all so Sharon, with twenty-five followers, can post *privately* to people she sees all the time a jankity-ass selfie with a litany of hashtags that include but are not limited to: #selfie #toocute #veryfirstdayofsummer #very #happydays #notthetvshow #but-wasntitgreatthough #television?

was adorable, but again, I didn't think much of it. After all, he was in Europe. I got home from the play and he was still awake, so we texted until he fell asleep on the tour bus. Shortly afterwards, I went to bed and woke up the next day to find a text message from him—a picture of a gorgeous sunrise in Italy. And on this went. We would text throughout the day until he fell asleep, and then when I woke up in the morning, I'd open iMessage and see there was a nice morning greeting and another picture from #BritishBaekoff. Then we'd text throughout the day, getting to know each other, coming up with inside jokes, etc. It was clear we liked each other, but I had no idea what it meant or where it could lead as he was on the road and I was about to leave America for two months to shoot *Ibiza* overseas, but I needed to find out. And I knew that staying in the texting zone for too long could be bad. So I suggested we Face-Time because I have dated enough to know that people can fake a personality over text. They can take their time to come up with a witty reply or look up something you're into, get a crash course in it, and then write you back. But in person or FT, you have to be present and connect. You have to be in the moment.

#BritishBaekoff was down, so I quickly got myself situated by putting a stack of books in the frame of my laptop camera to show that I'm smart, and I sat with one of my living room windows behind me so I could be beautifully backlit like Faith Hill in her classic "Breathe" music video. Not going to lie, I was nervous, but as soon as we started FaceTiming, all fears went away. I was swooning over his neck tattoo; he was laughing as I pretended to know much of anything about the UK, and we ended up talking for *two and a half hours*. That's right. We talked for the length of *The Shawshank Redemption* (#Callback) when it airs on TNT with limited commercial interruption. This texting/FaceTime routine continued for a few more days until I took a leap and offered to fly to Portland and see him on his next tour break. Lmao forever. Just a few weeks prior, I was all "hell to the no" about seeing him in Portland, yet there I was hunched over a trash can, trimming my pubes because I didn't want to be hanging out with #BritishBaekoff while in a swimsuit that's showing off my wild, down-there hair looking like it's doing its best Bernie Sanders/Doc Brown cosplay. #IHopeMyParentsHaveStoppedReadingThisBookByNow.

Long story short, #BritishBaekoff and I had such a magical weekend in Portland that he flew to NYC to be with me until I left for Belgrade, Serbia. And by the end of the New York trip, he DTR aka defined the relationship, and we officially became boos. AWW! Right? Of course!

However, just because the story of #BritishBaekoff and me getting together is sweet, it doesn't mean we're straight chilling in Happily-Ever-After land. We're in a long-distance relationship and only get to see each other every three to four weeks. We're workaholics with thriving careers and are constantly figuring out how to do the whole work-life balance thing better. Almost every time we part ways, I'm crying as though he's going off to war. It's not easy to physically be apart from the person you love for huge chunks of time. And it certainly isn't cheap to fly to see each other as much as we can. But we make it work. So, U2, if you're reading this in your book club (lol), please know that if #BritishBaekoff and I end up going the distance, be on the lookout for that Amazon Echo, which will be sent via the groundest of mail and will take approximately three weeks longer to get to you than it took Lewis and Clark to make their way across the cunch aka country because I'm too cheap for Amazon Prime.

*Addendum to This Addendum

And it's not #BritishBaekoff-related. Lol. Rude. ANYWAY! Remember the U2 concert. I went to in Cleveland with my sister-in-law, Liz? Great. Okay, while Bon-Bon, Liz, and I hung out, one of his assistants told him I was at the U2 after-party in NYC.

Bono stared at me for a beat. "Really?"

I couldn't tell what kind of "really" this was, so I guessed it was a "how dis heaux end up at my after-party" kind of "really." (Lol. He doesn't talk or *think* like that.) So I assumed it was not cool that I crashed the party and nervously explained, "Oh, yeah, I'm friends with Neyla and she invited me, but I was barely there."

Another couple of beats while he continued looking at me. Then he goes, "I can't believe you were there. You should've come over to me and said hi."

What. Ze. Fuq?!? But also, he can't possibly mean that. He's probably just being nice, like when I'm texting someone I don't care for and I write, "OMG! Hilarious! I am screaming and laughing so hard right now," but my face is so frozen that if I turned to the left, Idina Menzel would be chilling in the corner of my bedroom, belting out "Let It Go." Obviously, I did not say any of this (but I sure as hell thought it) and instead told him it seemed like his night and all his friends and his wife were there and I didn't want to be a bother.

"No, no, no," he continued. "You should have come over. It would've been so great to hang out."

Fuuuuuuuuuuuuuuuuuuuuuuuuuuuuuuuck. Bono wanted to hang out with me?!?! Like real one-on-one time? I couldn't believe it! I still can't! But I'm holding out hope he'll feel that way again and we'll chill. Perhaps if I grease the wheels a little bit and #BritishBaekoff and I send Bono the Amazon Echo now via next-day delivery, he might hit a sista up?

Acknowledgments

\

#RealTalk, I'm writing these acknowledgments and I'm not even halfway done writing the book yet. I had a bout of writer's block and decided to do a victory lap real quick, which is ignorant AF. But is anyone surprised by my ignorance at this point? Didn't think so. Alrighty, let's try to get rid of this writer's block by doling out some thank-yous, and I'm going to try to keep it short and sweet like sex with a Wall Street bro. #GreatStart-Pheebs. Sorry! I couldn't help myself. For real, for real, let's get this party started.

Da Fam

Mom & Dad—your support and love is incredible. It's so easy to walk this world (well, take Lyfts where the driver plays "Despacito" three times in a row) knowing you have my back. Also, after years of me badgering you, you finally agreed to FaceTime me. It has mostly been a mess as you've angled the camera at the tops of your heads, your elbows, or your ceiling fans, but it's the effort that counts. Love you.

PJ—Since we're both workaholics, we don't talk as much as we should, but whenever we hang out, it's always the best. Thanks for being an amazing big bro, and I love that us going to Cavs games is our new tradition. But for the love of Guy Fieri's frosted tips, can we please do pregame dining at places besides Wahlburgers? Love you.

Liz—We have FaceTime, spa days, and concerts. We have such a blast together, and I really wish I could get on board with *Harry Potter* and *Fantastic Beasts and Where to Find Them*, but I think us meeting in the middle (*Game of Thrones*) will have to suffice. You always make me laugh. Love you.

Olivia & Trey—You two are the cutest little nuggets. I'm so happy to be your aunt. Look out for each other and love each other even when you become teenagers. More importantly, your parents and grandparents are doing a hell of a job raising you. I know you'll hit that age where you'll be over them, but truly no one will love you better than them. PLUS! They have wiped your butts so many times for so many years whereas I moonwalk out of the room when your diapers start to smell like a landfill. They're practically Mother Teresa as far as you're concerned, so treat them like queens and kings, cool?

Friends

". . . How many of us have them? Friends!" Yeah, I think, legally, that's the most I can quote this song by Whodini without having to pay for it. My friends:

Acknowledgments

Ilana Glazer, Karen Asprea, Michelle Buteau, Jamie Lee, Baron Vaughn, Jessica Williams, Amy Aniobi, Abbi Jacobson, Naomi Ekperigin, Nore Davis, Alison Stauver, Josh Sussman, Joanna Solotaroff, Rachel Neel, Tig Notaro, David Lee Nelson, Maeve Higgins, Todd Weiser. You're all incredible, wonderful, complex, and beautiful people. I'm happy to know you, laugh with you, and we're lucky to be living our best lives.

#EverythingsTrash Crew

Robert Guinsler—As I always tell you, you're the best literary agent in the biz. I adore you so much. Your encouragement means everything. Your friendship is one I treasure.

Maya Ziv—It's been so great having you as my editor and Bitmoji partner. Thanks for allowing me to miss 28,000 deadlines and being totally cool with it. You knew I'd get it all done by the hairs on my yet-to-be lasered chin. Also, if you ever have a financial hardship, your curly hair would make for a nice weave, so remember that!

Kayleigh, Jason, Jamie, Amanda, and everyone involved with this book—You've made what can be an arduous process immensely enjoyable. Thanks for showing up every day and giving 100 percent. I'm a damn lucky broad to have you on my side.

Professional Team

Chenoa—Thanks for being my manager and wanting to work with me when most of the industry was treating me like room-temperature shrimp tempura. I appreciate the loyalty and the belief.

Acknowledgments

UTA Crew—Mackenzie, Tim, Ali, Natasha, and Heidi. Y'all are dope and legit down for whatever idea I throw your way. I know how rare that is and I ain't letting you go! You're stuck with me, so let's keep on making money together!

Glam Squad—Katya Sussman, you respect and celebrate my small titties, and I love you so much for that. For real, your taste as a stylist is second to none, you always make me look and feel good, and you have one of the kindest spirits. Delina Medhin, you are a makeup goddess. Thanks for working with me all those years ago when I could barely afford to pay someone to cover up my acne scars. Haha. I'm happy we do all this cool beauty stuff together. Plus, you have the cutest laugh. Nai'vasha Johnson, Nai'vash-vash! You always kill it in the hair department, and you make the most bomb-ass wigs. But besides making me look good, your positive energy is infectious.

Sechel PR—I love how six seconds after we started working together, you made my career about ten times better. The fact that you are an all-female crew is amazing and inspiring. But the icing on the cake is your fearless leader, Sam Srinivasan. Sam (in my Viola-Davis-from-*The-Help* voice), you is kind, smart, and important. In all seriousness, you are brave, fearless, funnier than me, and such a hard worker that you make me raise my game.

Mindy Tucker—I say this every time I see you, but you are the Annie Leibovitz of our generation. You give so much of your heart with each photograph you take. The comedy community is elevated simply because of your presence. Thanks again for another phenomenal book cover.

Acknowledgments

Mai—you came in the middle of what seems like a hurricane and became my assistant. And you have kicked major behind. Thank you for making me less of a hot mess. Totes preesh.

All the people who ever employed me, laughed at a joke, told a friend to check out my work, said a supportive word to me, bought something I've created, or even just thought something positive about me: thank you. I've been in this biz for ten years, and while it has been challenging, you've undoubtedly made this less lonely.

All the times I failed and all the folks who didn't hire me: thank you. You've not only taught me to be resilient, but you've forced me to be smarter, funnier, more business savvy, and to hold myself to a high standard, while also reminding me not to take all this seriously.

Last but not least, my true boo, #BritishBaekoff. You've changed my life. You're my best friend. I love you.

About the Author

Phoebe Robinson is a stand-up comedian, actress, and the author of the *New York Times* bestseller *You Can't Touch My Hair*. Most recently, she and Jessica Williams turned their hit WNYC Studios podcast, *2 Dope Queens*, into four one-hour HBO specials. Robinson has appeared on *The Late Show with Stephen Colbert, Late Night with Seth Meyers, Conan, Broad City, Search Party, The Daily Show*, and the *Today* show; she was also a staff writer on the final season of *Portlandia*. When not working in TV, she's the host of the critically acclaimed WNYC Studios interview podcast *Sooo Many White Guys*. She recently made her feature film debut in the Netflix comedy *Ibiza*.